# THE BROKEN COMMANDMENT

# THE BROKEN COMMANDMENT

by SHIMAZAKI TOSON
translated by KENNETH STRONG

UNIVERSITY OF TOKYO PRESS

UNESCO COLLECTION OF REPRESENTATIVE WORKS:
JAPANESE SERIES

This book has been accepted in the Japanese Series of the Translations Collection of the United Nations Educational, Scientific and Cultural Organization (UNESCO)

Translated from the Japanese original *HAKAI*

Published in English in Japan by arrangement with Orion Press


Published by
UNIVERSITY OF TOKYO PRESS
ISBN 4-13-087026-2
ISBN 0-86008-191-5


Printed in Japan

First paperback printing, 1977

Eighth paperback printing, 1992

The Japan Foundation Translation Series

# Contents

# Translator's Introduction

Thanks to the numerous translations published during the quarter-century since the end of World War II, Japanese fiction of the modern period is no longer a closed book to the Western reader. Yet its reputation is still that of a highly exotic plant, with a rare and subtle scent, no doubt, but alien in its very essence, and attracting—now that the thrill of the first sight of something so different has worn off—polite but not enthusiastic interest. An air of mystery hangs over the work of some of the most distinguished (and most translated) Japanese authors, such as Natsume Soseki, Kawabata Yasunari, and Mishima Yukio.[1] Some Western readers indeed, if they are frank with themselves, may admit to finding it even harder to "understand the Japanese" after reading a novel or two by one or another of these writers, all household names in their own country. That this should be so is hardly surprising, given the uniqueness of the Japanese cultural tradition; the mystery serves too as a useful reminder that despite the efficiency and speed with which Japan is being modernized ("futurized" might be a more appropriate term, now that Japanese technology is outstripping, in some fields at least, its Western counterpart), there remain profound differences between Japanese and Western modes of apprehending experience.

A few contemporary writers, it is true, such as Abe Kobo and Oe Kenzaburo, are expressing themselves in an idiom directly intelligible to members of any advanced urban and industrial society. The impact of Abe's *Inter Ice Age 4*,[2] for example, will hardly be less for English-speaking readers than for Japanese. But even in the earlier stages of Japan's modern century, when the gap between Japanese and Western experience was obviously far wider than is the case

[1] In this introduction, as in the translation of the novel, all Japanese names are given in the Japanese order, that is, with the surname first.

[2] Trans. E. Dale Saunders (New York: Alfred A. Knopf, 1970; London: Jonathan Cape, 1971; New York: Berkley, 1971). UNESCO Collection of Representative Works, Japanese Series.

today, some novels appeared that are nevertheless readily accessible to a reader used to Western fiction. Of these, Shimazaki Toson's *Broken Commandment* is probably the most memorable. In Japan its reputation is enduring. When it was first published in 1906, by the author himself, it created something of a literary sensation, attracting important reviews in some twenty-eight papers and journals at a time when novels were still widely held to have no function other than that of light entertainment, and running into five editions in its first year; it has not been out of print since. On the Western side, Donald Keene calls *The Broken Commandment* "the novel of the Meiji era which . . . has the greatest interest for the Western reader of today";[3] for Armando Janeira, it is "the first important novel inspired by deep humanist intention."[4]

The humanist intention of *The Broken Commandment* is apparent from even a brief summary of its plot. A young schoolteacher, a member of Japan's despised *eta*, or outcast class, has achieved his present position by concealing his lowly origin, as his father had commanded him, all through his years in school and teachers' college. The tension of having always to keep secret the truth about himself—of living a lie—increases, till finally friendship with an older fellow outcast, who is fearlessly campaigning against the discrimination under which the eta have suffered for centuries, impels him, in a famous scene, to reveal his origin—to break his father's commandment—and accept the consequences of his decision to free himself from the burden of his inheritance. But whether the implicit attack on a particularly Japanese form of social and class prejudice is to be taken as the sole, or even the main, intention of *The Broken Commandment* is open to doubt.

The novel is somewhat more complex than is evident at first sight. When it first appeared, most Japanese were puzzled by the "outcast" motif: though discrimination against the eta might have survived in some provincial

[3] Donald Keene, *Japanese Literature: An Introduction for Western Readers* (New York: Grove Press, 1955), p. 99.

[4] Armando Martins Janeira, *Japanese and Western Literature: A Comparative Study* (Rutland, Vt., and Tokyo: Charles E. Tuttle, 1970), p. 268.

areas, they persuaded themselves that essentially it was a feature of the feudal past, unknown in the new, modernized Japan. In this belief they were mistaken. Discrimination against the eta is not uncommon even today; in Shimazaki's time it was harsher and more widespread. Then, as today, most educated Japanese knew little or nothing about the submerged minority in the midst of their apparently homogeneous social organism, or did their best, in a compact of silence, to forget what little they did know.[5] Whatever Shimazaki's motives, therefore, his choice of such an unlikely topic—and at a time when the vast majority of his countrymen had little thought to spare for anything but the excitements of Japan's war with Russia, her first military encounter with a major Western power—was remarkable, to say the least. Who were these eta, this pariah class upon which *The Broken Commandment* threw its startling spotlight?

Officially, premodern Japanese society was neatly divided into four groups: samurai, peasants, artisans, and merchants, in descending order of respectability. Below these recognized classes were the *hinin*, or "nonpersons," consisting of "beggars, prostitutes, fugitives from justice, itinerant entertainers, mediums, diviners and religious wanderers who had fallen right out of the class system."[6] Below them, at the very bottom of the scale (though in later centuries they were sometimes considered to be equal, or slightly superior, to the "nonpersons") were the eta. As the name *eta* ("full of filth") implies, the members of this group were thought to be genetically impure; they were confined for the most part to occupations that as the result of a fusion of Shinto and Buddhist ideas had from early times been considered ritually polluting.

5 Professor Wagatsuma, the Japanese coauthor of the only comprehensive study of the eta to have appeared in English (*Japan's Invisible Race: Caste in Culture and Personality*, George De Vos and Hiroshi Wagatsuma [Berkeley: University of California Press, 1966]), was himself until the age of eighteen entirely unaware of the existence of the Japanese outcast community.

The outline of eta history given here is based upon the detailed information provided in *Japan's Invisible Race* and upon the pamphlet "Japan's Outcasts—The Problem of the Burakumin" (London, 1971), produced for the Minority Rights Group by Professor De Vos.

6 De Vos, "Japan's Outcasts," p. 4.

The first written reference to eta appeared in the thirteenth century, but by then they may well have existed as an identifiable group for several centuries. It was widely believed until quite recently that not merely did these outcasts look and smell different but also they were somehow less human, more "animal," than "normal" Japanese.[7] This sense of their being alien in some fundamental way to the majority around them gave rise from the late nineteenth century onward to some curious theories of the origin of the eta—that they are descendants of a Hindu or a Filipino tribe, of Koreans captured in some remotely distant war, even of a lost tribe of Hebrews. It now seems likely, however, that they are genetically as Japanese as the rest of their fellow countrymen.

Discrimination against them probably had its origin in religious taboos. From ancient times, Shinto, Japan's indigenous religion, emphasized the dangers of ritual pollution and laid down various avoidance practices concerning blood and death, so that those performing tasks related to childbirth, disease, and death, or working with the products of slaughtered animals, were kept from contact with the majority. The advent of Buddhism from China and Korea, with its sentiment of compassion for all living beings, strengthened in particular the notion that the slaughtering of animals and trades such as leatherwork were "unclean."

During the Tokugawa period (1600–1867), with its rigid social stratification and government edicts penetrating into every corner of life, the eta were more strictly segregated and discriminated against than before. Marriage with nonoutcasts was forbidden, and such contact as was unavoidable between eta and other Japanese was minutely regulated.[8]

[7] See Chapter 18 of *The Broken Commandment* and references elsewhere in the novel to eta as constituting an alien "race"—a term that until recently was used as loosely and unscientifically as it has been in the West.

[8] In addition to their hereditary pursuit of the "unclean" trades connected with the slaughter of animals, eta served the administration in certain occupations considered degrading because of their association with crime, e.g., *chori* (police minions, executioners) and *banta* (watchers over the bodies of executed criminals), whom Ushimatsu felt to be superior to the common run of outcasts (*The Broken Commandment,* p. 210).

When approaching the home of a commoner, the *eta* were required to take off their headgear and footwear before entering the courtyard; and they were not allowed to cross the threshold. Moreover, the privilege of sitting, eating, and smoking in the company of the commoners was denied to them; and in court, the *eta* were always seated in a lower position than that accorded to [commoners].[9]

There was a significant legal decision in 1859.

When an *eta* youth was killed in a scuffle between *eta* and non-*eta* gangs, Danzaemon, the *eta* leader in the Kanto district, brought the case before . . . the city magistrate. After careful reflection, the magistrate delivered the now famous judgement: an *eta* is worth 1/7 of an ordinary person. If you would have me punish the guilty party, let him kill six more of your fellows.

The following edict was issued in the year 1870 in the Wakayama feudatory:

The morality of the *eta* people is not good these years and they very often act viciously. Therefore, order them to abide by the following regulations:

(1) To walk at the edge of one side of the street and not to disturb passers-by, not only in the city, but also in their own community.
(2) Not to loiter except from sunrise to sunset, either in the city or in the suburbs. And also in their own communities, they are not to loiter arbitrarily during the night. On the holiday of Setsubun [holiday of the change of season] they are allowed to walk till five in the evening, but not later than that; on the last day of the year, not later than nine o'clock.
(3) They shall not eat or drink in the city.
(4) They shall not use umbrellas or headgear except in rainy weather.
(5) They shall not use any footgear, except sandals.[10]

In spite of these humiliating social impositions, by virtue of their monopoly of such trades as slaughtering and leatherwork the eta held a not insignificant position in the economic life of the country. In the course of time they established near monopolies in other industries, sandal weaving, basket making, and tea-whisk manufacture among them. Some, like Rokuzaemon in *The Broken Commandment*, became rich, wielding considerable power

[9] See also *The Broken Commandment*, pp. 87, 229.

[10] De Vos and Wagatsuma, *Japan's Invisible Race*, pp. 23–24, quoting from Ninomiya, Passin, and Donoghue. Passages from *Japan's Invisible Race* were originally published by the University of California Press and are reprinted by permission of the Regents of the University of California.

within their own communities. Danzaemon, the leader of the outcast community in Edo (Tokyo) in the final years before the Meiji Restoration in 1868, lived in a large mansion, controlled some six thousand eta households, and even set up a shoe-manufacturing business employing foreign technicians.

In August 1871, as one of the innumerable reforms that ushered in the modern period, the new government issued the Edict of Emancipation, abolishing the eta as such, partly out of a general desire to remove the old system of caste privilege and partly from the need to secure every possible source of revenue—one quid pro quo for the harsh treatment meted out to the eta had been that their land was tax free. Officially the eta now became known (as in *The Broken Commandment*) as *shin-heimin*, "new commoners." In fact, they were worse off than before. Social discrimination remained unaffected by the edict, and the loss of eta craft monopolies under the new economic system depressed even further an already downtrodden community. In a time of rapid and often upsetting change, eta were liable to be made scapegoats for feelings of resentment in neighbouring communities, feelings that culminated here and there in "eta hunts" and campaigns to exterminate the eta. The Mimasaka Riot was one of the worst of these incidents.

> On May 25, 1873, a farmer in Okayama Prefecture, long dissatisfied with the new government's policies, started a rumour that a stranger dressed in white was suspiciously wandering around trying to track down certain residents. The farmers gathered, armed with rifles and bamboo spears, and surrounded the house of the village head, demanding that he hand over the stranger, who they believed had gone into his house. The village head insisted that there was no such person. Still unconvinced, the villagers broke into the house and searched for the stranger. Unable to find anyone, the mob moved on to a neighbouring Buraku [eta hamlet] where they wrecked and burned fourteen houses. At the next village they destroyed the school building and a teacher's house. Then they split into two groups. One destroyed a school building and the home of the village head in an adjacent village, while the second group raided another Buraku. The groups merged at midnight and raided three more Buraku and set fire to the houses. Early in the morning the mob attacked a building of the prefectural government and also destroyed the houses of

> the officers. The government recruited 300 ex-samurai for protection, who started shooting and drove the mob away from the government buildings. The mob moved to other villages, destroying and setting fire to the houses of the village heads as they went. Many Buraku in the vicinity were raided. The mob increased in size, and on the fourth day, May 28, the whole district of Mimasaka became a scene of violence and destruction that lasted until June 1. Finally, 100 officials from . . . Okayama Prefecture, in addition to army troops from Osaka, arrived and subdued the riot. More than 400 individuals were arrested. According to official figures, 10 houses of government officials, 47 homes of village heads, 25 homes of policemen, 15 school buildings, and more than 300 Buraku homes were wrecked or burned. Eighteen Burakumin [eta] were reported dead and 11 badly injured. It was estimated that about 26,000 farmers joined the riot.[11]

A Ministry of Justice *Handbook of Japanese Customs and Folkways,* published in 1880, referred to the eta and "non-persons" as "the lowliest of all people, almost resembling animals." A reference to his school days in the same period, by an outcast who in the 1920s became one of the leaders of the modern eta liberation movement, shows that the portrayal of the ostracism of the eta boy Senta in *The Broken Commandment* is not a product of the author's fancy: "When I entered junior high school in 1883, I was the first child from Sakamoto [an eta village], and everyone was curious. . . . I was made to sit alone behind all the children in the class . . . nobody talked to me, or wanted to sit by me. . . . A teacher of a physiology class asked me if it was true that we [outcasts] did not defecate and urinate at the same time. . . ."[12]

Such, broadly speaking, was the position of the eta when Shimazaki wrote *The Broken Commandment.* According to the census of 1871, they numbered 383,000. Since in that year they officially ceased to exist as eta, they have not figured as a distinct group in any subsequent census; but the eta communities have stayed in being, their population apparently sharing in the overall national increase.[13]

In 1907 a national organization was formed for the first

[11] Ibid., pp. 36–37.
[12] Miyoshi Iheiji, quoted in ibid., p. 37.
[13] Some estimates put the present figure as high as three million.

time by the outcasts themselves, aimed at raising their status through self-improvement in "morals, manners, and sanitation." But little attempt was made to challenge society's hostility till the emergence some twenty years later of a more militant body, the Levellers' Association (Suiheisha), with its banner of "a crown of thorns the colour of blood against a black background of darkness." In 1905, when Shimazaki was working on his novel, a fighter for eta rights such as Inoko Rentaro in *The Broken Commandment* would have been a pioneer figure indeed; nor would his fate as Shimazaki describes it have been unlikely. Today the eta struggle for acceptance is gaining ground, aided by the climate of the times and by the mobility of modern industrial society. Yet discrimination persists, the contemporary situation of the eta parallelling in some striking ways that of the Negroes in the United States.

At the beginning of the twentieth century the modern Japanese novel, with one or two exceptions, had hardly begun to grow beyond the naïve political allegories and sentimental stories of the 1880s and 1890s. *The Broken Commandment* was not the first novel to display some social concern, nor was it the first to deal with the outcasts, but in its realism, its seriousness, and its humanism, however muted, it was wholly new. Yet the early Japanese critics, in playing down the eta theme of the story, were not influenced only by their ignorance of and lack of interest in the depressed minority. According to their interpretation of the novel (which is still generally accepted), its eta hero is primarily an embodiment of Shimazaki's own longing for inner, spiritual emancipation, an image that suggested itself to him from the life history of one particular eta that he heard from a friend: a symbol that by chance served his purpose, perhaps even better than he realized, but that could equally well have been replaced by some other figure burdened with Werther-like aspirations. A glance at the literary background and Shimazaki's life prior to his writing of *The Broken Commandment* may help to make clear why the novel has been taken in this way.

By the time Shimazaki was in his teens, the honeymoon period of reform with which the modern period began was over. For some two decades after the Restoration of 1868 the aims of the national modernizers and of those who dreamed of a spiritual liberation—a new individualism to replace the constricting codes imposed by the Confucianism that an authoritarian government had used for so long to mould education, morals, and social relations—had seemed to coincide: by the 1890s it was clear that they no longer did. (Now, nearly a century later, the intoxication of so many of the youth of late nineteenth-century Japan with a Western-inspired individualism may look very naïve, perhaps even ludicrously misguided, but the strength and sincerity of what they felt is beyond doubt.) This period saw the brief flowering of the Japanese version of Romanticism, associated above all with the poet and essayist Kitamura Tokoku (1868–94). Driven to despair by the widening and apparently no longer bridgeable gap between his sense of man's potentialities and the direction the society around him seemed to be taking, Kitamura hanged himself at the age of twenty-six. He had been Shimazaki's closest friend, the most formative influence on the first stages of his literary career. Shimazaki himself started out as a lyric poet. Like Kitamura, though with a streak of sentimentality Kitamura sought more strenuously to avoid, he spoke for the short-lived Romantic generation:

> At last the time for a new poetry has come.
> A beautiful new dawn is upon us. Some cry aloud, like the prophets of the distant past; some sing like the poets of the West: all are intoxicated with the brilliant light, the new voices, the dreams. . . . The imagination of youth has awakened from its long sleep, to revivify poetry with the living language of our people. Legends are reborn, nature takes on new colours. Before our very eyes, a powerful light has shone upon new emerging life, and upon death, the grandeur and decay of the past.
>
> Most of our new poets are simple, earnest men. Their art is childish, rudimentary; but there is nothing false, no mere ornament, in their work. The life of youth spills over from their lips, tears of true feeling stream down their cheeks. . . . For many, the flood of new ideas drowns all thought of food or sleep. The sorrow, the agony of our present age has driven many to madness.
>
> Forgetful of my own unworthiness, I too have joined in their chorus.

> Poetry is "emotion recollected in tranquillity." This is true of my poetry, which is a confession of conflict. Grief and pain remain in my poems. It is good, I believe, to speak out. To speak out, without faltering.
>
> I too have been saved, body and soul, by the little poetry that I have managed to achieve.
>
> Who can rest in the old life? To strive to open the doors to new life—this is the task, the duty of the young.
>
> Life expresses itself in energy; energy, in the speaking voice; the voice, in words. New words mean new life.[14]

Shimazaki had more reason than most to be keenly aware of both the "new life" to which the Romantics aspired and the "grandeur and decay" of the ideals of the past. His father, Masaki, as *shoya,* or headman, of the village of Magome in the Shinshu mountains—he was the seventeenth successive head of the family to hold this hereditary post—had been a person of some importance in the old order. Magome lay on the route of the Nakasendo, one of the five great national highways of the premodern period, and until the restoration of imperial rule in 1868 the Shimazaki house served as the local *honjin,* or officially designated stopping place for feudal lords and other dignitaries travelling to and from Edo. Masaki did not take kindly to the upheavals that followed the Restoration. He did advocate change, but he wanted the new Japan to return to the simpler pieties of her prefeudal past, not to adopt "modern," Western ways. Disappointment and frustration led finally to madness, and to his death in 1886. It was through a fictionalized portrayal of his father's turbulent life that Shimazaki Toson, many years later, was to explore the meaning, in human terms, of the vast changes Japan went through in the mid-nineteenth century—the only novelist close in time to those great events to attempt the task.[15]

Yet he can hardly have known very well this father, of whom he was the fourth and favourite son. For reasons that

[14] From the preface to *Toson shishu* [Collected poems of Shimazaki Toson], published in 1904.

[15] The novel is *Yoakemae* [Before the dawn]. Unfortunately it has not yet been translated, but Edwin McClellan provides an assessment of its stature, along with translated extracts, in his excellent *Two Japanese Novelists: Soseki and Toson* (Chicago: University of Chicago Press, 1969).

are not altogether clear—partly, it seems, because of the family's rapid decline in fortune after the closure of the Nakasendo Highway, and perhaps owing to domestic tensions (one of his elder brothers was illegitimate, and his father seems to have been involved in some extramarital entanglement)—Shimazaki was sent while still a small boy to Tokyo to live with friends of the family, and saw his father only once again before the latter died. The family who looked after him in Tokyo was kind, though obviously he must have discovered earlier than most what it means to be lonely.

At the age of fifteen, in 1887, a precocious interest in English led him to enter Meiji Gakuin, a Christian school where he had heard the language was well taught. Here he was exposed to what was for young Japanese of the time a heady atmosphere of emancipation; for the first time he heard of such notions as the dignity of the individual, of the importance of his own feelings, and of his right to express them. Like many of his contemporaries, he was baptized, and thought for a while of a religious, then of a political, career. Literature, however, soon proved a stronger attraction. Besides the great Japanese poets of the past, in particular Saigyo and Basho—the latter became a lifelong passion—he read fairly widely in such Western authors as Shakespeare,[16] Wordsworth, Byron, Goethe, and Dante.

A year after graduating from Meiji Gakuin, he was offered a post as English teacher at its sister institution, Meiji Jogakko (Girls' School). Emancipation, even in the tentative form that Japanese youth was then experiencing, brought

[16] The scene in *The Broken Commandment* where Ushimatsu hears his father's spirit calling through the night, though obviously derived in part from the traditional belief that the spirits of the dying visit their loved ones to say farewell, may owe something also to a memory of the ghost scene in *Hamlet*. It is often in such relatively trivial ways that the "influence" of Western literature on Japanese writers of the Meiji era (1868-1912) is to be observed. A comprehensive understanding of Dante or Goethe or Shakespeare was still lacking, much as in the West today our understanding of Asian literatures is still on a primitive level. Yet they did gain from these European heavyweights something invaluable—a sense of the *seriousness*, the splendour, of literature itself, which for many of them was a powerful element in their decision to take up writing as a career. Such a stimulus was badly needed, particularly by men who wanted to devote themselves to the writing of realistic prose fiction, an occupation that till then had been thought hardly worthy of a respectable, let alone a serious, man.

its inevitable complications. A brief romantic affair with one of his students, who was officially engaged to someone else, led to his resignation from the school after only one year. He tried to recover his peace of mind by spending nine months wandering at a leisurely pace about the country, as had been the habit of innumerable Japanese poets, Saigyo and Basho among them, for centuries. That same year, 1893, he joined Kitamura Tokoku and his small group of enthusiastic young Romantics in founding their journal, *Bungakukai* [Literary society]. For a while, under the spell of Kitamura's intense personality and with a ready-to-hand outlet for his literary experiments, his horizons must have seemed boundless. They were to close in upon him rapidly.

A year later Kitamura had hanged himself, the burning down of the old house at Magome had laid on Shimazaki's shoulders unexpected and unwelcome responsibilities, and, in the wider world, his country had embarked on war with China. But the stress of these events did not weaken the force of Shimazaki's Romantic impulse, though it may have delayed its expression. A move in 1896 to the peaceful surroundings of Sendai, in northeastern Japan, proved fruitful. During his ten-month stay in this old provincial capital, perhaps the happiest period of his life, he published *Wakana-shu* [A collection of young leaves], a small volume of lyric poems celebrating the joys and sadness of love, youth, and the seasons: rather naïve, but conveying even today the excitement, the vivid delight in a rediscovery of the external world and of the self, that marked *Wakana-shu* as the first clear utterance of Japanese Romanticism.

Three more such collections followed during the next five years, still primarily lyrical but including some less subjective sketches of incidents in the lives of ordinary people—a fisherman, a farmer, a blacksmith. For observing such lives Shimazaki had plenty of scope. In 1899, with his bride, he moved to a teaching post in Komoro, the boyhood home of his eta hero in *The Broken Commandment*. Here, on the edge of the Shinshu mountain country he had known as a boy, he lived and worked in relative obscurity for five years, developing slowly from an exuberant young Romantic into a deeply serious novelist, intent on discovering the truth about things and people, himself included, by steady contemplation of what he saw around him. Following Ruskin—he had published translations of parts of *Modern Painters* in 1896—he polished his prose style in numerous studies of the people of the region and their lives, published ten years later as *Chikumagawa no suketchi* [Chikuma River sketches].

But the ambition to write a full-scale novel was steadily growing. As avidly as ever, Shimazaki was reading Western models: Tolstoy, Dostoevsky, Ibsen, Maupassant, Flaubert. The appeal of lyric poetry weakened. Despite the success of his own poems, the weight of the native poetic tradition of elegance and subtlety, in conformity with rigid limitations of length, rhythm, and vocabulary, lay heavy; he had found it impossible to break entirely free of the old moulds. The novel, by contrast, seemed to allow a range and depth of expression that could do full justice to the "self-awakening" experienced by the Romantics.

Deliberately, Shimazaki prepared himself to write a "modern" novel. A commonplace enough decision, no doubt, yet at the time it must have seemed an agonizing choice. No prestige attached to the writer of the kind of fiction he had in mind, nor was there any likelihood of financial reward; and Shimazaki was as sensitive as any educated Japanese of his time to the feeling of frustration, of shame almost, at having to "bury oneself in the provinces," cut off from the metropolitan heart of a swiftly changing culture. One of his closest literary friends, Tayama Katai, went to cover the Russo-Japanese war as a correspondent. Shimazaki envied him greatly, but after one attempt to get a similar appointment, he decided to remain in his chosen backwater as what he later called, in a famous phrase that mirrors the unconscious Victorian earnestness of many outstanding men of Meiji, "a war correspondent in the battle of life" (*jinsei no jugun-kisha*). In this spirit he began early in 1904 to write *The Broken Commandment.*

The cost of his determination to go his own way was heavy. Shimazaki's salary, as a teacher in a provincial private school, was already low, and out of it he was helping the surviving members of the family to whom he was obligated for their care of him when he was a boy at school in Tokyo; it was lowered further when financial support from the local authority was sharply reduced, because of economic pressures caused by the war with Russia. Before long the whole family—three children already, the third born that same year—was suffering from undernourishment.

To say simply that Shimazaki ignored the hardships his obsession with the novel imposed on his family is probably unfair. It would be as true, and fairer, perhaps, in the context of the Japanese ethics of the period, to say that his dedication, even at the expense of his family, to the literary task he had set himself was proof of his "sincerity," that complex quality that in Japanese culture can produce on occasion both heroism and a harsh disregard of other people's welfare, in varying proportions. In Shimazaki's case there can be little doubt as to either the heroism or the harshness. In April 1905, deciding he needed to work full time on his novel if it were ever to be finished, he gave up the teaching post in Komoro and moved with his family to Tokyo. A week later his baby daughter died of meningitis. Already his wife was pregnant again, and was undernourished and suffering from frequent night blindness. They were living on money borrowed from a friend in Shinshu.

Eventually *The Broken Commandment* was completed. Unwilling to trust his novel to any of the commercial publishers, who in the literary climate of the day would be unlikely to take seriously such a work by an obscure poet with no connections in the literary establishment, Shimazaki published it with money borrowed from his father-in-law; when the binding was finished, in March 1906, he himself, in kimono and high wooden clogs, clattered through the streets of Tokyo trundling a cart loaded with the first few hundred copies to a bookseller in Kanda. Recognition was almost immediate. But the full price had yet to be paid. Within three months his two remaining daughters were dead, of dyspepsia and tubercular meningitis, and newspapers were advertising the novel as the book that had cost its author the lives of his children.

The subject matter of the novel was suggested to Shimazaki by the story of a brilliant young eta named Oe Isokichi, told him by a fellow teacher in Komoro. After graduating from Nagano Teachers' College, Oe became a teacher at a primary school, but was expelled ignominiously when it came out that he was of eta birth. Sympathizers on the staff at the teachers' college arranged for him to pursue more advanced studies in the comparatively liberal atmosphere of Tokyo. Eventually he returned to his old college in Nagano, this time to teach; but prejudice took over once more, and from here too he was expelled. After spells in various schools in other parts of the country, finally as a headmaster, he died in 1902, murdered, according to some accounts, by a fanatical hater of the eta.

Shimazaki's sympathy with outcasts who had to suffer this kind of humiliation, or even brutal attack, was genuine. Yet just as certainly this sympathy was not his chief concern in writing the novel. Eta critics have even objected that Shimazaki shows his own prejudice by dwelling too often on the ugliness, the ignorance, and the physical degradation of the outcasts. The reality of eta humiliation is dramatized only occasionally, and then only in a shadowy way, as in the expulsion from his inn of Ohinata, the well-to-do eta; nor does the eta hero show any sign of wishing to carry on the fight for liberation that his mentor has so heroically launched.

*The Broken Commandment* might have been a more satisfying novel, in traditional Western terms, if it were not deficient in these respects. But to judge it too harshly for this reason would be to miss the author's intention, and to underestimate the degree to which the novel, not least by its apparent defects, mirrors the society of its time. The latter point is particularly worth making in regard to the "happy ending," the wholly unexpected manifestation of a *deus ex machina* in the shape of an invitation to Ushimatsu to emigrate to Texas. At first sight this seems preposterous. But as Donald Keene remarks, this "ending vitiates the story for us, but it was perhaps the only possible one for Japan. I think it likely that in a European novel of the same date, it would be far more usual that the hero, offered the choice of a comfortable job in Texas or badly paid work as a battler for *eta* rights in Japan, would have chosen the latter. In this the

Japanese novel is realistic as European works are not."[17]

Serious suggestions for large-scale emigration of eta to the South Seas, Canada, Hawaii, Taiwan, Mexico, Australia, and the United States had been made since the late 1880s—the point being that discrimination was so deeply ingrained that even "liberal" Japanese could think only in terms of emigration as a solution to the problem. A serious fight for the emancipation of the outcasts *within* the country was so inconceivable as to seem to belong to the realm of fantasy. Twenty years after publication of *The Broken Commandment,* when the eta were forming their own militant movement, some of their leaders even toyed with the idea of "flying away like swallows" to the South Seas to improve their lot.[18]

To return to the author's intention. "The tragedy of one who has awakened," Shimazaki called *The Broken Commandment:* the tragedy of an early twentieth-century Japanese outsider, who by deliberate decision reached only after a long struggle achieves spiritual freedom, but at the cost of cutting himself off irrevocably from society. It is the inner freedom that interests Shimazaki more than any notion of the freedom of the individual within the social framework, or of the absolute dignity of the individual. In this respect, he and his eta hero are the forerunners of a long line of novelists and fictional characters in modern Japanese literature whose lives have revolved around their perception of themselves and their own immediate circle, rather than their relation, if any, with the changing society and culture of which they have been, as it were, nonparticipatory members.

Behind the "awakening" Ushimatsu lie several Western literary models, notably the Rousseau of *Confessions* and Dostoevsky's Raskolnikov. It is possible, as one Japanese critic early noticed, to equate at least five of the characters in *The Broken Commandment* with their "originals" in *Crime and Punishment*—Ushimatsu with Raskolnikov, Keinoshin with Marmeladov, Ginnosuke with Rasmihin, Bunpei with Rugin, O-Shio with Sonia. But Shimazaki was no slavish

[17] Keene, *Japanese Literature,* pp. 100–101.

[18] De Vos and Wagatsuma, *Japan's Invisible Race,* p. 43.

imitator. In a letter to a friend in November 1903, written just after reading *Crime and Punishment* and a month or two before starting work on *The Broken Commandment,* he concludes that Dostoevsky's achievement lay in the creation of a "modern tragedy of passionate thought."[19] Japanese literature was rich in emotion, short on intellect: Dostoevsky had fused the two into a perfect, organic whole, and it was this fusion that Shimazaki wanted to aim for in *The Broken Commandment.* Potentially, at least, and by Shimazaki's standards, Ushimatsu is a modern, self-conscious, and clear-thinking man. He knows how rational beings should behave, and slowly comes to realize that it is within his own power to free himself from the attitudes of subservience to which his birth condemned him.

Every word of Shimazaki's summing up of what he admired in Dostoevsky is relevant to *The Broken Commandment.* The Japanese bias toward emotion, with Shimazaki's own brand of lyricism, softens the harsh outlines of the story—too much so, no doubt, for some Western readers: Ushimatsu has at least his share of the tendency to gloomy or even mawkish introspection that balances the often lighthearted, hedonistic outlook of his countrymen. But that the tale should be a tragedy, in a peculiarly Japanese sense, is inevitable, given the role played by a character who has no counterpart in *Crime and Punishment* and whose influence is pervasive, though he never appears except as a corpse—Ushimatsu's father.

Through Ushimatsu's struggle of conscience to throw off the burden laid on him from boyhood, with wholly admirable intention, by the father whom he admires profoundly yet whose dearest wish he must in the end betray, Shimazaki effectively dramatizes the will of his generation to resist enslavement to the past. If there were any doubt about the strength of this determination, it is dispelled symbolically by the manner of Ushimatsu's father's death, murdered as he is by the prize bull of the herd he loves.[20] Yet the sequel to the killing, the long description of the slaughter—

[19] Shimazaki uses the English words "passionate thought."

[20] It has been pointed out by Japanese critics that images of wildness and primitive energy occur frequently in Shimazaki's poems.

ironically, by eta butchers—of the bull, the instrument of the father's end, is surely one of the most curious things in the novel.

The plot requires no such detailed account. Is Shimazaki implying—perhaps unconsciously—that while Ushimatsu may have succeeded in freeing himself from the authority of his father, the victory and the freedom may turn out to be sterile unless "freedom" is seen to have social implications beyond the narrowly personal, and the battle fought again on a much broader front? The point is not just academic. The authority of the "family" concept was all-powerful in Shimazaki's time, and survives in different forms today, in government as well as business life, offering valuable psychological support to the individual but operating not infrequently as a burdensome, coercive influence, as many writers—and more recently, film makers—have testified. Shimazaki himself was to take up the theme directly in his second novel, *Ie* [The house].

The interest of *The Broken Commandment*, therefore, lies partly in its attempt to articulate the difficult process of self-awakening in a young Japanese at a time when despite Japan's rapid transformation into a modern state, traditional and authoritarian attitudes remained predominant. The feeling of emancipation in the novel is far from complete. At the climax of the story, Ushimatsu's public confession of his outcast birth, Shimazaki makes him grovel before his pupils and colleagues—which may ring true, as a reflex action inculcated by centuries of oppression, but scarcely convinces the reader of the reality of Ushimatsu's hard-won independence of spirit. Nor does Ushimatsu ever confide in his friend Ginnosuke, though the latter would clearly not have rejected him had he done so.

But for all its inadequacies, *The Broken Commandment* remains a landmark in the development of the modern spirit in Japan. Ushimatsu's longings for a freer future reflected the aspirations of innumerable readers, most of whom probably knew little or nothing of the eta but had experienced in their own lives the conflict between the urge to "follow the world"—the solemn commandment laid on Ushimatsu by his father—and the resolve to fight its injustices, commended to him by his friend and mentor,

Inoko Rentaro. In style as in subject matter—its opening sentence, "Rengeji temple took in boarders," astonished contemporary readers, used to flowery diction, by its simple directness—and in its combination of the new realism with a poetic feeling for the austere splendour of the Shinshu landscape and compassion for the harsh lives of peasant and outcast, it opened new directions.

Later writers have explored particular aspects of the Japanese experience with greater subtlety and sophistication; few have attempted to probe as seriously into the problems that lie at the heart of *The Broken Commandment.* It deserves a place alongside the representative Japanese novels that are already well known in the West, such as Kawabata's *Snow Country,* Natsume Soseki's *Kokoro,* Tanizaki's *The Makioka Sisters,* Mishima's *The Golden Pavilion,* and Abe Kobo's *Woman of the Dunes.* Nor is it only a literary landmark. *The Broken Commandment* is as revealing as any Japanese novel of the psychology of a people who have changed much in the hectic century since they entered the modern world but remain even today largely conditioned by their unique history and culture.

For help in making the translation, I am indebted to the late Yanada Senji, Senior Lecturer in Japanese at the School of Oriental and African Studies, London, and to my wife, Sonoko Strong. In this introduction I have drawn freely upon critical and biographical studies by a number of Japanese scholars and critics, in particular Yoshida Seiichi, Hirano Ken, Ito Shinkichi, Senuma Shigeki, and Shibukawa Gyo. For permission to quote from *Japan's Invisible Race,* I am most grateful to Professors De Vos and Wagatsuma and to the University of California Press.

KENNETH STRONG

London, 1972

Note on pronunciation: Consonants in Japanese are pronounced approximately as in English, except that *g* is always hard, as in Gregory. Full value is given to double consonants. Vowels are pronounced as in Italian. Also as in Italian, the final *e* is always sounded. Thus the name Ginnosuke is pronounced Gin-no-su-keh.

# THE BROKEN COMMANDMENT

# Chapter 1

## 1

Rengeji temple took in boarders. The room Segawa Ushimatsu arranged to move into, after his sudden decision to change his lodgings, was a corner room upstairs in the priest's house, adjoining the temple. Rengeji was a venerable building, one of the twenty or more temples in the town of Iiyama in the mountainous region of Shinshu. It belonged to the True Pure Land sect. From the upstairs windows of the house, through the branches of the tall gingko tree, you could look out over a substantial part of the town. Not surprisingly, Buddhism having flourished here more than in any other part of Shinshu, the sight was like the past itself unfolding before your eyes—everything old, and everything, from the shingle tiles of the queer, squat northern houses and their wide downsweeping eaves protecting them against the snow to the soaring temple roofs and the topmost branches of the trees that showed themselves here and there above the mass of humbler buildings, seeming wrapped in a faint mist of incense. If anything in the panorama had a modern air, it was the white-painted building of the primary school where Segawa Ushimatsu taught.

A particularly disagreeable occurrence at his present lodgings had made him decide on the move. Certainly nobody would take this room at the temple if it were not so cheap. The paper that had been stuck over the walls was brown with dirt and age; there was no furniture or decoration, apart from an ancient *hibachi*[1] and a paper-mounted scroll hanging in the alcove. A priest's cell, in fact, solitary

[1] The charcoal-burning brazier that provides the only heating in the traditional Japanese house. It is usually round in shape and is made of wood, metal, or glazed earthenware.

and apart from the world. According as well as it did with his present lowly position as a primary school teacher, the room gave Ushimatsu a strangely cheerless, forlorn feeling.

This is what had happened at his present lodgings. A couple of weeks before, a rich man from the outlying district of Shimotakai—Ohinata was his name—had been staying there while waiting to enter Iiyama Hospital. It was not long before the hospital admitted him. The extra services he could so well afford—a special private room, a nurse to help steady him in his walks up and down the corridor—inevitably attracted attention, and soon some jealous tongue, nobody knew whose, began to put it about that the man was an eta, an outcast. The word spread instantly all over the hospital, and every patient was up in arms. Angry threats confronted the hospital director: "Turn him out—at once! If you don't, we'll go ourselves, the lot of us!" No amount of money can overcome prejudice of this kind. One evening soon after, taking advantage of the dusk, Ohinata had himself carried out of the hospital in a chair; he was taken straight back to the lodging house, where the doctor came to see him every day. But now it was the turn of the other lodgers to object. When Ushimatsu came home one afternoon, tired after his day's teaching, the place was in an uproar, with everyone clamouring for the landlady and complaining openly that Ohinata was "unclean. . . ." *Unclean!* The meaningless gibe infuriated Ushimatsu. Pitying—though only to himself—the unfortunate Ohinata and deploring the senseless inhumanity with which he was being treated, Ushimatsu dwelt long on the tragic fate of this outcast people, the eta. For he himself was one of them.

Anyone could see that Ushimatsu was a typical product of northern Shinshu, a well-built young man who had grown up among the craggy hills of Chiisagata. At twenty-two he had graduated with honours and a teacher's certificate from the teachers' college in Nagano. Thus thrust into the world, he had come straight to Iiyama. Now, two years later, he was known in the town as a devoted young teacher. That in reality he was an eta, a "new commoner," as the official phrase had it, no one had any idea.

"When will you be moving in, then?" asked the priest's wife as she entered the room. She stood before him, a woman of fifty or so in a brown *haori* coat, a rosary in her thin, pale hands. This nun, for such in a sense she was, though she was married and had never taken the tonsure, was a woman of some education, by the old standards at least, and to judge from the manner of her speech was not unacquainted with city life. A kindly nature showed itself in her expression. Murmuring half-audible *nenbutsu,*[2] she waited for him to reply.

Ushimatsu thought for a moment. Tomorrow, or even this evening, he wanted to say; but he could not afford the move yet. All he had at the moment was forty sen, and that certainly would not be enough—there was the rent to pay at the other place as well. No, he would have to wait another day, till his salary was due.

"I'll move in the day after tomorrow, in the afternoon."

"The day after tomorrow?" She stared at him, surprised.

"Is there any reason I shouldn't come then?" asked Ushimatsu.

"No, but that'll be the twenty-eighth, won't it? I thought you'd wait till the end of the month."

"That would be the usual thing, I suppose. I made up my mind rather suddenly, that's all," Ushimatsu said shortly, and changed the subject. He was still in a turmoil over what had happened at the lodging house, and was frightened of possible questions about it. It was his invariable habit, in conversation, to avoid any reference to the eta.

"Namu Amida Butsu . . . Namu Amida Butsu. . . ." The priest's wife was at her nenbutsu again. She showed no wish to probe any further.

## 2

It was five o'clock when he left Rengeji. He had gone to the temple straight from school and so was still in his

[2] An invocation, or prayer, much used in True Pure Land Buddhism. It consists of the three words "Namu Amida Butsu," sometimes translated as "Homage to Amida Buddha."

shabby Western suit, soiled with chalk and dust, and Japanese clogs, with a bundle of books and notebooks wrapped in a *furoshiki*[3] under one arm and his lunchbox in his other hand. Feeling rather ashamed of his appearance—as many workers do in a mixed crowd—he made his way back to his lodgings in Takajo Street. The eaves of the shops and houses were glistening in the sunlight that followed an autumn shower. Many people were out on the wet streets; some stood still and stared at Ushimatsu as he passed; others glanced at him contemptuously, as if to say, "And what might *that* be—oh, a teacher, is it?" Among them, perhaps, were parents of children in his own class. . . . Humiliated, angry, and suddenly despondent, Ushimatsu quickened his pace.

The bookshop in Honmachi Street had only opened a few days before. Outside, a big poster gave a list, in thick brushstrokes, of "Books just in from Tokyo." One title caught Ushimatsu's eye—a book he had been eagerly awaiting since seeing it advertised in the paper: Inoko Rentaro's *Confessions,* with the price listed against it. He stopped. Inoko Rentaro—the mere name was enough to excite him. Two or three young men were standing in the front of the shop browsing through magazines. Ushimatsu walked up and down several times, furtively clinking the coins in the pocket of his faded trousers—forty sen: enough for the book, anyway. But if he bought it now, he'd have nothing for tomorrow; and what about arranging for the move? Restraining himself, he started on his way again, but a moment later turned back and walked into the shop. He picked up *Confessions.* The book smelt slightly; it was printed on coarse foreign-style paper, between yellow covers. The choice of such a simple format, aimed at making the contents accessible even to the poor, gave a good idea of the kind of book it was. In our world today, in which so many young men read to learn, and at Ushimatsu's age, when the appetite for study is still insatiable, how could he deny himself the joy of reading, of learning? For our

[3] A large square piece of cloth, widely used in Japan for wrapping small objects to be carried by hand.

young men, indeed, knowledge is as food to the starving. Ushimatsu took out his forty sen and bought the book he had so wanted. All the money he had was gone; but what was material need, compared to his spiritual hunger?

Clasping his copy of *Confessions*—his excitement oddly deflated now that he had bought it—Ushimatsu was hurrying back to his lodgings when he ran into two of his school colleagues. One of them, Tsuchiya Ginnosuke, had been a classmate of his at college; the other was a young probationary teacher. He could see from their leisurely air that they were just out for a stroll.

"Segawa! Late, aren't you?" Ginnosuke called out as they drew near, tap-tapping with his fashionable stick. An open-hearted, sympathetic fellow, Ginnosuke at once noticed Ushimatsu's expression. In place of the usual cheerful sparkle a strange, unnameable anxiety clouded the deep, clear eyes. Maybe he's not well, Ginnosuke thought.

Ushimatsu told him how he had been looking for a new room.

"A new room? You're a great one for changing your lodgings—it was only the other day you moved in where you are now, wasn't it?" Ginnosuke spoke without malice; his smile was sincere. Just then he noticed the book Ushimatsu was holding.

"Show me!" he said, tucking his stick under his arm.

"This?" Ushimatsu gave it to him, smiling.

"Uh—*Confessions,* is it?" said the probationer, coming closer to Ginnosuke to get a sight of the book.

"You're still keen on Inoko, then." Ginnosuke looked at the yellow cover and glanced at the contents. "I remember now, I saw it mentioned in the paper. So this is it—not exactly showy, is it? With you, it's got beyond admiring his books—you worship the man himself." He laughed. "You're always talking about Inoko *sensei.*[4] In for another dose now, are we?"

"Don't be silly!" Ushimatsu laughed in turn, and took the book back.

[4] Literally, "teacher." A title of respect.

By now lights were coming on here and there as patches of evening mist settled over the town. After letting his friends know of his plan to move to Rengeji the day after next, Ushimatsu left them; but when he glanced back a moment later, Ginnosuke and the probationer were still standing on the street corner, gazing after him. Fifty yards farther on, and still the two had not moved, their figures hazy now in the dusk and the thin smoke drifting from evening fires.

## 3

The air vibrated with the boom of temple bells as Ushimatsu neared Takajo Street; it was time for the evening services. When he was a few paces from the lodging house, an abrupt warning was shouted to passersby—outside the gate, lanterns shone, and two bearers carried a covered chair into the dark street. It must be the rich eta trying to leave without being noticed, thought Ushimatsu sadly. He knew for certain that it was the eta when he recognized the rich man's attendant following the chair. Ohinata himself he had never seen, though they had been living in the same house; but the attendant, an eta like his master, going in and out with the bottles of medicine, had become a familiar figure. There he was now, very tall and the picture of faithful service, as with the skirts of his kimono tucked up into his sash and a protective eye on his master he gave directions to the chair bearers. Of low birth and status even for an eta, by the look of it, he passed by with an oddly cringing air and a slight bow, never dreaming that Ushimatsu was in reality an outcast like himself. The landlady was standing outside the gate calling goodbye. Inside, Ushimatsu could see, there was some sort of commotion; angry voices could be heard, their owners clearly meaning them to carry.

"Thank you, sir, thank you, and please take care of yourself!" said the landlady again, running up alongside the chair.

The occupant did not reply. In silence, Ushimatsu watched the chair being borne away.

"I told you so!" the boarders were saying to each other

triumphantly. When Ushimatsu, a little paler than usual, entered the house, most of them were still milling about in the long corridor that ran round the outside of the building, some fuming with self-righteous indignation, some venting their feelings by marching up and down noisily on the wooden floor, some ostentatiously tossing handfuls of salt out into the garden to purify it of the defilement caused by the eta's presence. The landlady had produced a pair of flintstones, from which she was attempting to strike a "cleansing fire."

Pity, fear, and a thousand other thoughts and feelings jostled violently in Ushimatsu. Driven from the hospital, driven from his lodging, cruelly humiliated—with what bitterness the man in the chair must have cursed his fate as he was carried out, silent, into the street. But Ohinata's destiny, inevitably, was that which all eta had to face sooner or later; and was not he himself an outcast, an eta? Miraculous, how he had managed to come safely all this way through years of study and of teaching, without fear, thinking and acting like any normal human being. . . . Out of such thoughts rose a picture of his father, who lived alone up there in the mountains, hermitlike, tending his cattle. Ushimatsu remembered the cowherd's hut at the foot of Mount Eboshi.

Muttering "Father, father," he walked to and fro across his room. Suddenly some words of his father's came back to him. When he left home for the very first time, his father, deeply concerned for his only son's future, had given him much advice. It was then that he had told him about their ancestors: how they were not descended, like the many groups of eta who lived along the Eastern Highway, from foreign immigrants or castaways from China, Korea, Russia, and the nameless islands of the Pacific, but from runaway samurai of many generations back; that however poor they might be, their family had committed no crime, done nothing dishonourable. One thing more he added: that the only way—the only hope—for any eta who wanted to raise himself in the world was to conceal the secret of his birth. "No matter who you meet, no matter what happens to you, never reveal it! Forget this commandment just once, in a moment of anger or misery, and from that moment the world will have rejected you forever." Such had been his father's teaching.

It was as simple as that. *Tell no one:* that was the whole commandment. At the time, so thrilled was he to be going away to study, Ushimatsu had hardly taken in his father's words; those were the days of dreams, when it was all too easy to forget the commandment. Then suddenly he had grown up, become aware of himself; it was like leaving the agreeable novelty of a neighbour's house for the half-forgotten discomfort of one's own. Now he saw for himself the need for secrecy.

## 4

For a while Ushimatsu lay motionless on the *tatami*[5] floor, thinking; but he was tired and soon fell asleep. When he woke, the oil lamp was diffusing its forlorn light, and his supper lay ready on the little table in the corner. He was still in his Western clothes. He had slept an hour or more, he supposed. Outside he could hear the rain. Sitting up, he pulled the table toward him, glancing as he did so at the cover of the book he had bought. He took the lid off the rice tub and sniffed: cold boarding-house rice, a mixture of different lodgers' leftovers. Ushimatsu sighed. He pushed the table away, lit his last cigarette, and opened *Confessions.*

Inoko's ideas, it was widely said, gave expression to the "new torment" being endured by the lowest class in Japanese society. Some people objected to what they called his extreme fondness for self-advertisement. True, he was incapable of writing about anything but himself: hence the peculiar sense of nervous tension running through all his work.

Yet nobody who had once read him could deny the appeal of his books, combining as they did a vigorous philosophy with the most delicate observation. Not content with unwearying study of the lives of the poor, of the workers, of the so-called "new commoners," so as to reveal

[5] Thick mats made of compressed straw. They are laid from wall to wall in a Japanese room, like a fitted carpet.

the springs of pure water among the murkiest strata of society, he depicted their condition from every possible angle, repeating over and over anything that might at first be difficult to accept, until he could be sure it had sunk deep into the reader's consciousness. His viewpoint was, strictly speaking, that of the psychologist rather than that of the philosopher or economist. As for his style—his ideas stood out like a row of boulders, the more forceful for their stark, unambiguous clarity.

But these were not the only reasons why Ushimatsu admired Inoko's writings. The fact that this fighter for the oppressed had been born an eta moved him deeply—secretly, indeed, he idolized him as a rare fellow outcast who had pioneered a way to rise above their humiliating destiny. Inoko had inspired him to resent fiercely the irrational contempt in which all eta, human beings like anyone else, were held by society. So it was that Ushimatsu bought every book of Inoko's, read every article of his that appeared in the journals. The more he read, the more he felt himself drawn irresistibly toward a new world. His true self-awakening as an eta had begun.

This new book began with the words "I am an outcast." A vivid account followed of the ignorance and squalor to which the eta had been reduced, with portraits of many fine eta men and women whom society had discarded merely because of their eta origin, and bittersweet recollections of the writer's own struggle—from the frustration of his early search for spiritual liberation, and tortured doubts in the face of society's contradictions, to his finding at last of new life, like a long night giving way to the dawn sky.

New life—for Inoko, it had grown out of a chance catastrophe. The secret of his eta birth (he was of an old outcast family from Takato, in southern Shinshu) had been disclosed by a couple of students at Nagano Teachers' College, where he was teaching philosophy at the time; it was before Ushimatsu, who came from the same district as he did, entered the college. One of the teachers an outcast . . . shock alternated with doubt as the rumour spread. Many refused to believe it, though for differing reasons: a man of such character, they said—or a man of such looks, or such brains and education, according to the speaker—just *couldn't* be an eta. But a few of his colleagues, jealous of his popularity, clamoured for his expulsion. If there were no racial[6] prejudice, there would have been no massacre of the Jews at Kishinev, no talk in the West of a "yellow peril." In a world where reason bows to force, who would stand up and declare it was wrong to expel an eta? When Inoko finally admitted his origin and took his leave of the many friends he had made among his colleagues, not one showed the smallest sign of sympathy. With his departure from the college, Inoko abandoned "learning for learning's sake."

All this was described in detail in *Confessions.* Several times Ushimatsu put down the book and shut his eyes, overcome with sympathy. As he went on, it grew more difficult to read. Sympathy is a curious thing: it has the paradoxical effect sometimes of making it harder to grasp the real thoughts and feelings of its object. Also Inoko's writing was of the kind that drives you to think, rather than just to read on simply for the pleasure of the style or story. Eventually Ushimatsu found himself reading with his thoughts concentrated not on Inoko's narrative, but on himself.

That his own life had been so peaceful so far he owed to the surroundings in which he had grown up. He was born in Mukai, an eta settlement in the town of Komoro, into a family that provided the hereditary "headman" of a clan of some forty eta households scattered among the uplands of Kita-Sakuma. Until the Restoration his ancestors had served for generations as prison warders and policemen of the lowest grade. His father, besides being exempted from tax in return for overseeing the clan, received a small stipend of rice; and being the man he was, he made sure of sending Ushimatsu to primary school even when he was forced by increasing poverty to move out to Chiisagata. When Ushimatsu started to attend the village school at Nezu, he

[6] Shimazaki's indiscriminate use of the terms "race" and "class" in relation to the eta is perhaps explained by his classifying them, as did Ushimatsu's father, into the descendants of (a) foreign castaways and (b) runaway samurai. See Introduction, p. x.

was just an ordinary boy—it never occurred to anyone that this attractive little fellow might be an eta child.

Finally his father settled in the hamlet of Himekozawa, his uncle and aunt moving in with them. Not a soul in the district knew them, nor was there any need for them to speak of their history, so that in time they grew used to the new environment, Ushimatsu being the first to forget the old days. When the time came for him to go to Nagano for further education, as a scholarship student at government expense, any talk of their former life seemed to him to have to do only with a distant past, with generations he had never known.

But now old memories had revived. The terror he had known as a boy of seven or eight, when he often was jeered at and stoned by other children, awoke within him once more. Dimly he recalled even earlier days at Komoro; glimpses too of his mother, who had died before they moved. *I am an eta*—what turmoil these few words stirred in Ushimatsu's young mind. . . . Reading his hero's *Confessions,* instead of admiration he felt only bitter pain.

# Chapter 2

## 1

Payday being on the twenty-eighth of the month, on that day the faces of the school staff were noticeably more cheerful than usual. The moment the big bell rang for the end of the last lesson, all the teachers hastily got their books together and left their classrooms. Clamour in the corridors, a surging wave of boisterous children swinging empty lunchboxes and sandal bags, throwing haversacks over shoulders, laughing and shouting as they started for home. Finishing his lesson with the fourth-year class of the upper school, Ushimatsu pushed his way through the two-way flood to the staff room.

The principal was in the visitors' room. He had been moved to Iiyama only recently, simultaneously with the appointment of a new District Inspector of Schools, and was therefore newer to the school than Ushimatsu and Ginnosuke, who were thus a potential thorn in his flesh—like the younger in-laws whose carping a wife may have to face in her husband's family. Today the new inspector, along with three members of the town council, had been visiting the school. During his short tour of the classes, what the inspector had to say to the principal mainly concerned educational topics—proper surveillance of the teachers, modifications in the daily lesson plans, repairs to blackboards, desks, and chairs, improved hygiene to deal with the widespread incidence of trachoma among the pupils. Now that the inspection itself was over, the conversation widened. White eddies of tobacco smoke slowly filled the room. A janitor bustled in and out, and tea was evidently on the way.

Education, according to the principal, meant rules. To him, the inspector's directives were the commands of a superior officer—besides which, he himself had always believed in military-style discipline for children, an attitude that was reflected in the daily life and activities of his school. "Like clockwork" was his watchword, the supreme precept he expounded to the pupils, the spirit behind every instruction he gave to his staff. The airy doctrines so often on the lips of teachers too young to know the real world he dismissed as mere useless tinsel, irrelevant to the serious business of life. Insistence on these principles had brought success, at least in his own estimation, for the powers that be had awarded him a gold medal inscribed *In recognition of meritorious service*. This medal, token of his life's achievement, stood now upon the table in the visitors' room, the eyes of the company focussed on its golden glitter. One of the councillors was admiring the purity of the gold, another calculating its weight, the third working out its cost. Title, 18 carat; diameter, 1 inch; weight, nearly 3 ounces, was the final joint estimate. The letter of commendation that went with the medal praised the principal's great contribution to education in the prefecture, "in recognition of which, in accordance with the terms of the Education Endowment Ordinance, we hereby award him a gold commemorative medal."

"Really, Principal, this award honours not only you but everybody concerned with education in the district," said one of the councillors, a white-bearded old gentlemen, very politely.

Another, who sported gold-rimmed spectacles, followed at once with, "Some of us would like to give a little party to mark the award. Would you honour us with your presence this evening at the Miuraya, Principal? We very much hope, of course, that the inspector will come too—"

"I'm obliged to you for thinking of it," said the principal, rising from his seat and bowing. "An award like this is the highest honour an educator can wish for, and I am very pleased of course, little though I have done to deserve it. One is painfully aware, indeed, of one's unworthiness—"

"Don't say that, Principal. It reflects on us, when we've come to ask you to a party to celebrate," put in the third councillor, a thin, bony fellow, rubbing his hands as he spoke.

"It won't be a big enough feast for you to feel you ought to refuse," pleaded white-beard.

The principal's eyes sparkled with pleasure. Trying unsuccessfully to conceal his feelings, he fidgeted for a moment, alternately sticking out his chest and working his shoulders up and down, then turned to the inspector.

"Will you be able to go?"

The inspector smiled magnanimously. "Since they are so kind as to invite us, it would hardly be polite to refuse."

"Just so, precisely. Well then, I shall hope to see you all this evening, gentlemen, and will keep my proper thanks till then." The principal bowed. "My regards to your colleagues, if you please."

Anyone not familiar with how things work in the country will find it difficult, I daresay, to understand fully the principal's position. The first essential for anyone who goes into a country district to teach is exactly the kind of canny, this-worldly circumspection practised by this principal. A man who eschews all vulgarity, preferring to let his mind dwell forever on the lofty visions he contemplated at college, will not last a single day as a country headmaster. A true principal must cultivate the influential families of the district, hastening to offer them his congratulations or his condolences as occasion may demand; at public gatherings he must take his place with the Shinto and Buddhist priests; he must learn to take the local wine, and to speak the local dialect without sounding too ridiculous—and by the time he has qualified in all these respects, he will inevitably have forgotten his academic ideals and adapted himself to the ill-educated yokels among whom he moves. A "clever educator" usually means one who has built up a strong position for himself by collusion with the town councillors or other local bigwigs.

The three councillors took their hats, and the principal went out to see them off.

"Please be sure to bring the inspector with you, Principal. You'll come straight from school, won't you?"

"Very kind of you. Thank you, gentlemen." The principal bowed.

## 2

"Janitor!" the principal shouted down the corridor.

The pupils had all gone home by now. The classroom windows were shut; even the tennis court on the playground was deserted. Only an occasional burst of laughter from the staff room, and fragments of a melancholy tune played on a harmonium in an upstairs classroom, disturbed the silence.

The janitor came padding up in his straw sandals. "Did you want something, sir?"

"Mm. It's after hours, but I'd like you to go down to the town office again if you would, and hurry them up—bring the money back with you as soon as it's ready. Everyone's waiting."

This order given, the principal went back into the visitors' room. The inspector, puffing at a cigar, was deep in the newspaper. With a word of apology for his momentary absence, the principal drew his chair over to where the inspector was sitting.

"Look at this," said the inspector affably, holding up the paper. "There's a detailed report of the award here. You're a model educationist, it says. It gives the letter of commendation too, the whole text. And your life history into the bargain."

"It's gone down quite well, I must say," the principal said complacently. "People talk about it wherever I go. The most unlikely folk know all about it and go out of their way to congratulate me."

"Splendid."

"It's all thanks to you, of course—"

"No need to be ceremonious," the inspector cut him short. "We help each other, don't we?" He laughed. "It's an honour for our party, though, this award, and I can guess what it means to you."

"Katsuno's very happy about it too."

"My nephew? I know he is. He wrote me all about it, quite a long letter. I felt I could see him smiling there in front of me, he was so full of the good news. He's devoted to you, you know."

Katsuno Bunpei, the inspector's nephew, had only recently been appointed to the school after passing the exams for his teacher's certificate. Being fairly new to the school himself, the principal made much of Bunpei, so as to get him on his side. As far as length of service went, Ushimatsu was now the senior teacher, and he and Ginnosuke, the other young graduate from Nagano Teachers' College, were more popular with the pupils than the principal himself, whose display of favouritism to Bunpei did nothing to alter their position in this respect.

"What a contrast with Segawa," said the principal, lowering his voice.

"Segawa?" The inspector frowned.

"Let me explain. It's not as though the award had been given to a complete stranger, someone he'd never met before—you'd think even Segawa would be pleased for my sake, wouldn't you? Not a bit of it. He says—mind you, I haven't heard him say it myself; obviously he couldn't say this sort of thing to me face to face, anyway—it's a big mistake, he says, for a teacher who's been commended or given a medal to think he's done something marvellous, as if he's a hero or something. A medal's only a medal, perhaps;

worthless from his point of view, I daresay. But it's a sign, a token: what makes me pleased and grateful is not the bit of gold but what it stands for." He laughed. "Aren't I right, Inspector?"

The inspector sighed. "So he's at it again. Where does he get those ideas of his?"

"Times change. Maybe you and I are a bit out of date. It doesn't follow that our modern young friends are always in the right, though." The principal smiled derisively. "What's certain is that it's going to make things awkward for me if Segawa and Tsuchiya carry on the way they've been doing up till now. I won't be able to run the school as it should be run if the teachers aren't united. I'd be much happier, I must say, if I had Katsuno as the senior assistant instead of Segawa."

"If that's how you feel, we can probably find ways of putting things right," said the inspector with a meaning look.

"How, for instance?"

"We could transfer him, and put in somebody else—somebody you preferred—in his place. There are other possibilities of course—"

"Yes, but even a transfer won't be easy without some excuse. He's so popular with the pupils, and if we don't watch our step—"

"Of course. We can hardly tell him point-blank he's got to go, when he's done nothing wrong. If we're too subtle, on the other hand, we'll have people suspecting something, and we don't want that." The inspector changed his tone. "It's not for me to speak highly of my nephew, but he'll be a great help to you, I'm sure. Segawa's no better than he is. What is it that's so special about Segawa, anyway? Why do the children make such a hero of him? It doesn't make sense to me. Sneering at other people's honours, indeed! What *does* a man like Segawa respect, if that's his attitude?"

"Inoko Rentaro and his ideas, for a start."

"Inoko—the eta?" said the inspector with a grimace.

The principal sighed. "It's frightening to think of the young people reading books like his. Unhealthy, they are, unhealthy! So many of the new books coming out are corrupting. That's why we have this crop of abnormality, young men behaving like madmen. . . . We can't hope to understand the way the young think nowadays."

# 3

There was a knock on the door of the visitors' room. Abruptly the two men fell silent. Another knock.

"Come in!" the principal called out, getting up from his chair. The inspector stared after him as he went to open the door. It would be a messenger, he supposed, from the councillors who were giving the party. But it was an elderly teacher who came in, followed by Ushimatsu. The principal and the inspector glanced at each other.

"You're engaged, sir?" asked Ushimatsu.

The principal smiled. "Nothing special. We were just talking of you, as it happens."

"Mr. Kazama here wishes to see the inspector, sir. He has a request he'd like to make to him in person." Gently Ushimatsu pushed his colleague forward.

Kazama Keinoshin was an old teacher—old enough to be Ushimatsu's father—whom the changing times had long ago left behind. Slowly, nervously, in a formal haori coat of black cotton over a soiled kimono and cheap *hakama* skirt, he shuffled up to where the principal was sitting. Declining years make a man timid, and if the inspector were to show himself even a little unsympathetic, he would shut up like a clam.

"You've some business with me, you say?" The inspector's tone was intimidating. Keinoshin hesitated, fidgeting, till the inspector could contain his irritation no longer and began pulling out his watch and tapping the floor with his shoes.

"What is it? How can I know what's on your mind if you don't tell me?" Impatient, the inspector stood up.

Falteringly, Keinoshin began. "There's something I wanted to ask—"

"Well?"

Silence filled the room again. Ushimatsu felt a surge of pity for old Keinoshin as he stood there, head bowed, trembling slightly, unable to get the words out.

The inspector was clearly not going to wait much longer.

"I'm a busy man. If you have anything to say, have the goodness to say it without wasting any more of my time."

Ushimatsu couldn't bear it. "You don't need to feel such constraint, Mr. Kazama. . . . It was something to do with your retirement, wasn't it?" After a moment he turned to the inspector. "May I ask you on his behalf, then? When a teacher retires for the reasons for which Mr. Kazama is retiring, is it possible for him to be considered for a pension?"

"Certainly not," said the inspector coldly. "Look at the regulations under the Primary Schools Law. You'll find them clear enough."

"I know what the regulations say, but—"

"How can anything be done that isn't provided for in the regulations? If a man has to give up working because he's in poor health and hasn't got the strength to do the job properly, I have no authority to make him stay on, and a teacher qualifies for a pension only if he's worked a full fifteen years. Mr. Kazama's still six months short."

"Couldn't you help him even so? Half a year can't make much difference."

"If we once started making exceptions there'd be no end to them. Mr. Kazama has to retire 'for personal reasons,' he says, but everybody can think up 'personal reasons'—it wouldn't be only him. No, you'd best forget about the pension, Mr. Kazama, and make the most of your retirement to get well again."

After this rebuff there was nothing more Ushimatsu could do. Sadly, he turned back to Keinoshin. "Perhaps you should put your case yourself, Mr. Kazama?"

"No. After what the inspector has said there'd be no point in speaking on my own. I suppose I've nothing to do but forget about the pension, sir, like you said."

Just then the janitor arrived from the town office with a heavy-looking parcel in a cloth wrapper. The inspector took his hat and was shown out by the principal.

# 4

The teachers were assembled in the staff room. It was Saturday, and in the eyes of these men and women waiting to receive their salaries, a more pleasurable day even than the Sunday that would follow it. Most of them, exhausted by the daily round of long hours of teaching in big classes, felt little interest in education. Some even loathed the children. The probationary teacher, the youngest of all, who had just passed his exam at the end of the special course in reading, writing, and arithmetic, and as yet had barely learned to smoke, was cheerful enough, for he had a long vista ahead of him; but the old ones, all but superannuated, sunk in reminiscence or in envy of their juniors, with no trace of dignity save in their wispy beards, would have struck even an ignorant stranger as pathetic. Some waited with no thought but to convert into saké the reward of their month-long labours.

Ushimatsu was starting back to the staff room with Keinoshin when the janitor stopped them in the corridor.

"Mr. Kazama, the man from the Sasaya's here to see you. He's been waiting quite a while."

"What's that—the Sasaya, you said?" He smiled ruefully.

The Sasaya was a cheap eating house and saké shop on the outskirts of Iiyama that sold the local brew, warmed up, to the peasants—and provided Keinoshin, as Ushimatsu had long known, with a refuge where he could forget the cares of the floating world. From Keinoshin's forlorn expression, Ushimatsu guessed that the man must have chosen payday to come and dun the old teacher for his drinking debts.

"He didn't need to come to the school, though," muttered Keinoshin. "All right—tell him to wait," he said to the janitor and hurried off with Ushimatsu to the staff room.

The late October sunlight lit up the big room, criss-crossed with patterns of tobacco smoke. One knot of teachers stood below the notice board, another by the timetable; most were arguing noisily. Ushimatsu stopped in the doorway and glanced round the room. Katsuno Bunpei, he noticed—the inspector's nephew—was leaning against the grey wall talking to Ginnosuke. Bunpei, with his brand-new Western-style suit and sober tie, everything about him just so, smart and prepossessing: his beautifully groomed black hair, the glow of youth in his cheeks, his quick, probing, restless eyes. What a contrast with the burly Ginnosuke, with his close-cropped hair, red cheeks, and sleeves nonchalantly rolled up, his talk punctuated with easy laughter. The eyes of the women teachers were fastened on Bunpei.

Ushimatsu did not envy Bunpei his smart appearance. What did worry him was that this new teacher came from the same district as himself. Knowing Komoro and its surroundings as well as he clearly did, he would almost certainly have heard the name Segawa, and supposing—it was perfectly possible, the wide world unhappily being smaller than it seemed—he were to come across someone who knew that the head of the clan was an eta . . . but would anyone be likely to speak of it after all these years they had lived away from Komoro, up in the mountains? Just supposing the worst came to the worst and he did hear it, Bunpei wasn't the one to let a piece of information like that go to waste. . . . With so much ground for suspicion, he must be on his guard against Bunpei. A dozen warning visions took shape before Ushimatsu's anxious eyes.

Soon the principal finished checking the money the janitor had brought. It was already divided up; Ushimatsu helped the principal distribute it, setting out each teacher's October salary on his or her desk.

"Tsuchiya—a present for you!" He lined up several piles of 50-sen coppers, already sealed, on Ginnosuke's desk, then a packet of silver and some notes.

"That's a mint of coppers you're giving me!" Ginnosuke laughed. "I won't be able to lift 'em at this rate. By the way, it's today you're moving, isn't it?"

Ushimatsu smiled but made no reply. Bunpei took up Ginnosuke's question. "So you're moving, are you?"

"Segawa's going vegetarian[1] from tonight, you know!"

Hiding his embarrassment with a laugh, Ushimatsu hurried over to his own desk. Monthly repetition could not

[1] That is, is moving to a temple, where the diet would be vegetarian.

dampen the elation in every teacher's face as he received his salary. One shook his bag of silver; another wrapped his pay in his furoshiki and dangled it to feel the weight; one woman smiled to herself as she ran her hand over the pocket in her hakama skirt where she had put her money for safety.

Suddenly the principal got up importantly from his chair. The buzz of conversation round the room stopped. Clearing his throat, the principal reported in formal, machinelike tones the retirement of Mr. Kazama. On November the third, the Emperor's birthday, after the conclusion of the ceremonies proper to the day, he proposed to hold a tea party in honour of their colleague and in recognition of his years of devoted service. A chorus of approving voices from the teachers greeted this announcement. Keinoshin stood very straight and bowed, then sat down again with a dejected air.

The teachers began to get ready to go home. While many of them crowded round Keinoshin with words of sympathy or encouragement, Ushimatsu slipped out. Some moments later, though Ginnosuke looked everywhere for his friend—the corridor, the visitors' room, the janitor's room, the porch—he was nowhere to be found.

## 5

Ushimatsu walked quickly home to his lodging, more cheerful now that he had been paid for the month. Yesterday had been a gloomy day indeed; he had gone without his daily trip to the public bath, bought no cigarettes, thought of nothing all day but the move to Rengeji. Who can smile when his pocket is empty? The joy of lighting his cigarette now, when he had paid every sen of his rent and was ready to leave the moment the carter came, was inexpressible.

He wanted the move to attract as little attention as possible. What would his landlady think, though, of his bolting so suddenly? Suppose she decided there was some connection between him and Ohinata and that he was refusing to stay on because of the way Ohinata had been forced to leave? What could he have said if she had cross-examined him about his reasons for moving—as she might well have done, seeing that she took offence so easily? He couldn't help feeling guilty, since he was moving without any obvious reason; a slip of the tongue on his part, and he would be in a worse state than if he had never thought of moving at all. But no: personal reasons, he had said, and that was enough, surely. Here he was suspecting her and imagining the worst, but she was used to seeing lodgers come and go and had been less put out than he had feared when he told her.

While he was still ruminating, the carter arrived. They got all his baggage—book box, desk, wicker trunk, and bedding roll—onto the small handcart. As he walked out of the gate, lamp in hand, the landlady said goodbye.

When he had gone two or three hundred yards down the street, following the carter, Ushimatsu glanced back toward the lodging house and gave a deep sigh of relief. The road was bad, the carter slow. Ushimatsu walked on in silence, thinking of how dramatically his life had changed and brooding sadly on the destiny he had inherited. Loneliness, despair, the absurdity of it all; an indescribable welter of sensations assailed him, and with them a flood of memories, stirring unfathomable depths. It was a dreary evening, with the flavour already of November; the damp autumn air lay over the houses like thin smoke. Here and there yellowing leaves from the roadside willows drifted idly to the ground.

On the way they ran into a small gang of boys parading through the streets with a big paper flag. They were playing at bands, marching in time to a merry cacophony from drum and flute and singing for all they were worth. Ushimatsu recognized them: they were boys from the lower school. Following behind them, and singing no less loudly, was a cheerful, heedless drunk. The shambling step gave him away at once—it was Keinoshin.

"Hey, Segawa—take a look at my band!" Keinoshin pointed to the boys in front of him, who responded with a shout of laughter to their teacher's pathetic show of dignity. A whiff of saké-laden breath came Ushimatsu's way.

"Ready, are you?" Keinoshin raised both hands like an orchestra conductor. "Now listen, everyone. Up till today I was your teacher. From tomorrow I won't be your teacher anymore. I'll be your conductor instead—see? A-ha-ha-a. . . ." His laugh dissolved in hot tears.

With another shout, the guileless musicians resumed their march. Keinoshin stood gazing after them for a while. Then he came and joined Ushimatsu.

"Oh well, I'll walk with you to the corner there." He was trembling. "What are you doing with a lantern, Segawa, when it's hardly dark yet?"

"Me?" Ushimatsu smiled. "I'm moving house."

"Moving, are you? Where to?"

"Rengeji."

Keinoshin lapsed into silence. The two walked on together, each wrapped in his separate thoughts.

"Ah," Keinoshin began again, "I envy you, Segawa. You're still young, you see. 'Bright prospects for a brilliant career,' as the saying goes—that means you youngsters. I'd like to be young again, just once. . . . A man's finished when he's old, like me."

## 6

The carter was as slow as ever. Ushimatsu and Keinoshin sauntered on, still talking. As they were nearing a crossroads, the carter stopped to wipe the sweat from his forehead and drink in the cold air. A watery grey mist veiled the sky; only the western horizon gleamed still with a faint yellow streak of light. The streets were rapidly darkening. One house was already lit up, though it was hardly time for it yet. The name Miuraya could clearly be made out on the signboard under the eaves.

The sound of conviviality emanating from an upstairs room intensified the cheerless, lonely mood of the two passersby in the street below. The revelry was evidently at its height. A geisha was dancing, to judge by the shadows moving on the paper windows; several samisen twanged in unison, their querulous melody punctuated intermittently by spirited drumbeats. The girl whose voice they caught now and then rising above the music would be one of the performers. A geisha, holding her skirt clear of the muddy street, hurried past them into the Miuraya, followed by an attendant carrying her samisen; she too must have been summoned to the party upstairs. They could easily distinguish the laughing voices, among them those of the principal and the inspector, made oblivious of time—or so it sounded—by much food and drink.

"Cheerful, aren't they, Segawa?" said Keinoshin in a low voice. "Big party, by the sound of it. What's on tonight, I wonder."

"Don't you know?" Ushimatsu was astonished.

"No, I never know anything."

"It's a party for the principal—because of his getting that medal."

"Mm, so that's what it is."

Clapping followed the end of a samisen piece. Cups of saké were being exchanged, it seemed. As the voice of a young servant girl called on the geisha to "keep the gentlemen's cups filled," Ushimatsu and Keinoshin turned into a side street, and the sounds of revelry faded.

While they were talking, the carter had gone on ahead. Keinoshin alternately sighed, hummed, and broke now and then into a despairing, hysterical laugh. When he started chanting, "The floating world is like a dream," in a low voice, making up his own tune as he went along, Ushimatsu too found himself sinking into a strangely despairing mood.

"Voice wants tuning." Keinoshin sighed again. "The saké's worn off too, worse luck." He groaned like an animal as he walked on.

"Where are you going, Mr. Kazama?" Ushimatsu asked out of pity.

"Me? Going to see you as far as Rengeji—that's where I'm going."

"Rengeji—why?"

"You wouldn't understand why. No, I'm not explaining now, either. We've known each other a long time, you and I, but it's only the last week or two we've begun to be friends. Someday I'd like to have a nice long talk with you, Segawa."

Keinoshin left him abruptly the moment they reached the great gate of Rengeji. The priest's wife came out to welcome Ushimatsu. The carter had already come and gone, she told him, and Shota, the temple servant, had taken his belongings up to his room.

To Ushimatsu, new as he was to temple life, there was something bizarre about the mingling of the smell of fish grilling in the kitchen with the smoke of temple incense.[2] A young acolyte passed Ushimatsu's door on his way to the temple hall, perhaps on his way to lay some offering on the altar. The sliding windows had been freshly repapered, which made the room look much pleasanter than when he had seen it before; and soon the bath would be ready, their "health bath," as they called it, with an infusion of dried radish leaves. As he sat at the brand-new table inhaling the delicious fragrance of the bowl of beancurd soup before him, Ushimatsu discovered an unexpected homelike warmth within these ancient walls, which at first had seemed so monastically austere.

# Chapter 3

## 1

It was unlikely that Ginnosuke would ever find out the secret of Ushimatsu's birth. At the teachers' college in Nagano they had been the closest of friends, united by the intimacy of dormitory life and endless talk together—Ushimatsu's discourses on history, his favourite subject, or on the beauties of the grey landscape of Chiisagata, being matched by Ginnosuke's on his native village on the shore of Lake Suwa and on the fascinations of plant collecting. For both, these memories they shared were as fresh as ever. Indeed, whenever Ginnosuke thought of Ushimatsu he could not help wondering at the changes time had worked in his friend compared with what he had been in the old days, when time and time again, side by side in the dining

[2] Ushimatsu evidently had not realized that not all Buddhist priests are necessarily vegetarian, particularly in the tolerant True Pure Land sect.

hall, they had sniffed together the same crude brew of rice and barley. That air of melancholy: if you wanted proof that he had lost all his old cheerful disposition, it was there in his eyes, in the way he walked, in his tone of voice. But why? Why should he have withdrawn so deeply into himself? Ginnosuke was puzzled. There must be some reason, and he longed to help his friend.

The day after Ushimatsu had moved being Sunday, in the afternoon Ginnosuke went to call on him. On the way he met Bunpei. Together they climbed the mossy stone steps inside the temple gate. To their right were the priests' quarters, to their left the bell tower, and straight ahead, at the end of a path along which a few late autumn flowers still bloomed, the temple hall. Between the bell tower and the temple hall stood a small hexagonal building—a sutra library, its steep tiled roof, white walls, and pillars in the Chinese style testifying at once to the glory and to the decline of a former age. Under the yellowing gingko tree Shota, the temple servant, was bent over his broom, absorbed in his task of sweeping fallen leaves.

"Mr. Segawa, please?" Ginnosuke asked. Shota bowed very low. He dropped his broom and hurried off, barefoot as he was, to the priest's house to see if Segawa was in.

But Ushimatsu was already calling out to them from his window, through the upper branches of the gingko tree. "Come on up!"

## 2

Ginnosuke and Bunpei followed Ushimatsu up the dark stairway to his room. The autumn sunlight seeping into the room through the gingko leaves turned everything yellow—the faded wallpaper, the scroll hanging in the alcove, and the rows of books and magazines below it. With the cold air from the open window an agreeable freshness flowed into the little room with its archaic, cell-like atmosphere.

The copy of *Confessions,* open but turned face downward on his desk, caught Ushimatsu's eye. Pushing it hastily to one side, as if anxious they should not notice it, he offered them a white blanket to sit on in place of cushions.

"You've a mania for moving," said Ginnosuke, looking round the room. "When once a fellow gets the habit of moving, like you, it seems he wants to make a regular thing of it. Your last room was better than this, wasn't it?"

"What made you want to move, anyway?" asked Bunpei.

"Too much noise in that boardinghouse." Ushimatsu tried to sound casual, but embarrassment showed unmistakably in his expression.

"The temple's quieter, certainly," said Ginnosuke nonchalantly. "But what was it people were saying—that eta was turned out of the place, wasn't he?"

"Yes, that's the story," chimed in Bunpei.

"That's what started me thinking," Ginnosuke went on. "Maybe it was some trivial unpleasantness like that that made you decide to leave?"

"How d'you mean?" Ushimatsu asked in turn.

"That's where you and I are so different." Ginnosuke laughed. "I was reading an article in a magazine the other day about a man who was mentally ill. Like this, it was. Someone left a dead cat on a bit of waste ground next to the house the man was renting. When the man discovered the cat, he moved to another house that same day—without talking it over with his wife even. With the mentally ill, apparently, quite trivial things—like the sight of a dead cat, for instance—are often motive enough for moving." He laughed. "I'm not saying you're mentally ill, Segawa. But to look at you, you do seem to be off-colour physically. Aren't I right? That's what made me think of the dead cat when I heard about the eta being turned out—maybe it was the eta business, coming on top of your not being well anyway, that made you feel you wanted to move."

"Don't be so silly." Ushimatsu laughed, but unconvincingly.

"No, I'm serious." Ginnosuke looked closely at his friend's face. "You're pale, you know. Why not see the doctor?"

"I'm not ill, that's why," Ushimatsu replied with a smile.

"There are plenty of sick people around who don't know they are sick." Ginnosuke was not to be deterred. "And you're one of them. What about your not sleeping at night, for instance? It's obvious to me there's something wrong with you."

"Obvious, is it?"

"Of course. Delusions, hallucinations, nightmares, that's the trouble. The man I told you about was so sick that the sight of the dead cat touched off a whole set of hallucinations, and it's the same with you. What's a dead cat? Nothing. An eta gets turned out of a lodging house. What's so unusual about that?"

"That's the trouble with you, Tsuchiya—always jumping to conclusions," Ushimatsu cut in. "Once you've decided how things are, you'll listen to nobody else."

"You moved so suddenly, that's all." Ginnosuke changed his tone. "But you'll be able to get more work done here, that's for certain."

"I've been interested for some time in finding out more about temple life," said Ushimatsu.

Kesaji, the maid, came in with a teapot.

## 3

Few even among the Japanese can be as fond of tea as the people of Shinshu. It is in the nature of these dwellers of the cold mountain country to love the drink, and most households make a point of enjoying it together four or five times a day. Ushimatsu was no exception. Pouring three strong, hot cups and offering two to his guests, he then put his own cup to his lips and revived as he inhaled the aroma of the green leaves. After a pause, he began to speak of his new life at the temple.

"Listen—I tried the temple bath last night. It was marvellous, after working all day. I thought to myself, when I opened the little window and saw the asters flowering just outside, this is the joy of temple life, to be able to sit in your bath where it's so quiet you can hear the grasshoppers chirp. Different from the lodging house, all right. It felt like coming home."

"True, there's nowhere so dreary and vulgar as a lodging house." Ginnosuke lit a cigarette.

"There're all kinds of other things too," Ushimatsu went

on. "The rats, for instance—swarms of them. I couldn't believe it."

"Rats?" Bunpei leaned forward.

"They came right up to my pillow last night. Not exactly pleasant, if you're not used to them. There were so many that I spoke to the priest's wife about it this morning. You'll be amused at what she said—according to her, it's only charity to feed them and let them be. Better that way than keeping a cat to kill them, anyway. They're not such bad creatures if only you give them enough to eat. Look how well behaved *our* rats are, she says. Which isn't far wrong, if you put it like that. The rats here aren't the least bit afraid of humans. They even run around in broad daylight. No, a temple's not like other places—I've learnt that much."

"What a story!" Ginnosuke laughed. "She's an odd character, by the sound of it."

"Not exactly odd, just a bit more religious than most. She's neither a regular nun nor the kind of temple wife who's only there to look after the priest. She's not quite the ordinary housewife, either. It's the first time I've ever met a True Pure Land priest's wife."

"Who else is there?" asked Ginnosuke.

"A young acolyte, a maid—oh yes, and Shota, the old servant, the one who was sweeping the leaves when you came. No one calls him anything but Simple Sho, though. He's a bit weak in the head. It's his job to strike the big bell outside five times a day—at dawn, eight o'clock, noon, sundown, and ten o'clock at night."

"What about the priest?"

"He's away at the moment."

So Ushimatsu recounted what he had seen and heard thus far at Rengeji, till finally he came to speak of O-Shio, Keinoshin's daughter, who had been adopted by the priest and his wife.

"Kazama's daughter, you mean?" said Bunpei, knocking the ash from his cigarette. "The girl that came to the Friends of the School meeting the other day?"

"Yes, that was her," replied Ushimatsu, recalling the meeting Bunpei spoke of. "She must have left school the year before Ginnosuke and I came."

# 4

That day being the anniversary of the death of the former priest of Rengeji, they were busy in the temple kitchen preparing the *shojin*[1] dishes appropriate for the occasion. It was customary for the present priest to take a special meal and recite the sutras once a month in memory of his predecessor; but since this particular day was the thirty-third anniversary of his death, the priest's wife had said she would be cooking rice with chestnuts, the dead man's favourite dish, to offer to his spirit, and would like the lodger to have some too. The assistant priest's wife was helping her.

When everything was nearly ready, the priest's wife, always ready for a chat, left the other women to watch the cooking and came up to Ushimatsu's room. In her eyes, Ushimatsu, Ginnosuke, and Bunpei were so many children. Old-fashioned though she might be, she was very knowledgeable in her way and found no difficulty in keeping up with the young men's talk. She liked, on occasion, to speak of religious matters, and told them now of the vigil that would take place on the twenty-seventh of December, the yearly commemoration of the death of Saint Shinran, founder of the True Pure Land sect. On this winter night parishioners of both sexes would gather in front of the shrine and talk of old times; the priest would give a sermon, intone a sutra, and read from the lives of holy men, till at midnight all would share in a vigil supper.

After murmuring several nenbutsu, she went on to ask them about Keinoshin's retirement. Her husband had done his best to help Keinoshin, she said. The priest had urged him again and again to give up drinking, and more than once even got him to sign a pledge of abstinence, but each time he slipped back. He knew very well he would pay for it if he went on drinking, but the disease had proved too much for him. Because of this weakness he had grown shy of calling at the temple, and now, apparently, he could not bring himself to come at all. O-Shio must be so sad for her unhappy father.

[1] Vegetarian—therefore purificatory—food.

"So he's had to resign after all, has he?" The priest's wife sighed.

"That's why it was then," said Ushimatsu. "I met him yesterday when I was on my way here, and he took it into his head to come with me as far as the gate—said he couldn't tell me why, though. The moment we got here, he turned tail. He was quite drunk."

"Came here, did he? He can't forget his daughter, I suppose, no matter how drunk he gets. That's what it is to be a parent. . . ." The priest's wife gave another sigh.

All this talk had prevented Ginnosuke from saying what was really on his mind. Still, it would be a pity to go home without ever mentioning it, when that had been the whole point of his coming; and in any case they would be sure to invite him to share the rice with chestnuts, so he decided to stay on, in the hope that he would get a chance to speak later in the evening. Anxiety for his friend filled his thoughts.

As this was a special occasion, supper was served in the big room downstairs. They were waited on by the acolyte, in a white kimono—evidently he had just finished the evening sutra readings in the temple hall. The light from the well-trimmed oil lamp played on the incense smoke as it rose and faded into the night air and threw changing patterns on the high wooden ceiling. The yellow robe hanging from a hook on the ancient wall would be the priest's, no doubt. The three young men were intrigued by the unfamiliarity of everything in the room. Ginnosuke in particular was in fine form, chattering away and laughing often; they could hear him in the kitchen, so the priest's wife could not help listening to their talk even before she joined them. Later O-Shio came in to listen too. She sat close to the priest's wife.

Bunpei suddenly came to life. It was his nature to blossom out in quite a startling way at any party where there were women present, and even his voice sounded different now from when they had been on their own upstairs. As he began to talk, inspired by the company, the light in his eyes adding to his natural charm, he convinced all his listeners he was a fascinating character. Now and again he glanced with a special interest at O-Shio. She was listening intently to the conversation, stroking her hair occasionally or adjusting the skirt of her kimono. Ginnosuke, who noticed nothing of all this, turned to O-Shio.

"It was the year before we came that you graduated, wasn't it?"

The priest's wife also turned toward O-Shio.

"Yes." The girl flushed, shyness accentuating her youthful beauty.

"There's a graduation photograph of your class at school," said Ginnosuke, smiling. "A fine lot of young ladies you've all turned into. Two years back, when we first came, some of you still had runny noses, I shouldn't wonder!"

Laughter filled the room. O-Shio's cheeks reddened again. Only Ushimatsu sat silent by the lamp, deep in thought.

## 5

"I'm worried about Segawa. Anybody can see he's terribly down about something." Ginnosuke turned to the priest's wife for confirmation. "Don't you think so?"

"Well, he certainly doesn't look too cheerful," she answered, cocking her head.

"Three days ago," said Ginnosuke, looking at Ushimatsu, "on the day you came here looking for a room, we met in the street, remember? You looked so preoccupied, I stood there staring after you, wondering what it was all about and hoping you weren't getting yourself into a state reading Inoko again. I noticed you had a copy of his *Confessions* with you. You shouldn't read books like that, you know."

"Why not?" Ushimatsu straightened up.

"Because it doesn't do to let yourself be influenced by him so much."

"What's wrong with being influenced?"

"Nothing, if it's a good influence, but in this case it's not. Look, it's since you started reading Inoko that this change has come over you. Given that he's an eta, there's nothing surprising about him feeling the way he does, but surely there's no need for anyone who's *not* an eta to imitate him. He's so morbid, puts everything in such an extreme way."

"Are you saying it's wrong to sympathize with the poor and the workers?"

"No, not wrong. I admire his ideas myself. But to brood over other people's misfortunes, as you seem to be doing, that's going too far. Why *do* you read so much of this kind of thing, Segawa? Why are you forever thinking, thinking —and what is it you're thinking about, anyway?"

"Me? The same kind of things as you, I suppose. Nothing very profound."

"There must be *something*. If there wasn't some good reason, you wouldn't have changed so much."

"Have I changed?"

"Certainly you have. You're nothing like the lively fellow I knew at college. That's what makes me think—you're not naturally the melancholy type, it's just that you dwell on things too much. So why not broaden out a bit, take up other interests—develop the positive side of yourself? I've been meaning to say this for quite a while. I've been worrying about you, you see. If you're ill, of course, it's up to you to see a doctor."

The talk lapsed, and there was silence in the room for a while. An air of abstraction came over Ushimatsu. When it faded a moment later, he was noticeably paler.

"What on earth's the matter?" Ginnosuke stared at him in astonishment. "Marvellously silent you've turned all of a sudden."

Instead of answering, Ushimatsu only laughed. Ginnosuke laughed with him. O-Shio and the priest's wife had been listening attentively to the two young men, looking from one to the other as they spoke.

"Have you read *Confessions,* Tsuchiya?" Bunpei asked.

"No, not yet."

"Or anything else of Inoko's? I haven't read a line of him myself."

"Let's see, I've read *Labour*—oh yes, and *Modern Thought and the Depressed Classes:* I borrowed that from Segawa. He's a powerful writer, there's no doubt about it. Goes deep, too."

"Where did he get his education?"

"The Higher Teachers' College in Tokyo,[2] wasn't it?"

"I remember hearing that when he was living in Nagano, his hometown was so proud of a local eta having gone so far in the world that they invited him back to give some lectures. When he got there, though—it wasn't far from Nagano—he was turned away from the inn. He was so disgusted, he left Nagano not long afterwards. He carried on with his studies after he'd left the college, though, didn't he? An odd character to come from an eta background."

"He's an amazing man."

"It's how an eta could make his mark in the intellectual world that's always puzzled me."

"They say he's consumptive. Maybe illness has something to do with it."

"Consumptive, is he?"

"People with that kind of disease are always more serious-minded. Staring death in the face makes a man think non-stop. There's a kind of urgency in Inoko's writing that's characteristic of consumptives. Plenty of famous men have had illness to thank for their success."

"Tsuchiya will see these things from the physiological angle." Bunpei laughed.

"It's not so ridiculous, you know. Illness is a philosopher, you might say."

"In that case, it's Inoko's illness, not the fact that he's an eta, that makes him write those books of his!"

"Isn't that the only explanation that makes sense? How else would an eta produce such lofty ideas?"

While Ginnosuke and Bunpei were talking, Ushimatsu sat silent, staring at the lamp. The heartache that he could not wholly hide, at odds with the youthful colour of his cheeks, intensified the air of dejection in his otherwise manly face.

Tea was served, and the three young men turned to other subjects. The priest's wife entertained them with news from her husband, who was away on a journey. The acolyte, who had sat down against a pillar in the adjoining room, was nodding sleepily. From somewhere in the yard outside the kitchen came a slow series of faint, dull thuds: Simple Sho pounding rice.[3] The evening wore on.

[2] One of the two such institutions in Japan at the time. The other was in Hiroshima. Both enjoyed high prestige.

# 6

After his friends had gone home, Ushimatsu walked back and forth in his room, increasingly disturbed. Recalling all they had said, every subtle movement of feeling he had read in their faces, he shivered. The insult to his fellow outcast, Inoko, whom he so revered, left the bitterest taste. Just because he was an eta, they had implied, the man and his work were to be dismissed out of hand—the absurdity of this kind of talk, apart from anything else, was enough to infuriate Ushimatsu. But no tears, no arguments, however deeply felt, no ideology, however passionate and powerful its attack, could break down such prejudice; so it was that great numbers of the "new commoners," honourable, law-abiding citizens, had been ostracized from birth, buried alive in a world that hardly knew of their existence.

Racked by such thoughts, Ushimatsu could not sleep. He lay with his head on the pillow, his eyes open, brooding on his life hitherto. The rats appeared again. The patter of their feet on the straw mats making sleep still more difficult, he lit the oil lamp again, turning it very low, and set it by his pillow. The tiny creatures, darting nimbly like shadows in and out of the wall in dark corners of the room, jerking their long tails, oblivious of the alien being so close to them, at once annoyed and amused him. Their faint, squeaky cries matched the autumnal loneliness of the night within these ancient, austere walls.

Every thought brought new anxiety. Maybe the very actions which he had meant to divert any possible suspicion had on the contrary invited it—the more he thought about it now, the more careless and lacking in foresight he seemed to have been. Why hadn't he stayed on at the lodging house when Ohinata was made to leave? Why had he come scurrying here to Rengeji? Why, whenever anything new of Inoko's came out, must he go out of his way to announce it with such ill-concealed pride? Why did he have to defend Inoko, and so make people think there was some connec-

[3] The special rice cakes used in Japanese New Year celebrations are made from a particular variety of rice that has been pounded to a glutinous state in a mortar.

tion between the eta writer and himself—why should he bring up Inoko's name at all? Why didn't he take more care to conceal his buying of Inoko's books? And having bought them, why couldn't he have the sense to read them only when he was alone in his room? Exhausted with worries that led to no clear conclusion, Ushimatsu spent a tortured night, his body restless and his mind wandering in dark places.

By morning, though, he had decided: nothing could be done about the past, but in the future he would have to be far more cautious. He would never refer openly to Inoko's work again, never speak of his character, never even mention his name. This was the only way to guard against discovery. His father's commandment struck home with new force. *Tell no one!* Life and death hung on those words. Compared with this single precept, all the commandments and austerities that black-robed disciples of the Buddha imposed so painfully upon themselves were as nothing. Buddhists who betrayed their Master incurred nothing worse than the name of apostate; an eta who betrayed this commandment of his father's was utterly and permanently ruined. What eta who wanted to make anything of his life would be so mad as to reveal by his own choice the secret of his origin?

Ushimatsu was twenty-three. A fine age, when you thought of it. The more he longed for his life to continue as it was now, the more insistently the bitter knowledge of his eta-hood forced itself upon his consciousness. In Ushimatsu's eyes the small pleasures of his present position took on a special attractiveness. Come what may, that one vital commandment he would never break.

# Chapter 4

## 1

Out in the country it was the busy harvest season. Everywhere groups of peasants were working furiously in the fields; here and there the rice had been reaped and dried already, and wheat sown in its place. Now was the time for farmers to win their reward for their year's labour—quickly, before the snow came. The plain on either side of the lower reaches of the Chikuma River resembled a battlefield.

Directly after coming home from school Ushimatsu had gone out for a walk, with the idea that it would help him get his usual spirits back. He made his way to the end of Shinmachi through a few fields of mulberry trees, whose leaves were just beginning to turn, and came unexpectedly upon a corner of the open country. Sitting in the shade of a huge pile of bundles of straw and stretching his feet out on a bed of frost-withered grasses, he drank deeply of the country air and felt life reawakening within him. He watched the peasants: men and women, husbands and wives, parents and children, all were working with a dogged intensity, veiled from head to foot in a continuously rising cloud of yellow dust. The sounds of hulling and threshing mingled with the rhythmic pounding of rice by wooden mallets on the dry, hard earth. White smoke rose in several places. A flock of sparrows would soar up, twittering, then swoop down to settle all over the field.

The autumn sun burnt down fiercely, making the peasants' work hard beyond words. The women wore hats of straw; the men had wrapped strips of cloth round their heads. It was an unusually parched, windless day; their whole bodies streamed with sweat. As Ushimatsu was watching them in the brilliant light that bathed the countryside, a boy of thirteen or fourteen appeared beside the pile of straw. From his sunburnt forehead and gentle expression Ushimatsu recognized him at once as Shogo, Keinoshin's son. The boy was in his own class. Every time he saw him, Ushimatsu could not help thinking of his father, the pathetic old teacher.

"Where are you off to, Kazama?" he asked.

"To see—" Shogo faltered. "Mother's out in the fields."

"Your mother?"

"Over there—look, sir, there she is!" Shogo pointed her out, reddening a little. Ushimatsu had heard some talk about Keinoshin's wife but had no idea that that was she working in the field, right in front of him. In an old smock with a brown sash, cotton half-gloves of dark blue, and a hat of plaited straw, she was busy on the thresher, her body swaying back and forth as her foot worked the treadle. All the women of north Shinshu are tough and dogged, better workers than their men, as often as not; but even so, there could not be many teachers' wives who would willingly work out there in the fields, pitting themselves against the bitter extremes of Shinshu weather. Circumstances must have left her no choice, Ushimatsu thought sadly. Shogo was pointing again: that man with the mallet, next but one to her, was Otosaku, an old peasant they had known for many years, and the woman between him and Shogo's mother, shaking the winnowing tray above her head in front of her—she was Otosaku's wife. With every shake of the tray a cloud of yellow dust from the husks enveloped them all like smoke. The young girl at his mother's side, Shogo went on, was O-Saku, his stepsister.

"How many brothers and sisters have you?"

"Five."

"That's plenty, isn't it? Let's see, there's your sister O-Shio, Susumu in the lower school, O-Saku—and who else?"

"Two more little ones, a brother and a sister. Big brother went for a soldier—he's dead."

"I see."

"Big brother who died, big sister who went to the temple, and me—we had the same mother."

"What happened to her?"

"Not here anymore." Shogo ran off; his stepmother was calling.

## 2

"Shogo! How old are you going to be before you decide to make yourself useful?" Ushimatsu could hear her saying. Shogo was standing nervously in front of his stepmother; he seemed afraid of her.

"Just think, you're in the fourth year at school, aren't you?" she said angrily. "Can't you see how we're slaving here in all this dust, with so much to do we even had to ask

Otosaku here to lend a hand? You ought to have come out to help straight after school without being asked. Whoever heard of a fourth-year boy still dreaming of nothing but locust catching? Lazy brat!" She stopped the thresher. Otosaku's wife, too, paused in her work; glancing sympathetically at the boy, she tightened her apron, shook herself to get rid of the dust, and wiped the greasy sweat from her face. Rice husks rose in a yellow mound on the mat in front of her. Otosaku straightened his bent back; leaning on the long handle of his mallet, he stared up at the deep blue above him, drinking in its freshness.

"Hey, O-Saku!" Keinoshin's wife was scolding again. "You're a girl, why can't you behave like one? A pair of good-for-nothings you are. I'm sick of you both, my own children and all. . . . Look at Susumu! He's more use than the two of you put together."

"Susumu's not working!" Shogo retorted.

"What d'you mean, not working?" The mother's voice trembled with anger. "He's minding the little ones, isn't he—that's more than you're doing! And you, Shogo—I've only got to open my mouth for you to start contradicting. Your father's too soft with you, that's why you won't listen to a word I say. . . . You're so cheeky, you make me hate you! Give you the least bit of rein, and there's no knowing what you'll get up to. You've been whining to that sister of yours at the temple, I suppose? That why you're so late coming? Sneaking off without telling me, you little—"

"Mrs. Kazama!" Otosaku couldn't bear it any longer. "Won't you forgive him today, for my sake? You'd best not be so cheeky, Master Shogo. If you're not going to do what mother tells you, you can't expect me to put in a word for you afterwards."

Otosaku's wife went up to Shogo and whispered something to him, her hand on his shoulder. Then she put a mallet into his hand and led him over to her husband. Otosaku lifted his mallet and began hulling again, this time with Shogo as his partner; the two fell quickly into a common rhythm, shouting old work cries to match each movement as they brought the mallets down on the rice, then swung them again above their heads. The two women went back to their work.

So Ushimatsu learnt, from this chance glimpse of Keinoshin's family, that neither O-Shio nor the luckless Shogo were Keinoshin's children by his present wife. He realized that the wife must feel bound to labour like this for her husband's sake because he was so poor, that it was the burden of their five children, and Keinoshin's misfortune, that made her so touchy and short-tempered. The knowledge made him pity Keinoshin all the more.

Ushimatsu had recovered at least some of his composure. Once again he could see clearly, think clearly. All kinds of memories crowded through his mind as he sat gazing at the country scene—of innocent childhood days when he had lain as he lay now, sprawled by the edge of rice fields, watching the harvest; of the slopes of the Eboshi range, and the patchwork of fields and stone walls climbing up them from the valleys below; of raised footpaths between paddy fields, fringed with autumn-tinted reeds and camomile and every kind of mountain weed and wild flower; of days spent netting locusts and chasing woodmice, while autumn winds sent yellow waves sweeping over the fields, and of evenings whiled away by the fireside, listening to ghost stories and old legends of men bewitched by foxes and badgers, or laughing hilariously at tales of untamed peasant love. Those early days, before he knew he was an eta; they belonged to another age, another world.

He went over his years of study at the college in Nagano—those years of laughter and boisterous fellowship, when still he knew little of the world and thought of himself as a man like other men, never doubting the worth and dignity of his fellows, never himself the object of such doubt. He remembered the old woman in the cake shop outside the main gate, where he would go for goodies when the lot fell on him—this was the way they shared expenses—to keep his friends supplied; the late nights in the dormitory, when the students, noiseless after the lights-out bell, would slip out of bed the moment the warden's footsteps died away at the far end of the corridor and talk on far into the small hours, huddled together in the dark; the boyish happiness that set him shouting for sheer joy when he had climbed the hill to Ojoji temple and stood by the Karukayas'[1] grave. . . . How utterly his life had changed. The memory of past happiness only accentuated his present depression. Ushimatsu sighed—why should he have grown so nervous, so suspicious, he asked himself, looking up at the sky. Suddenly a small cottonwool-like cloud, emerging without warning from the blue void, caught his attention. He watched it, letting his thoughts drift on till weariness overtook him and he fell asleep, propped against the bundles of straw.

## 3

When he woke, the light was already fading. Some of the peasants were making their way home along the raised paths; groups of rough, ungainly figures passed where he lay. Some carried mattocks, others sacks of grain; some of the women, young mothers with babies in their arms, hurried past their men. The long cruel labour of the autumn day was over at last.

Some, though, were still working, Keinoshin's people among them. Otosaku had started for home, his back bent and his legs stiffened under the weight of a huge bale. The two women and Shogo were finishing the hulling and winnowing, and packing the grain into sacks.

A sudden cry of "Mam-ma! Mam-ma!" made them all turn round. Shogo's brother Susumu was running toward them, dragging his small sister by the hand and carrying his baby brother, screaming his head off, on his back.

The mother took the baby and put it to suck at her breast.

"Susumu! Where's father gone?"

"Dunno."

His mother sighed, wiping her eyes with her sleeve.

[1] A father and son about whom many well-known tales are told. The father, a thirteenth-century provincial lord, is said to have left home to become a Buddhist priest after seeing a dream in which his wife and mistress, in the shape of snakes, were engaged in mortal combat. Years afterwards his son sought him out, but the father, having given up all worldly ties, refused to acknowledge him. Later, however, he relented, and the two lived together at Ojoji temple in Nagano.

"What's the good of working, I can't help feeling, when I think of your father—"

"Mother, look what Saku's doing!" Susumu shouted, pointing at his sister.

"What!" His mother spun round. "Who's been opening that bag—who's been opening that bag without asking mother?"

"Saku's been stuffing herself—I saw her!" screamed Susumu.

"Stupid girl, what's to be done with you?" the mother barked suddenly. "Bring me the bag—bring it here at once!"

O-Saku, a seven-year-old, stood with the bag in her hand, too frightened by her mother's anger to move.

"Let us have some, mummy!" Susumu and his other sister were whining. Shogo ran over to his mother and joined in.

The mother snatched the bag from O-Saku. "Show me—it's half empty, you little wretch! No wonder you were so quiet. The moment my back's turned, you're up to your tricks. It's stealing, gobbling them up all by yourself like that, without asking. You're a thief! Get away with you—a thieving child's no child of mine!" She took out some of the few rice cakes that were left in the bag and gave one each to the three other children.

"Can I have one?" O-Saku held out a hand.

"You—when you've hardly finished eating the ones you stole!"

"One for me, mother!" Shogo pleaded. "You gave Susumu two, and me only one!"

"You're his big brother, aren't you—you shouldn't be so greedy."

"But you gave him such big ones—"

"If you're going to complain, give me back the one you've got. When will you learn to take what your mother gives you without grumbling?"

His cheeks bulging with one rice cake, Susumu held up the other in triumph. "Shogo's a fool—stupid Shogo!" he shouted.

Shogo's face darkened. Darting forward, he clouted his brother on the head. Undaunted, Susumu hit back with a swipe at Shogo's ear. Oblivious of everything but their quarrel, the two brothers faced each other like two wild beasts, their shoulders stiffened and poised for combat. When Otosaku's wife ran over to separate them, they both burst out crying.

"Why do you have to fight over it—you're brothers, aren't you?" said their mother angrily. "You'll drive me out of my mind if you go on like that, the pair of you."

The more Ushimatsu heard as he watched this scene from his seat in the shadow of the heaped-up bundles of straw, the deeper the pity he felt for the whole unfortunate family. The evening bell sounded from Rengeji. Ushimatsu got up and left the field.

Again the bell of Rengeji echoed through the lonely late-autumn air, tolling consolation to the peasants after their long day's labour and a summons to enjoy the rest they had earned. The few who still remained in the fields hurried to finish their tasks. Patches of mist formed over the opposite bank of the Chikuma River; already the peaks of the Kosha range had faded into the darkness, and only the fields stood out in the dying light from the sun as it sank beneath a russet sky, hidden by the mountains. Dusk enfolded the woods and clusters of farmhouses beyond. If only one could enjoy the beauty of such a scene to the full, free of care and mental suffering, what a time of bliss youth would be! The more painful Ushimatsu's inward conflict, the deeper his sense of such beauty, of external nature as a living force permeating his very being. A single star appeared in the southern sky, its bluish gleam enhancing the splendour of the twilight landscape. Absorbing the spectacle about him as he walked, Ushimatsu dwelt yet again on his own past and the uncertain future.

"But what if I *am* different?" he told himself defiantly as he took a narrow path across a bean field. "Even as an eta, I belong to society—eta or no, like any other man I have the right to live!" Momentarily heartened by the thought, he looked back. Keinoshin's family was still working. The white of the towels the two women had wound round their heads stood out in the failing light; sounds drifted through the quiet, chilling air, of mallets pounding, of orders to gather up and bind the straw. Someone straightened and looked in his direction—Shogo? Figures and faces were no longer distinguishable, as insubstantial as moving shadows.

## 4

"Been a long day," the mountain folk say in place of "Good evening." On his way back Ushimatsu exchanged these words with each peasant he met. Passing the Sasaya, the little eating house with a sign advertising saké and cheap single-dish meals, he repeated the greeting to a man sitting on a bench outside—who turned out to be Keinoshin.

"Segawa!" Keinoshin stopped him. "Couldn't have met you at a better place. I've been wanting to have a nice long talk with you. You're not in a hurry, are you? Keep me company, just for this evening, Segawa! It does a man good to talk in a place like this once in a while—and there's things I want to tell you—"

Thus pressed, Ushimatsu entered the Sasaya with Keinoshin. Pedlars came in here for rest and refreshment during the day, peasants in the evening. A log fire was blazing in a big hearth in the middle of the room; a row of old saké bottles, no doubt filled with the local brew, stood against the wall. But since it was the busiest season of the year for the peasants, none of them could afford to stay for long. One such, still in his working sandals, was taking long pulls at a glassful of saké, but he soon went out, leaving Ushimatsu and Keinoshin alone by the fireside.

"What'll you take tonight?" the woman of the place asked them as she hung an iron pot on the hook over the fire. "We've bean stew—how would that suit you? Or fried bullheads, fresh from the river?"

"Bullheads?" Keinoshin licked his lips. "Fine! And we'll have the stew too—that'll make a real meal of it."

Keinoshin was quivering with thirst. When sober he was dull and listless, spoke little, and looked positively ill. He could not have been much over fifty, though, and did not in fact look any older—his hair was still quite black. Ushimatsu felt closer to him than before, after seeing and hearing his wife and children out in the fields. Logs crackled in the fire; already the pot had begun to bubble, giving off an appetizing aroma. The woman served them from it with two bowls of stew filled to the brim, and hot saké in an old-fashioned china serving bottle.

"Segawa," Keinoshin began, his hand shaking as he poured the saké, "how long is it since you came to Iiyama?"

"Getting on to three years now."

"As much as that, is it? Seems like it was only a few months ago. Time goes so fast—no wonder I'm getting old, while you young ones dash ahead. Even I had my time once, Segawa: tomorrow, tomorrow—I was always dreaming of tomorrow—and now the bell's tolled fifty. . . . My family were Iiyama samurai. When I was little, I served the lord of our fief as a page; then I was sent to Edo City, till the Restoration, that is. What changes there've been! Change, change—look at the castle ruins down by the river. What do you and your generation think of those stone walls, or what's left of them? I'm so overcome when I see all that ivy creeping up them, I nearly choke. Almost every castle you go to, it's the same; nothing but a few ruins, and mulberry trees planted where the samurai used to drill. That's how low samurai have sunk. The ones who've kept their heads above water have only managed it by teaching school or clerking in government offices; that's all they could do. There's nothing so useless as a samurai—and I'm one of them, Segawa." Keinoshin laughed cheerlessly. Draining his saké cup, he licked his lips, then held the cup out to Ushimatsu.

"Exchange cups, shall we?"

"Let me fill yours up again," said Ushimatsu, his hand on the bottle.

"No, you drink from my cup first—then I'll drink from yours. I didn't think you drank at all, though. Made a big mistake, didn't I? Tonight's the first time I've seen you show your mettle, Segawa!"

"I'm no drinker. Three cups is my limit."

"Drink this one, anyway. I couldn't talk like this to anyone else. Twenty years now I've been teaching—fifteen since I qualified—twenty years of doing the same thing over and over. You'll laugh at me, I daresay, but toward the end I didn't know what I was teaching, standing there in the classroom in front of them all. It's true, though. Happens to every teacher who does the job for any length of time. What are primary school teachers—in the lower school, anyway—but labourers who've picked up a few snippets of learning? Day in, day out, the din, the struggle to keep the classroom tidy and a horde of children in order, working long hours for a miserable salary—I can't help wondering how I've kept going for so long. You'll think it's stupid of me to retire now. Stupid I may be, but even *I* know well enough I'd get a bit of a pension if I could hold on for another six months. But I can't: that's the devil of it. . . . Tell me to go on working, and you might as well be sentencing me to death. My wife's worried, of course. How can we live if you give up teaching, she says—wants me to get myself a job at the bank as a ledger clerk or something. I ask you, Segawa—how could I cope with anything new when I can't even do the job I've done for twenty years? All my energy's gone. There's just nothing left in me, Segawa. A carthorse kept at work with the whip till it drops: that's what I am, Segawa—a carthorse!"

## 5

Keinoshin stopped abruptly as a boy stepped in from the street. The woman was busy at the sink, in a clatter of pots and dishes, but hurried over to the door when she saw who the boy was.

"Hallo, Shogo lad!"

The boy looked worried. "Is father here?"

"Aye, he's here."

Keinoshin frowned. Getting up, he led the boy over to the fireplace from the semidarkness where he had been standing, just inside the entrance, and looked at him intently.

"What is it—anything the matter?"

"Mother says—" Shogo hesitated. "M-mother says will you come home early this evening."

"Mm. Sent you after me, did she? At it again," Keinoshin mumbled.

"Aren't you coming home, father?" asked Shogo timidly.

"I'll come when I'm ready. Tell your mother I'm busy

with Mr. Segawa, and I'll come home when I've finished." Keinoshin lowered his voice. "What's your mother doing, Shogo?"

"Clearing up the chaff."

"Still working, is she? Wasn't she upset when she sent you—you know, like she usually is?"

Shogo didn't answer. He stared at his father, childish pity in his eyes.

"Your hands look cold," Keinoshin said, taking the boy's hands in his own. "Here, take this"—giving him a coin—"and buy yourself a persimmon or something. Don't tell your mother or Susumu, mind you. Off you go, then! I'll be back soon, like I said. All right?"

Crestfallen, Shogo went out.

"You remember how I went with you as far as the temple gate, the day you moved to Rengeji?" Keinoshin started again. "I can tell this to you, Segawa, though I couldn't to anyone else. I've behaved badly toward the temple, and the priest is very angry with me: so long as I go on drinking, he says, he won't have anything to do with me. My daughter, whom the temple family adopted, and Shogo, and the boy I lost—my eldest, the one that joined the army—these three I had by my first wife. Her family were Iiyama samurai, like mine. We were still comfortably off when I married her, and she died before I'd sunk as low as I have now, so whenever I think of her I can't help remembering how things were in the old days—it was the happiest time of my life. One drink, and I'm back there. It's got to be a habit with me now. After all, what is there left to enjoy but memories when you're getting old? She chose the right time to die, beyond a doubt. We're funny creatures, though: the woman you marry when you're young will always seem the best, I suppose. But with her, it was her character. She wasn't stiff-necked like my present wife. Relied on her husband in everything, she did, trusted him absolutely in the old-fashioned way. My daughter O-Shio's the same kind of girl. Her eyes—whenever I look at her, it's her mother I see. . . . Not only me, either. People often mention the likeness and go on to talk of the old days . . . you can see they don't take to my present wife. To be frank with you,

Segawa, I didn't want to let the temple have my girl. But staying on at home wouldn't have done anything for her. I was so sorry for her, with a home like ours. Rengeji was very keen on having her, too. The priest and his wife have no children, and here in Iiyama, unlike other places, people have a real respect for priests and their families—so I finally let her go."

The more he heard, the more sorry Ushimatsu felt for Keinoshin. For all his down-at-heel, defeated air, there was a trace of samurai dignity about him still.

## 6

"My life's been such a failure." He sighed. "Failure—can you imagine what bitterness the word holds for me? Some people say I'm poor because I drink, but if you ask me, I drink because I'm poor. I can't go a single day without drinking. When I started drinking, I drank to forget my troubles, but now it's the other way round: I drink to make myself feel the pain. Sounds silly, I suppose. If I miss the saké for just one evening, my mind goes numb . . . it's only when I'm drinking and letting the misery of it all sink in that I feel alive at all. There's a lot more to tell, if I'm going to talk of what I ought to be ashamed of. . . . Before I got the job here at Iiyama School, I used to work at Shimotakai, out in the wilds. It was there I married my present wife. She was born there—she can work, too, like the country-woman she is: grabs hold of the rice with one bare hand when it's stiff with frost and cuts it with the other, she does—*I* can't do that. If I tried, I'd be ill in no time. She can stand it, though. Poverty too—she's tougher, she can bear it better than I can. 'We can't afford to care what people say or think anymore,' she said to me. 'I'll turn peasant myself!' and so she did . . . started all by herself—the stupid woman. There's a fellow called Otosaku who used to serve my family in one way and another in the old days. He and his wife have been helping her—repaying the kindness they had from my father, they call it. But she's not making a success of it, or so I tell her, but she won't listen. Being a samurai, of course I know nothing about that kind of thing—how much rice per field goes in rent, how much crop you get for each bag of seed, how much fertilizer you need each year—how many square yards there are to the acre, even. I don't know how much land my wife's renting, either. It's her idea, I gather, to teach the children a bit of farming, and turn peasant herself in the process. That's what's always making trouble between us. Not that you could ever expect an ignorant woman like her to do much for the children's education. It's the children we fight over. We quarrel because we have children, or maybe the children come when we make it up after a quarrel, I don't know which. I've had enough of children. When you've already got so many, you wonder how you could ever cope with another. It'd only make the lot of you that much poorer, but then it comes, and what can you do? When my third girl was born, I told my wife to name her O-Sue,[2] then maybe we wouldn't have any more —but she'd hardly got up again when another was on the way, a boy this time: Tomekichi,[3] we called him. Can you imagine it, five kids snivelling round you from morning till night? It's more than a man can bear, I tell you. The sheer, grinding misery of it—I really pity any poor family I see nowadays with a horde of children, because I know what it means. It's hard enough to feed five. Heaven knows what'd happen if we had any more."

Keinoshin laughed. Hot tears dropped on his threadbare sleeve. "I've done my best, though, Segawa." He ran his hands over his head. "What about Shogo, by the way? He's in your class. The way he is now, d'you think he'll come to anything? I wish he were a bit livelier. He's such a crybaby, more like a girl than a boy. His brother Susumu's always teasing him. It's not that I specially like one or dislike the other—they're both my own, after all—but they are different, and somehow I can't help feeling sorry for Shogo, all the more because he's not so strong. Susumu's my wife's favourite. For her Shogo's just a nuisance. She never stops scolding him, and if ever I try to butt in, she takes it the wrong way, tells me to keep my mouth shut. I let her have

[2] *Sue:* end, final. A name incorporating this word is not uncommonly given to the youngest child of a family.

[3] *Tome:* stop; *kichi:* good fortune.

her own way and just look on. I try to keep away from her as much as I can, though. If I didn't sneak out for a bit of drinking on my own now and then, I couldn't keep going. If I do say anything once in a while, she barks out she wasn't so poor when I married her—and that shuts me up, you see: I sold all the kimonos she brought with her for drinking money. . . ." He laughed. "How futile a life like mine must seem to you, Segawa!"

Keinoshin's recital of his troubles had the paradoxical effect of cheering him up. The saké took effect quite quickly that evening: his talk grew gradually vaguer and more repetitive, till the words ran together in inarticulate mumbling.

The two got up from the hearth, and Ushimatsu paid the reckoning. It must have been past eight when they left the Sasaya; darkness had blanketed the almost deserted streets. Occasionally a drunk stumbled into them, groping—a woman muttering to herself as if she were demented, a man who seemed to have forgotten where he lived. Keinoshin walked precariously, in constant danger of falling, his eyes too dimmed with drink to reflect even the starlight. Deciding there was nothing for it but to see him home, Ushimatsu walked at his side, now supporting him with his right arm, now getting him to hold on to his own shoulders like a baby clinging to its mother's back, now putting both arms round him to help him keep his balance. When at last he got him to his house, Keinoshin's wife, with Otosaku and his wife, was hard at work outside in the cold, dew-laden air. The moment Keinoshin's wife saw the pair approaching, she called out to Ushimatsu: "*Acha-maa!* You've had a hard time of it, I can see!"

# Chapter 5

## 1

The morning of November the third, the Emperor's birthday, brought an exceptionally severe frost, a warning of the approach of the long winter that the mountain country must endure. The window of Ushimatsu's room was completely clouded over, as if with smoke. This year, the twenty-fourth of His Majesty's reign, the official ceremony in commemoration of the imperial birthday was to be held at the school. Ushimatsu took his formal haori coat and hakama skirt from his wicker trunk and put them on, finishing with the sleeveless overcoat he had worn at last year's ceremony.

The sunshine was streaming into the northward-facing corridor as he came down the dark stairway. As the frost began to melt, leaves drifted from the trees in the sunlit courtyard between the temple and the priest's house; the gingko, more susceptible than the others to the onset of winter, had already lost the last touch of yellow from even its topmost branches. Leaning against the corridor wall, O-Shio was watching the frost-bitten leaves flutter to the ground. Ushimatsu, filled with compassion for her father and his misfortunes, found himself looking at the girl with a new interest.

"O-Shio! Would you tell them in the kitchen I'm on watch at school tonight? If they could pack me something for supper, I'll send someone from school to fetch it."

O-Shio stood away from the wall. With the timidity common to young girls, she seemed to shrink a little from Ushimatsu. He looked at her, trying to find some resemblance to her father: that forehead, the set of her hair—no, it was Shogo who took after the father; O-Shio must have inherited the dead mother's features, as Keinoshin had said.

"I—I'm afraid you must have found father a nuisance the other evening," said O-Shio hesitantly, reddening a little.

"Not in the slightest," Ushimatsu replied with unfeigned sincerity.

"My brother came yesterday and told me about it. It must have been so awkward for you. With father being like that, we give people so much trouble."

Evidently she could not forget her father for a moment. He noticed the gleam of melancholy deep in her soft black eyes; her cheeks were red and swollen from weeping. Ushimatsu turned the collar of his overcoat up over his ears, put on his hat, and left Rengeji.

On the way he found in the inside pocket of his overcoat, all crumpled up, an old pair of wool-lined gloves. Smoothing the creases, he put them on; a bit on the small side, but they did help to warm his hands. Their musty smell awoke memories of other imperial birthdays—last year, the year before, the year before that: festival days when still he had learnt so little of the world that he never stopped to think of anything that was not gay or amusing. The gloves were as they had been, faded but otherwise unchanged. But consider the changes *within* a man—what would become of his own life, for instance? What of himself in a year's time, on the next imperial birthday—no need to look so far ahead, what of himself tomorrow? By turns elated and depressed by this train of thought, Ushimatsu walked toward the school.

Rising Sun flags had been hung out along the streets, as befitted the day; most families, one sensed, would be spending this most solemn of festivals quietly at home. Groups of boys and girls chattering gaily were hurrying to school along the still-frosty roads, the boys at their most mischievous age but with an oddly grown-up and dignified air on this one day of the year in their ceremonial uniforms. The girls wore new hakama skirts of brown and purple.

## 2

Marching in step, the pupils climbed the stairs to the hall where the ceremony to mark the sovereign's birthday was to be held. Ginnosuke, Bunpei, and Ushimatsu marched at the head of their respective classes, the second, first, and fourth years of the upper school; Keinoshin, now officially retired but attending as a guest, followed wistfully behind his former class.

In the midst of the general mood of excitement and rejoicing, something had shocked and saddened Ushimatsu—the announcement in a Tokyo paper that Inoko Rentaro's illness was now serious. It had caught his eye just before the ceremony was due to start, so he had had to stuff the paper in his pocket without reading the details. Some men were born to live lives that were short in time but long by any other reckoning—lives of incessant, restless activity. Rentaro must be such a man, thought Ushimatsu. The paper said his condition was "grave." Burning himself out before he could set the world on fire? Sympathy for the older man, his fellow eta, crowded all other feelings from Ushimatsu's mind. He longed to look again at the article, but for the moment that was impossible.

Combined with the official birthday celebrations there was to be a ceremony in honour of the local members of the Red Cross Society. Many of those in the hall had commemorative emblems of red and silver shining on their chests. Twenty or so priests lined one wall; the sense of incompleteness resulting from the absence of just one, the incumbent of Rengeji, was immediately felt, underlining the peculiar status of temple religion in Iiyama. A centre of interest was Takayanagi Risaburo, an up-and-coming politician who would soon be standing a second time for election to the Diet. The teachers were ranged together by the organ.

"Attention!" Ushimatsu's voice rang out, brisk and dignified, and the official ceremony began. Among the pupils, Ushimatsu—now the senior assistant teacher—was better liked than the principal. His command "Bow—low!" sent an indescribable vibration of feeling through their young breasts. Then came the singing of "May Thy Glorious Reign," during which the principal unveiled the imperial portrait; and the reading of the Rescript on Education, followed by massed shouts of "Banzai! Banzai!" echoing and reechoing like thunder. The principal's speech came next. His gold medal displayed squarely on his chest to enhance his dignity as a prominent educator, he took as his theme the duties of loyalty and filial piety. Then followed the song "The Emperor's Birthday," and last a brief speech of greeting by Takayanagi on behalf of the invited guests, this a polished performance by a veteran orator. The people of Shinshu have a weakness for eloquence. Takayanagi's remarks, though hardly more than a string of formalities, had his audience enchanted. A mood of peace and joy pervaded the hall.

As soon as the assembly was formally closed, Ushimatsu's class crowded around him, jostling, asking him questions, or just jumping up and down. Some pulled on his hands, others took turns ducking under his hakama, any trick they could think of so as not to let him go. In the third-year class there was an eta boy called Senta, who was always on his own, carefully avoided by his classmates. There he was now, on his own as usual, leaning forlornly against the wall watching the others play. Even on this festival day, poor lad, he could not join in the fun. Ushimatsu bit his lip. "Come on—don't be scared!" he longed to call out to the boy. But the other teachers were looking. Like a fugitive, Ushimatsu slipped away from the milling crowd of boys and girls.

Though the sharp frost that morning had bared most of the trees in the yard, autumn colours still lingered on the cherry. Standing in its shade, entranced too by the whispering of the wind in its branches, Ushimatsu took the newspaper from his pocket. Rentaro's condition was critical. . . . While not all of Inoko's ideas might be acceptable, the writer said, one couldn't help admiring the courage of an eta who had raised himself from such depths and fought so hard for his convictions. One's sympathy was therefore all the more acute on learning that he was suffering from the same dread disease that had carried off before their time so many men of promise. Not that it was impossible to guess at the reason why he had succumbed; too often this tragic illness went with the intense, almost fanatical seriousness of the kind that made itself felt in his writing. Indeed, the writer of the article himself, for similar reasons, was all too familiar with the contents of the medicine chest, etc., etc.

Time and again the wayward shadows on the ground delighted Ushimatsu. Beauty was born again in the dead leaves, touched by sunlight and the autumn breeze.

## 3

The tea party for Keinoshin began at eleven o'clock. When he had met O-Shio before leaving the temple earlier that morning, Ushimatsu thought at once of her unhappy father; now, with Keinoshin in front of him, sitting in the seat of honour, his thoughts reverted to the girl as he had seen her leaning against the ancient wall of the corridor. Keinoshin's speech was a long string of reminiscences. Pity kept Ushimatsu listening; no one else bothered to lend an ear to the old man's meanderings.

At last the tea party was over. Bunpei was going out to the courtyard for a game of tennis, when the principal called him back and took him to his own room. From where they sat down, facing each other by the window looking on to the playground, they could hear excited shouts from the tennis enthusiasts, Ginnosuke among them.

"No need to get too mad on sport, Katsuno. Talk to me for a while, will you?" The principal's tone was very friendly. "Tell me, what did you think of the speeches?"

"Your speech, sir?" Bunpei put his racket across his knees. "Very impressive, I found it."

"Really? Made 'em think a bit, eh?"

"I can truly say it was one of the best I've ever heard."

"It's nice to hear someone say that." The principal smiled. "As a matter of fact, I spent all yesterday evening working on it. How did you like my definitions of loyalty and filial piety—the way I explained the characters?[1] I took a lot of trouble over that, I can tell you, consulting dictionaries and reference books. How did it strike you?"

"A speech with that amount of work behind it always carries weight."

"But you were the only one who listened seriously, I daresay. The rest are an empty-headed, dreamy lot. No ear for solid good sense. I even heard some of them congratulating Takayanagi. . . . They shouldn't have had to listen to him and me together."

"What more can you expect of people so ignorant?"

Bunpei's remark dissipated the look of mortification that had momentarily clouded the principal's face.

So far, the principal had appeared to be talking as he was in order to avoid saying the one thing he had called Bunpei in to hear, but now he came to the point. What he wanted to discuss with Bunpei was how to get rid of Ushimatsu.

"The trouble is," he said, lowering his voice, "so long as we've people here like Tsuchiya and Segawa, outsiders who

[1] That is, the two ideographs for "loyalty" and "filial piety."

don't fit in with the rest of us, there'll be no proper unity in the school. Tsuchiya won't be staying long, anyway He's as good as got a post as an assistant at the Agricultural College. He'll go without any prompting from me. Segawa's the awkward customer. Once he's out of the way, Katsuno, the school will be ours, yours and mine: I want you to take his place, you see. Your uncle and I have talked it over, and he's of the same opinion. Well, what about it? Any bright ideas as to how we could squeeze him out?"

Bunpei could find no reply.

"Look how the boys idolize him—it's 'Segawa sensei! Segawa sensei!' all day long. He goes out of his way to make himself popular, and when a teacher does that kind of thing, there's likely to be a reason for it. What do you think, Katsuno?"

"I'm afraid I don't understand."

"To put it bluntly—this is between the two of us, mind you—Segawa's aiming to get control of the school for himself. I'm sure of it."

"He can't be!" Bunpei laughed, but did not take his eyes from the principal's face.

"You don't think so?" The principal sounded less certain.

"But it's far too early for him even to think of it—they are still so young, both he and Tsuchiya."

At the word "young," the principal sighed. A tennis ball bounced near the window; another match had begun. Bunpei listened in spite of himself. Glancing at the youthful face opposite him, the principal sighed again.

"What d'you suppose Segawa's brooding about all the time?"

"Brooding?" said Bunpei with an air of surprise.

"Every time I look at him he seems to be far away, racking his brains about something. Maybe the new age we live in makes people think too much. It looks very odd to me, though."

"But with him it's something different that's on his mind, I think—not what you were saying, Principal."

"If so, that makes it all the odder. His kind has such different ideas from people of my generation. Anything that appeals to me he turns up his nose at, and things that seem trashy to me fascinate him. Do you think that just because the generations are so different we can't work together? Is there such a gap between us?"

"*I* don't think so."

"That's what I like about you. Don't let him and his ways infect you, Katsuno. I've a mind to do what little I can for you in the future. In a hard world, the more we help each other the better, don't you think? We've got an outsider among us. I'm not saying we've got to decide what to do about him here and now. Just think it over—you may hit on something—and if you get word of anything special about Segawa, let me know."

## 4

Outside, another burst of applause. Bunpei went out with his racket to join the sportsmen. Getting up from his seat, the principal opened the window. A game was in progress. In spite of his ageing appearance, the principal was not old enough to be aware of any weakening of his physical powers but he detested all games, and tennis in particular, which was so popular among the young, aroused in him all the old-fashioned Oriental contempt for such childish pastimes—contempt that showed in his expression now as he watched from the window.

The sun had dried out the ground; the players were aflame with the thrill of the sport. Ginnosuke, with one of his boys, had challenged Bunpei and his partner, but the combination quickly proved too much even for the tennis-mad Ginnosuke; roundly defeated, he and his partner dropped their rackets and walked off the court as the crisp air echoed with their opponents' cries of "Game!" and excited applause from the spectators. Two or three women teachers, leaning from a classroom window, joined in the clapping. Several of the boys who had been watching rushed forward to grab the rackets. The first to pick one up, though, was Senta, the eta. Seeing who it was, the others ran up and tried to snatch it from him, but he held on to it for all he was worth, his face burning with resentment at being set on so unjustly. So far, so good; but when he stood his ground, waiting, no partner would come out to join him. "Nobody coming?" shouted the pair on the other side of the net, impatient to start. Exchanging glances, the boys jeered at Senta, exulting in his humiliation as he stood awkwardly out there on the court. Not a single one would partner him.

Ushimatsu threw off his haori and picked up the remaining racket. Laughter broke the tension. The women teachers smiled from their window. The principal looked on with a new interest, presumably anxious for his favourite Bunpei not to lose to Ushimatsu. With the afternoon sun behind them, Bunpei and his partner had the advantage from the start.

"One–zero!" called Ginnosuke, who was acting as umpire.

Ushimatsu and Senta had lost the first point. The boys lining the court smiled derisively, enjoying Senta's defeat.

"Two–zero!" from Ginnosuke again. Another point lost. "Two–zero!" the boys repeated, just loud enough for Ushimatsu and Senta to hear.

Their opponents—Bunpei and a young probationary teacher, the one Ushimatsu had run into on his way back from going to look at the room at Rengeji—were not novices and made a well-balanced pair, while Ushimatsu's partner had hardly begun to learn.

"Three–zero!" Riled, and seemingly obsessed even in the game by the need to save the pair of them from defeat in this confrontation of outcasts versus "citizens," Ushimatsu urged his weak partner to keep trying.

Ushimatsu's turn to serve. He took his stand on the line facing Bunpei for what could be the last point. His first ball grazed the net.

"Net!" called Ginnosuke. Ushimatsu served again.

"Fault!"

The last chance. Furious by now, Ushimatsu summoned all his strength for his last, critical serve, staking his destiny, as young men will in that time of dreams, on the outcome of a game.

Bunpei's return was masterly. Carefully avoiding Ushimatsu, he placed the ball where Senta, who was already confused, was least expecting it—with the sun shining full in his face, the boy never even saw it coming.

"Game!" The boys who had tried to snatch Senta's racket clapped and danced in triumph. Even the principal, to his surprise, found himself shouting congratulations to Bunpei.

"A zero game, Segawa—too bad!"

Too crestfallen to heed Ginnosuke's remark, Ushimatsu picked up his haori and left the sports ground. Going round into the yard behind the school, where there was no one to see him, he stopped suddenly. How could he forgive himself? Rentaro, Ohinata, and now Senta . . . linked together, the three names made him shiver with fear. Always, to spite him, wisdom dawned too late. . . .

# Chapter 6

## 1

Ushimatsu and Ginnosuke stayed on at school that evening because they were both on night watch. Keinoshin, suddenly disconsolate after the festivities were over, could not bring himself to go home; supper over, he stayed talking in the duty room till the clock on the wall struck eight, then nine, with the two young teachers, their own lives hardly begun, still listening with a smile to the old man's querulous ramblings.

Unlike the day, the night was cold, hinting at the severity of the morning frost to come. When Ushimatsu went out to do his rounds, Keinoshin did not budge from the hibachi but went on talking with only Ginnosuke to listen. After twenty minutes or so Ushimatsu came back. Blowing out his lamp at the door, he hurried over to the hibachi.

"Cold's not the word for it! I'm numb all over. It's the bitterest night we've had this year. Feel this!" He put an icy hand on Ginnosuke's wrist.

"Hey, you're frozen!" Jerking his hand away, Ginnosuke gazed at his friend with concern. "You're looking pale, Segawa. Anything the matter?" he found himself asking again.

"Just what I was going to say," nodded Keinoshin.

Ushimatsu shivered, as if at some sudden recollection. For a moment he hesitated—but with the other two staring at him so intently, it was impossible to keep silent.

"An incredible thing happened just now. . . ."

"What d'you mean, incredible?" Ginnosuke frowned.

"It was when I was walking round the outside of the building. I'd just passed the vaulting-horse on the playground when I heard somebody calling. There was nobody anywhere near, though—I had the lamp with me . . . the voice seemed familiar, somehow, and no wonder, as I realized after a moment: it was my father's."

"The world's a queer place, right enough," said Keinoshin wonderingly. "What did it say, this voice of yours?"

"It kept repeating, 'Ushimatsu, Ushimatsu.' "

"Called your name, did it?" Keinoshin's eyes widened.

Ginnosuke laughed. "Don't be ridiculous. Segawa's been having hallucinations."

"No, it was real. I'm sure of it," Ushimatsu insisted.

"But how could it be? It must have been some other sound you mistook for your name."

"You can laugh, Tsuchiya, but it *was* my name, I tell you. It wasn't the wind, it wasn't a bird—and of all voices, would I be likely to mistake *that* one? It *was* him—my father."

"You're joking—having us on."

"Nothing'll convince you, will it, Tsuchiya? But I'm serious. I heard it with my own ears—"

"That's just it—I don't trust those ears of yours. Your father's away on his farm up in the mountains, isn't he? And you talk of hearing his voice, down here in Iiyama! You're fooling, Segawa."

"Didn't I say it was incredible?"

"Incredible—like the old fairy tales, eh? We know better than to believe in that sort of thing nowadays."

"But, Tsuchiya," put in Keinoshin, "that's too sweeping. There may be exceptions—"

"Trust an old fogy like you to say that!" said Ginnosuke with good-humoured irony.

Suddenly Ushimatsu stiffened, as if he were hearing again the voice he had described. His face grew paler, and a strange, indefinable fear showed in his eyes; they knew now he was not joking.

"There it is again—outside the window! It's so strange . . . I'll go and have another look. Be back in a minute!" He ran out into the dark.

Ginnosuke was anxious about his friend, Keinoshin awe-struck. His *father's* voice, of all things. . . . Surely it must be a sign, an omen?

"Come to think of it, it's worse if we just sit here worrying—why don't we go after him?" suggested Keinoshin.

"Good idea." Ginnosuke got up from the hibachi. "There must be something the matter with him. Nerves, if you ask me. Hold on a second, I'll fix a lamp."

## 2

Deep in thought, Ushimatsu made his way to where he believed the voice came from. The light from the window of the duty room shone feebly on a corner of the play-ground; everything else—the school building, the trees—was invisible, wrapped in darkness and silence, as if in hiding. It was a windless night, piercingly cold. No one who does not know at firsthand the severity of the upland climate can imagine the bitter chill of these Shinshu nights.

Again he heard his father's voice. . . . Ushimatsu stopped, peering through the faint starlight: no sign of any human shape, no sound. What was it that was deluding him on this bitter night, when even the prowling dogs were silent?

*"Ushimatsu! Ushimatsu!"* Again . . . he shuddered, distraught and feverish. It *was* his father's voice, hoarse but still resonant, calling to him from the distant valley of Nishinoiri, beneath the peaks of Eboshi. . . . He looked up. Like the earth, the sky was at rest: voiceless, soundless. The daytime breeze had died, the birds vanished; nothing remained but the cold gleam of the scattered stars and the awe-inspiring spectacle of the Milky Way, trailing like a wisp of smoke across the majestic heavens. As his gaze lingered on the sea of indigo above him, it seemed to dissolve into a vision of the world beyond; he heard it again,

his father's voice calling his name, echoing through the cold, starry spaces in search of his son. But what did it mean? Ushimatsu walked about the yard, bewildered. Why, why this calling of his name? Ushimatsu remembered the commandment, his father's solemn words. . . . Perhaps it was only natural for a father's love to sense, even at a distance, the spiritual struggles of his son? A plea to keep their secret always, never to forget what it had cost his father to raise his family thus far—from the cowherd's hut on the mountain slopes? Or was it all mere fancy, a fabrication of his own anxiety? In a daze of fear and doubt prompted by these imaginings, hardly conscious of what he was doing, Ushimatsu answered the call: "Father! Father!"

"Ah, there you are!" Ginnosuke appeared suddenly, with Keinoshin behind him. Lantern in hand, he peered at Ushimatsu's face, then into the darkness round them. Ushimatsu told them he had heard the voice again.

"There you are, Tsuchiya—I told you so," said Keinoshin, shivering with cold and fear.

Ginnosuke laughed. "Nonsense. It's nerves all right. Segawa's so—so touchy these days. That's why he's hearing things."

"Think it's nerves, do you?" Ushimatsu said, reflectively.

"Look, when people see things that aren't there, hear things when nobody's spoken, it's proof they're upset, nervy. Voices, visions—they're nothing but hallucinations, born of fear."

"Hallucinations?"

"Bogies, bugbears of your own invention, if you like. Aural hallucinations—sounds a bit odd, but that's what you've been having tonight."

"Maybe."

For a few moments none of the three spoke. No sound broke the silence all around them. Suddenly, from the vast loneliness of the starry sky, Ushimatsu heard again his father's voice.

*"Ushima—a—tsu! Ushima—a—tsu!"* It grew fainter, like the cry of a bird in flight, and faded at last into the enveloping silence.

"Segawa!" Ginnosuke shone his lantern again on his friend's face, which had grown paler still.

"I heard it again."

"Just now? I heard nothing. There wasn't any voice."

"Wasn't there?"

"What d'you mean, 'wasn't there'? If there wasn't, there wasn't. That's all there is to it." He turned to Keinoshin. "Did you hear anything?"

"No, nothing." Keinoshin was equally definite.

"See? Neither of us heard anything—only you. Proof again it's your nerves." Once again Ginnosuke's lantern swept the darkness round them. The sky was a mirror now, reflecting only the pale glimmering of the stars; the earth, a huge black shadow. No shape that might have spoken came within the lantern's beam. Ginnosuke laughed. "I wouldn't believe it even if I heard it, or saw it, for that matter, whatever it was—not without touching it first. It's just as I've been saying all along. You hear these voices of yours because you're in bad physical condition, and for no other reason at all. Which reminds me—it's freezing. I'm not standing out here any longer!"

## 3

That night Ushimatsu lay sleepless on the tatami floor of the duty room, thinking still of his father and of Inoko. Ginnosuke began to snore within seconds of getting into bed; gazing at his friend's face on the pillow beside his own, Ushimatsu envied him his easy, peaceful sleep.

Well on into the night, he jumped out of bed, turned up the oil lamp, and started to write a letter to Rentaro. A letter to *him*, even though it was only to ask how he was and wish him a speedy recovery, had to be written where and when there was no chance of his being seen. Several times he stopped, glancing at Ginnosuke; but his friend lay with his mouth open like a dead fish, sunk in sleep.

Rentaro was not a total stranger. They had met once, on a friend's introduction, and had begun to get to know each other a little through letters they exchanged two or three times earlier that year. But Rentaro looked on Ushimatsu simply as a well-wisher, never dreaming that he was an eta like himself. Ushimatsu, for his part, hesitated to reveal his secret and felt himself for that reason under a kind of shamefaced constraint in his dealings with Rentaro, so that even in the letter he was writing now he could not express himself freely. The reason *why* he felt so drawn to Rentaro—if he were to tell him *that*, there'd be no need to write of anything else. . . . He would have told, if he could. But he could not: this was the flaw in Ushimatsu. So the letter finished as it had begun—as a commonplace letter of sympathy to a sick man. A spasm of guilt struck him as he signed it. Tossing the brush aside, he sighed, and crept between the cold sheets. No sooner had he begun to doze than nightmare after nightmare crowded upon him.

Next morning Simple Sho from Rengeji turned up at the school with a message for Ushimatsu, insisting on seeing him in person; so Ushimatsu went out to the main entrance to meet him. Sho handed him a telegram. Hastily Ushimatsu broke the seal and read it:

FATHER DEAD

Dazed, refusing to believe what he saw, he read the words again. It was true: *his father, dead.* The telegram was from his uncle in Nezu.

COME HOME IMMEDIATELY

the message ended.

"Terrible, terrible! What a shock for you, sir. . . . Yes, I'll go back and tell the mistress right away," said Simple Sho, a childish horror of death in his halfwit eyes.

Though he was well on in years, Ushimatsu's father had always been exceptionally healthy, never catching so much as a cold, even in the bitterest of the mountain winter, and outdoing much younger men in strength and endurance. The life of a cowherd—the words have a romantic, pastoral ring, but the work itself is beyond any ordinary man, especially up there on the pastures of Nishinoiri: "Old Segawa can stand it up there, who else?" people would say. A man cannot live for years in that remote valley on a knowledge of cattle alone. Even if he can endure the cold, the loneliness will wear him down. Anyone born under the warm southern sun lacks the stamina for a mountain cowherd's life. The mountain folk of northern Shinshu are different; and Ushimatsu's father, in particular, frugal, sinewy, and hard-working as he was—for him the hardest labour was never just "work"—had his own private reason for preferring seclusion from his fellow men. Always prudent, it was not only on Ushimatsu that he enjoined concealment. He himself took care to attract as little attention as possible, hoping for nothing, praying for nothing but his son's success; for Ushimatsu's sake he had exchanged the floating world for these remote mountain slopes, to spend months on end alone with his cattle, contemplating the smoke of distant charcoal burners' fires. The saké he bought with the little money Ushimatsu sent him every month was his great pleasure, enabling him, as he often said, to forget both hardship and loneliness.

That this father of his, this man of iron, should have died so suddenly—no word of any illness, even. . . . The telegram gave no details. Each year his father would go up to the cowherd's hut in the early spring, as soon as the snow began to melt, and not return to their cottage in Himekozawa till the valleys were buried once again in snow. It was just about now that he was due to come down for the winter, but the telegram did not say whether he had died at home or up at Nishinoiri.

Ushimatsu remembered the voice he had heard in the night, and how it had grown fainter and more distant, as if saying a last farewell. Even Ginnosuke was dumbfounded for a moment when Ushimatsu showed him the telegram, staring at it and at Ushimatsu in turn.

"You said you had an uncle in Nezu?" he said at last. "He'll have seen to everything, I suppose. But what a blow for you, Segawa! You'd better go and get ready to leave right away. We'll take care of your work here." Sincerity shone in Ginnosuke's face. He said nothing of what had happened the previous night. "Death is a fact, nothing mysterious about *that,*" was all that could be read in this young botanist's eyes.

The principal came to school precisely on time. Ushimatsu told him of the telegram and asked leave to start for home at once, since Ginnosuke had agreed to take his classes.

"A great shock for you, of course, my dear Segawa," began the principal ingratiatingly. "Don't worry about school. Tsuchiya and Katsuno will cope between them. Fancy, your father dead—I shouldn't have thought it possible. . . . You'll come back and give of your best to the school again, I'm sure, as soon as the mourning's over. The success we've had is partly due to you, you know. I can't tell you what an encouragement it is to me to have you on our staff. Someone was speaking so highly of you the other day—I felt I was being praised myself! I depend on you a great deal, you see." His tone changed. "But journeys cost money, more than one thinks. I've some cash here, as it happens, so I could give you an advance. How about it, Segawa? No need to be shy about asking: it wouldn't do if you ran out, would it?"

The principal was exceptionally friendly, but to Ushimatsu's ears his cordiality seemed forced.

"Don't forget to put in your notification of absence—rules, you know!" the principal added.

## 4

Ushimatsu hurried back to Rengeji. The priest's wife and O-Shio ran out to meet him, to ask about the telegram. Staring at him as the dreadful news sank in, the two women listened to his strange tale of the night before, investing it as women will with terrors of their own imagining. Agitatedly they recalled similar "coincidences," of which stories abound—portents of death, visitations from the souls of the dying, spirits flying through the night.

"But, Mr. Segawa," the priest's wife said suddenly. "I'm forgetting—you surely haven't had anything to eat yet."

"No, how silly of us," put in O-Shio.

"Then you get your things ready, and I'll see to your breakfast. Such a pity I've so little in the house, and you going off on a journey. . . . Shall I grill some salted salmon?"

Almost in tears by now, the good lady bustled about the kitchen, muttering nenbutsu incessantly. Years of temple life had had their effect on this untonsured nun, making her susceptible nature yet more tender and easily moved.

Ushimatsu went upstairs to get ready. The occasion being what it was, there was no need to take either presents or luggage. He changed into the hand-woven padded kimono his aunt had given him, and was tying on his leggings for the journey when Kesaji, the maid, followed by O-Shio, came up with his breakfast. Used as he was to eating on his own, with the rice tub set down beside him so that he could help himself as often as he wanted, for Ushimatsu the prospect of being served by O-Shio was at once embarrassing and agreeable. He pulled the table toward him and started on the bowl she had already filled. There was less constraint than before in O-Shio's manner. No longer so nervous of him, and less reserved now that she knew of his genuine sympathy for her father, she asked him all kinds of questions as she served him. One such question concerned his mother.

"Mother? She died when I was seven," said Ushimatsu simply, as a man should. "It's so long ago, I hardly remember her. Really I don't know what it's like to have a mother. Or a father, for that matter. I've spent so little time with him these last six or seven years. . . . My father was getting on, though—he was older than yours. It's healthy people like him, maybe, who go quickest when they do get ill. So you see I haven't had much to do with my parents. But it's been the same with you, O-Shio, hasn't it?"

O-Shio grew tearful. She had not lived under the same roof with her father since that spring—she was twelve then —when she was adopted by the temple family; and her mother, like Ushimatsu's, had died when she was a child, so that she too had seen little of her parents. Recalling her family's decline, O-Shio blushed and bent her head.

Watching her, Ushimatsu could imagine her dead mother. "Whenever I look at her, it's her mother I see," Keinoshin had said; when she was young, the woman who "relied in everything on her husband, trusted him absolutely in the old-fashioned way" must have been exactly like the girl before him—affectionate, easily moved to tears, her expression changing so often that you felt you were looking at someone different every time you glanced at her. Like O-Shio, she must have appeared plain one minute, enchanting the next, now pale and seemingly lifeless, now gay with all the freshness and innocence of youth, a touch of red unfolding in her white cheeks with the naturalness of a flower. So he imagined O-Shio's mother to have been in her youth: with the beauty and character natural to a girl of northern Shinshu, and most apparent to a northern Shinshu man like Ushimatsu.

His preparations for the journey made, Ushimatsu went downstairs to drink tea with the others. The priest's wife presented him with a wooden rosary as a journey gift. In a pair of straw sandals woven by Simple Sho, to farewell bows from Sho and the women, he walked out through the high temple gateway.

# Chapter 7

## 1

Ushimatsu would never forget the loneliness of that journey. Compared with the last time he had gone home, in the summer of the year before last, he felt himself to be utterly changed. Two years—not long, perhaps, but for Ushimatsu time enough for the great crisis of his life to have begun. Some, in different circumstances, go placidly through the world, changing but only unconsciously: for Ushimatsu the inner convulsion had been both violent and deeply felt. For the moment, at least, there was no need to be on his guard. Drinking freely of the crisp, dry air as he walked along the bank of the Chikuma River, he gave himself up to brooding on his uncertain destiny and wondering at the upheavals it had brought him so far. The waters of the Chikuma, a muddy yellowish green, flowing silently toward the distant sea; the squat willow trees, leafless now, cowering on its banks; river, trees, mountains—the unchanged landscape intensified his gloom still further. Sometimes he all but threw himself down by the roadside to weep in secret among the dead grasses, in the hope of lightening even a little his burden of near-despair. But he could not; his heart was too heavy, too tightly locked in darkness to be able to seek such easy relief.

Groups of travellers drifted past him, some with tear-stained faces, haunted by the memory of better days, haggard like starving dogs; some walking barefoot, in grimy kimonos, looking for work; a sunburnt father and son on a pilgrimage of penitence, chanting a sad hymn, the hardships of their journey transmuted into austerities of saving power; a company of strolling musicians in slatternly hats of straw, masquerading as innocent victims of the world, begging as they strummed a love song on their samisen. Ushimatsu watched them all, comparing their lot with his own: how wretched his life, how enviable their freedom!

Yet even for him every step away from Iiyama seemed a step toward freedom. Gradually, as he tramped the grey earth of the Northern Highway in bright sunshine, now climbing gentle hills, now winding through fields of mulberry or straggling villages, sweating, his throat parched, socks and leggings white with dust, Ushimatsu began, paradoxically, to feel refreshed. Branches of persimmon trees by the roadside sagged under their load of ripening yellow globes; in one field, soy pods swelled; millet heads drooped, full-eared, in another; in others, already harvested, green shoots of wheat were sprouting. He heard farmers singing, birds chirruping—for the joy of "little June," as the mountain dwellers call their Indian summer. Free of mist, that day even the high peaks of the Kosha massif revealed themselves in their splendour; from the valleys between them, blue smoke climbed into the sky from charcoal burners' fires.

Just past Kanizawa, a ricksha with a fashionably dressed passenger overtook Ushimatsu. He recognized Takayanagi Risaburo, the politician who had made that speech at the imperial birthday celebration the day before. This was the time of year, he recalled, when prospective Diet candidates began to work up publicity for themselves and their views; Takayanagi was no doubt off on a country tour to prepare the ground for the next election. Riding past with a pompous air, he gave Ushimatsu a supercilious glance but did not speak to him. Two or three hundred yards farther on, he looked back again; but Ushimatsu took no particular notice.

As the sun climbed gradually higher, the plain of Minochi unfolded before Ushimatsu's eyes, spreading out on both sides of the Chikuma, its sandy topsoil, washed down from upstream, testifying to the violence of the spring floods. Fields stretched away as far as he could see, interrupted here and there by clumps of zelkova trees. Plain and mountains seemed to be inhaling the deep blue November air, witnesses to nature's vitality even in the months of withering and decay. Ushimatsu hurried on, eager to make the best speed possible upstream, to Chiisagata, to Nezu, drawn always by the blue skies that shone like a sea of light above his beloved home.

It was two o'clock in the afternoon when he reached Toyono, where he had to catch the train. Takayanagi, after arriving earlier by ricksha, had apparently been waiting for the same train; a few minutes before it was due he came out of the tea house near the station. Where was he going, Ushimatsu wondered. Takayanagi looked at him, evidently asking himself the same question about Ushimatsu; yet he seemed to be taking care their eyes did not meet, as if he were somehow anxious to avoid him. At the ceremony the day before they had only seen each other, had not been introduced, and neither made any move to speak now.

A warning bell rang; the waiting passengers pressed through the barrier. Belching black smoke, the train, which had come from Naoetsu down on the coast, drew into the little station. Takayanagi pushed through the crowd, opened a door, and disappeared inside. Ushimatsu chose a compartment near the engine. Amazed, he recognized one of its occupants.

"Inoko sensei!" He took off his hat and bowed. Inoko too looked overjoyed at this chance meeting.

## 2

So here he was, face to face by pure chance with the man who for so long had not been absent, waking or sleeping, from his thoughts; who was looking at him now, obviously glad to see him again, and surprised, it would seem, at his new look of maturity. His eyes shining with affection and respect, Ushimatsu explained the reason for his journey. So sudden, so unexpected, and with the innermost feelings of both men revealing themselves so unfeignedly, the meeting had that special beauty that flowers now and again in a friendship between one man and another.

The tall, rather pale woman sitting on Rentaro's right put down the newspaper she was reading and looked at Ushimatsu. And a stout, well-dressed elderly gentleman in the corner, who had been gazing at the mountains through the window, turned to look first at him and then at Rentaro.

Having read of his illness in the paper and written to him to express his sympathy, Ushimatsu was surprised and delighted to see Rentaro so well, with no sign of the emaciated appearance Ushimatsu in his anxiety had imagined. The broad forehead, lined by an inflexible will, the jutting cheekbones, and above all the eyes, burning with a fierce, nervous light, reflected the heroic spirit within. Maybe his lack of pallor was misleading—consumptives often have bright cheeks—but from what Ushimatsu saw, he could not believe the man opposite him was as ill as the paper had said, in great pain and retching blood. . . . He told Rentaro of the article.

"They said it was that bad, did they?" Rentaro smiled. "Somebody heard a message wrong, I suppose—I have been bad, and they must have assumed I still was. The papers often make mistakes like that. Don't worry on my account. I'm well enough to travel, as you can see. I wonder who blew the thing up so?" He laughed.

Rentaro was on the way home from Akakura Spa, where he had been convalescing. He introduced his companions. The quiet, refined-looking lady on his right was his wife; the portly gentleman was a Shinshu lawyer and politician named Ichimura, well known for his eloquence and forthrightness, who was about to put himself forward as a prospective Diet candidate.

"Mr. Segawa, is it?" said the lawyer with an easy friendliness, smiling pleasantly as he introduced himself.

"Ichimura and I got to know each other quite by chance," said Rentaro, "but we're close friends now, as you can see, and I owe him a great deal. He's been such a help with getting my books published."

The lawyer shook his massive head vigorously. "No, the debt's on my side, I assure you. Inoko's my junior in years, that's true, but in everything else I sit at his feet." He sighed. "All the men of real character and spirit nowadays are young. Look how old *I* am, and all my life as good as wasted: it makes me ashamed to think of it." The regret in his words was genuine, unmarred by any trace of envy of more gifted, original minds. Born on Sado Island, it was only ten years since he had settled up here in the mountain country. Passionate by temperament, impetuous alike in good and evil, he had known every kind of trouble, pleaded for every kind of client, and in a long political career had experienced at firsthand all the struggles for power, the short-lived dreams of parties and factions, the pains of imprisonment as a "political"; had tasted, in short, all the sweets and bitters society has to offer, to become at last what he was now—a man of compassion, ally of the weak and the poor. Who can fathom heaven's dispensations? What stranger than that this politician should have for his friend, in his declining years, an educated, talented eta—an outcast?

Ushimatsu gathered that Ichimura had embarked on a speech-making tour to Komoro, Iwamurata, Usuda, and other centres and was determined to make the trip on foot up to his own Chiisagata, to present himself to the electors there. Rentaro was accompanying him, partly to support his friend on the platform, partly to deepen his own study of social problems. That night he would be staying at Ueda with Ichimura. Sometime in the next two or three days, Ushimatsu was thrilled to hear, he hoped to get up as far as Nezu.

"You're teaching at Iiyama at the moment?" Ichimura

asked. "Iiyama—one of the other candidates is from there, isn't he?" Set a thief to catch a thief—and politicians to track each other down. Ichimura's question followed immediately on his hearing that Ushimatsu was from Iiyama. Takayanagi was travelling on the same train, Ushimatsu told him. He seemed to find the news puzzling for some reason, tilting his head and repeating several times, "Where can he be going, I wonder." Then he laughed. "But this is what makes going by train so interesting—you've no idea who you're travelling with."

No one can sense so clearly as a sick person whether the feelings of others are genuine or feigned. Receiving as he did so much pretended sympathy from the healthy and fortunate, it was a relief for Rentaro to have with him such genuine friends, and he seemed deeply appreciative, in particular, of Ushimatsu's sincerity, which showed itself in the tone of everything he said. His wife took from her basket some persimmons she had bought through the window at the last station. Picking out some of the reddest and most juicy-looking, she offered them to Ushimatsu and the lawyer. Rentaro took one too, and inhaling its autumn fragrance, began speaking of his experiences at Akakura Spa and of his trip out to the Echigo coast, interrupting himself to extol the freshness of the Shinshu persimmons compared with what passed for fruit in the markets of the capital.

Groups of peasants boarded the train at every stop. Loud laughter and peasant talk, unconstrained by city manners, filled their compartment. Up here in Shinshu even the trains, unlike those of the Tokaido line, were old and crudely built, resembling the mountain cottages among which they ran. The higher they climbed, the more violent the lurching from side to side and rattling of windows, till the passengers could no longer hear one another talk. The Chikuma River, which down at Iiyama lapped as smooth as oil against its banks, had changed to a torrent, throwing up silver waves as it sped down the narrow valley bottom. Currents of crisp, invigorating air from the windows signalled their approach to the highlands.

Soon the train arrived at Ueda. Most of the passengers

got off here, including Rentaro and his wife and the lawyer.

"We'll see you at Nezu," Rentaro promised. Sadly Ushimatsu gazed after him as he walked away.

Suddenly alone in the compartment, Ushimatsu leaned against the cold iron pillar in the aisle, closed his eyes, and pictured to himself once again the chance meeting that had just ended. To tell the truth, he was somehow disappointed. For all the frankness and cordiality Rentaro had shown him, Ushimatsu still sensed in the older man's manner a reserve, an indefinable coolness. How could it have been, he wondered, when his admiration for Rentaro was so deep, so genuine, that Rentaro had failed to respond? With a touch of envy he recalled the intimacy the lawyer enjoyed with his friend.

Then the truth dawned on him. His sympathy for Rentaro, his admiration for him, the strange sense of frustration in his relationship with this man, all arose from the simple fact that he himself, like his hero, was an outcast; and so long as he kept this secret, though he were to talk himself hoarse on any other subject, his deepest feelings would never touch any corresponding chord in Rentaro. How could he expect otherwise? Suppose he *were* to tell him—how much lighter would be his burden then. . . . Amazed and delighted, Rentaro would take him by the hand: "You too?" In that moment each spirit would recognize itself in the other; together they would enter on a far more profound relationship, sharing the same tragic destiny. . . . That was it. Rentaro, at least, he *must* tell! Ushimatsu pictured to himself the joy of their next meeting. . . .

## 3

It was nearly evening when the train drew into Tanaka Station. Passengers bound for Nezu had to walk the three miles or so from here, climbing up across the mountainside. As Ushimatsu stepped down onto the platform, he noticed Takayanagi getting off too—an imposing figure, as befitted a Diet candidate. Yet there was a curiously preoccupied, almost melancholy air about him, along with the obvious hunger for power and show. Now and then he looked round almost furtively; Takayanagi was still avoiding his glance, Ushimatsu noticed. Evidently he *was* anxious they should not meet. Where was he going, he wondered again. Takayanagi hurried through the barrier to mingle, almost as if he were looking for somewhere to hide, with the little crowd of countryfolk who had come to meet him. Then, fugitivelike, with his head sunk deep in his overcoat collar, still surrounded by jostling peasants, he set off in the direction Ushimatsu was about to take.

When Ushimatsu turned off the Northern Highway to take the narrow track where it led through a mulberry plantation, Takayanagi and his party were no longer in sight. As he climbed higher, up a path between paddy fields terraced with stone walls, a broad, smooth slope spread out before him, sweeping up to the mountains, to Mount Asama and the three peaks of Mount Sanpo, and dotted here and there with a straggling hamlet or a pine wood, each one the focus for Ushimatsu of precious memories. Far below, deep in the valley, the Chikuma gleamed in the evening sun. A bank of purple-grey cloud hid the Hida mountains to the west, a region untrodden by man since time began. But for the clouds, their snowy peaks would have shone like silver in the dying sunlight, a panorama of astounding grandeur. Ushimatsu had always loved mountains. As he walked the uneven, rocky path, gazing now at the spectacular slope above him, now at the no less spectacular valley below, and thinking of the simple life and ways of the mountain dwellers of Shinshu, the tide of young blood within him seemed to rise in instinctive response from every corner of his body. Iiyama lay now beneath a distant sky. Drinking deep draughts of the air the mountains themselves exhale, for a while he knew once more the joy of self-forgetfulness.

He watched the sun sink down in glory upon the mountaintops. The mountains themselves changed their colours in the gradually thinning light, from red to purple, from purple to grey; slopes and foothills darkened, and shadows spread from valley to valley, as the last rays lingered on the peaks. In another corner of the sky Mount Asama trailed its streamer of grey smoke flecked with yellow, like a smouldering cloud.

Ushimatsu's absorption in the splendour around him did not last long. With Araya left behind, another village met his gaze, with the mountain rising behind: a checkerboard of earthen and whitewashed walls wrapped in dusk, and dark twisted shapes projecting between one cottage roof and another—persimmon branches, surely—Nezu it was, at last! Here even the voice of a peasant singing on his way home could touch Ushimatsu to the quick. Here it was that his father had come from the town, from Komoro—to hide; at this thought, the evening landscape lost its charm. The sheer joy of coming home mingled with despair; his legs began to tremble. Nature could console, but only for the briefest moment, for with every step he took toward Nezu his awareness of what he was, of himself as an eta, an outcast, a *chori,*[1] weighed more heavily upon his spirit.

When he entered the village that was the second of the two homes he had known, it was quite dark. His father had moved with his family to this particular place partly because the village was within easy reach of the cattle pastures, and partly because he could rent a bit of land here for next to nothing—the fields Ushimatsu's uncle was working now. Always cautious, he had chosen to settle on the outskirts of the village, where he would attract the least possible attention: Himekozawa hamlet, Nezu Village, Chiisagata District, Nagano Prefecture—such was Ushimatsu's second home, a hamlet of fifty households.

## 4

His father had died away from home, in the cowherd's hut up at the Nishinoiri pasture grounds. Ushimatsu's uncle had been waiting till he came so they could go up to Nishinoiri together. Sitting him down by the fire to rest a little after the journey, he talked of the dead man in the kindly, selfless way Ushimatsu remembered so well, while his wife listened, sobbing, and the fire burned briskly in the

[1] Used here as another name for the eta. See Introduction, p. x, n. 8.

hearth. Neither old age nor illness had caused Mr. Segawa's death: his end had been sudden, a sacrifice, one could say, to his work. With a natural love for cattle and long experience as a cowherd, he was universally trusted, not least by the owner of the pasture grounds, and no one could suspect this veteran of the pastures of any mistake or oversight. But none can foresee how life will treat a man: tragedy had come suddenly, its instrument a bull that had lately been introduced to the herd. Even a normally placid bull may turn fierce for a while, or even run amuck, when let loose among the cows: much more so a naturally boisterous crossbreed. Maddened by the freedom of the broad pastures and the lowing of the cows, the habits imposed during its breeding forgotten, the bull had disappeared from the pastures, reverting to the wild beast it was born to be. Three days, four days passed, and still it did not come back. Ushimatsu's father had gone out each day to search for it, wading through marshland, tramping from hill to hill, calling it by name till late in the evening, but to no avail.

Yesterday morning he had set out once again—without his dinner, which normally he would take in his haversack whenever he had far to go—but had not come back at the expected time. Puzzled, the man who worked for him went up to the Nishinoiri hut as usual with the salt for the cows. When he got there, the cows came crowding round as if they were especially glad to see him—and there among them, trying to look innocent, was the bull, its horns dyed red with blood. Horrified, with the help of a couple of other men who happened to be up in the pasture, he caught the beast. It was tired by then and made no great show of resistance. The man then started to look for Mr. Segawa, and found him at last, lying moaning in a thicket of bamboo. He managed to carry him on his shoulders to the hut but could do nothing for him, the wound was so deep. So he hurried down to the village with the news. Mr. Segawa was still conscious when his brother reached the hut; he had died at ten o'clock last night. Today the villagers had gone up to the pasture grounds to prepare for the farewell vigil at the hut that night. They would be waiting now for Ushimatsu.

"So there we are." Ushimatsu's uncle glanced at his nephew. "I asked your father before he died if there was anything he wanted to say. The pain was bad, but his mind was clear enough, I could see. 'I've spent my life minding cows, and I've always wanted to die for them,' he said. 'There's nothing else—except for Ushimatsu. I'm anxious about him. There have been hard days, I won't deny. It's for his sake I've stuck them out. There's something I've kept reminding him of all through. When he comes home, tell him *not to forget. Not to forget*—that's all. . . . ' "

Ushimatsu bowed his head as he listened in silence to his father's dying words.

"That wasn't all," his uncle went on. " 'Don't hold the funeral down in Nezu,' he said. 'Bury me up here on the mountain where I belong, under the grazing. And don't let them know in Komoro that I'm dead—don't tell them, brother!' I promised, and that pleased him, by the look on his face—he smiled a little. A while later—he was still watching me—the tears started streaming down his cheeks. He didn't speak again."

This account of his father's last moments moved Ushimatsu beyond words. "Bury me on the mountain." "Don't tell them in Komoro!"—all for *his* sake. Behind the words he felt afresh his father's extraordinary caution and his fierce, unwearying resolve, a decision once taken, to persist in it to the end. With his son he had been more than strict, almost cruel. Even now, after his death, Ushimatsu still stood in awe of his father.

After resting awhile he set off for the Nishinoiri pasture. His uncle, who went with him, had seen to everything: the village office had certified the death, a coffin had been made; the priest of Joshin-in temple in Nezu had been asked to officiate at tonight's vigil and was up at the hut already. Everything was prepared for the funeral tomorrow. Ushimatsu had only to present himself at Nishinoiri, nothing more.

It was about a mile and a half to the foot of Mount Eboshi, by the lonely hill path over Tazawa Pass. The darkness was impenetrable; they could hardly see where to tread on the rocky ground. Lantern in hand, Ushimatsu led the way. When they had left the last of the village dwellings behind, the path grew steadily narrower till it was no more than a line of footprints among rotting leaves. They climbed several small ridges before coming down through a valley and onto the sweeping uplands, close by the cowherd's hut.

## 5

The little hut was crowded with villagers. Light shone through cracks in the wall; the dry sound of the priest's wooden gong mingled in the mountain air with the plashing of a stream, adding to the quiet, lonely sadness of the scene. The hut itself was little more than a shelter from the rain and dew, a thatched roof over rough walls. Save for an occasional foot traveller taking the shortcut by way of Tonoshiro Hill to Kazawa Spa, no stranger ever came this way. Nishinoiri witnessed only the harsh lives of a handful of charcoal burners, forest rangers, and cowherds.

Putting out his lantern, Ushimatsu entered the hut. The old priest of Joshin-in, a group from Himekozawa who had been helping with the funeral arrangements, some peasants and their wives, old friends of Ushimatsu's father—all greeted Ushimatsu with kindly sympathy. The smoke of incense, picked out by the flickering light of a taper, cast a haze over everything in the room. The body lay in a crude, makeshift coffin. White cloth had been draped around it, and the memorial tablet placed in front, among offerings of rice dumplings, chrysanthemums, water, and sprays of aniseed leaves. After the first reading from the sutras, at a sign from the priest the mourners came one by one to stand before the coffin and pay their respects. Tears streaked their faces. Ushimatsu followed his uncle; bowing, he looked upon his father in the dim candlelight and took his earthly farewell. His lonely cowherd's life ended, the figure in the coffin seemed to be waiting for the moment when he would lie deep beneath the grazing grounds. How his face had changed—cold, pale, bloodless! Ushimatsu's uncle believed in the old ways. To help the dead man's spirit on its journey, he had laid out on the coffin lid a peasant's hat of woven sedge, straw sandals, a bottle of saké, and a knife to ward off evil spirits.

Before long the sutra readings began again. The priest struck his gong. A confusion of sounds, at once sad and jarring—the priest intoning, voices recalling stories of the dead man, guileless peasant laughter, the munching of food—gave Ushimatsu no chance to rest. The talk among the mourners went on all night. The dying man had asked them not to send word of his death to Komoro, and in any case it was seventeen years or more since he had left the town; so no message was sent, and no one came from Mukai. Ushimatsu's uncle was obsessed with fear of what might happen if word did reach Komoro that the old eta chief was dead and some awkward visitors came up in consequence. According to him, his brother's choice of the pasture as a grave had been thought out long ago. If his body were taken to one of the temples in Nezu, it would be all right if the funeral were accepted by the priest like any ordinary peasant's funeral, but there was always the terrible possibility that the body might be turned away. Custom ordained that eta had no right to burial in an ordinary cemetery. Ushimatsu's father knew this very well. For his son's sake he had endured the lonely mountain life, and for his son's sake he had chosen to be buried in the pasture. Even so, Ushimatsu's uncle was desperately worried; his one thought was to get through the funeral without incident.

The following afternoon the mourners gathered again in and around the hut. The owner of the pasture, the dairyman who kept his cattle there, and everyone else who had heard of the death came to join in the last rites. The grave had been prepared near a small pine tree on top of a hill. Presently the time came for the committal, and the body of the old herdsman was carried out from the hut he had known so well. Behind the coffin walked the priest, with two mischievous-looking acolytes; Ushimatsu followed with his uncle. The women all had white cloths wound round their heads. Each mourner wore what style of dress he chose: some were in formal cloaks with their family crest, some in homespun; as is the way among these mountain folk, almost none wore a hakama, the long divided skirt that is expected of city dwellers on such occasions, their lack of display matching the austere life of the dead herdsman. In no special order, without ceremony, its only escort the grief of sincere hearts, the little procession walked in silence up the hill.

The service at the hut had been simple too. Yet the humble mourners, with so many memories of the dead, had heard a solemn music in the plain rhythm of drum and bell and cymbals, a moving elegy in the mechanical chanting of the requiem and the sutras. After lighting a stick of incense and offering a final prayer, many had gone home. Now the coffin arrived at its last resting place. A mound of earth lined the grave; all round it the late-flowering daisies had been trampled flat by the gravediggers. When the remaining mourners, Ushimatsu and his uncle among them, had thrown in their handfuls of earth, the rest was shovelled in. It struck the lid of the coffin with a rumble like that of an avalanche, the clay sending up such a pungent smell as to awaken thoughts that were hard indeed to bear. Steadily the grave filled till a mound grew over it like a little hillock. Ushimatsu watched, sunk in thought. His uncle too was silent. *Do not forget!* his father had commanded once more with his dying breath; and now, vanished from the world, he lay deep under the earth of the pasture.

## 6

The funeral was over. Leaving the owner of the pasture to look after the grave, and the young herdsman who had worked under his father to take care of the hut, the mourners started back to Himekozawa. Ushimatsu wanted to take with him the black cat his father had kept at the hut, but it refused to leave its accustomed home. When he offered it food, it would not touch it; nor would it come when he called it. They could only hear its pitiful mewing from under the veranda. Beast though it was, it missed its dead master. How would it live up here in the mountains, they wondered, when the snow began to fall. "Poor creature—maybe it'll turn wild," said Ushimatsu's uncle.

One by one they started back. Ushimatsu and his uncle made their way over to the cattle pen first. The young herdsman went with them, carrying salt to put out for the cows where they were grazing. A wan November sun gave the Nishinoiri pasture an even more remote and desolate air. Young pine trees grew here and there along the way. Wild mountain azaleas, which the cows would not eat, bloomed everywhere among the grasses in spring but now stood withered and bare. Everything reminded Ushimatsu of his father. He remembered how toward the end of May two years before he had visited him in the pasture. It was the season, he remembered, when the horns of the cattle were beginning to itch, and these withered azaleas had been in full bloom, a wild profusion of reds and yellows. He remembered the children gathering spring herbs. He remembered the cooing of the turtledoves, the delightful breeze blowing over the lilies of the valley and bringing with it the scent of early summer. He remembered how his father had pointed out to him the new green on the hills and explained how well suited the rich grassland of Nishinoiri was for grazing cattle: a diet of such greenery with a little salt and water from the mountain streams was sufficient to cure almost every sickness that affected them. He remembered, with the old fascination, the stories his father had told, of cows that herded together according to their breed, of jousts with horns when a new member sought admission to the herd, of the sanctions that cattle, like men, apply to one another, of cows that had ruled the pasture like queens.

Ushimatsu's father had retired early to these mountain slopes, but a longing for fame and position burned within him all his life. In that, with his passionate nature, he was quite unlike his diffident, unassuming brother. The fierce resentment that drove him to the mountains because his birth made it impossible for him to work his way up in the world never left him. Nothing in his own life had gone the way he wanted, but for his son, and his son's children, he had long ago determined that things must be different. They were to be given the chance to live out his dreams—the sun could rise in the west before this resolve of his would change. *Go, my son! Fight, make your way in the world*—his father's spirit lived in these words. As Ushimatsu thought over that lonely life, he felt with a new force the passion and the hope in his father's dying message.

The sharpened sense of the cost of the commandment into

which his father had poured his whole life, his very spirit—his last, urgent breath—the unspoken communion, the flow between them, as of his father's very lifeblood—all these sensations, with the fact of death itself, left Ushimatsu shaken to the depths. Death is mute; yet it spoke now with greater power than a thousand words, to make him meditate upon his own life and destiny.

When they came to the cattle pen, Ushimatsu could look back at the work his father had left. Six miles and more of natural pasture, and the great herd, some standing, some lying asleep, scattered among the pines. The shed was at the eastern end of the long plateau. Within a rough stockade a number of still-hornless calves were grazing. The young herdsman, very mindful of his duty as host, made a fire with dead grass for them to warm themselves and went round collecting fuel to build it up. The mourners who were left had been up all night, and the day too had been tiring. At last exhaustion made itself felt; some of them half dozed around the fire, the smell of burning leaves in their nostrils. Ushimatsu's uncle put out heaps of salt on rocks round about for the cows to lick. Ushimatsu watched with a wistful tenderness the animals his father had known and cared for so well. A black cow flicked its tail, a brown cow with a white face and belly shook its ears, a brindle calf mooed; with quivering nostrils, eager for the salt but not knowing what to make of so many strangers, the nearest of the herd circled the little heaps at a distance. Some, greedier than the rest but still staring at the suspicious figures before them, edged a little closer. Ushimatsu's uncle laughed; Ushimatsu and the others laughed too. With such entertaining companions, they felt, even this lonely mountain life might be bearable.

Presently they took their leave of the ground where Ushimatsu's father would rest forever. The high peaks—Eboshi, Kakuma, Azumaya, Shirane—all disappeared behind them. As they passed the Fuji shrine, Ushimatsu turned back to look again at his father's grave, but by then even the cow pen was out of sight. He could see, beyond the long, bleak stretch of pasture, a single thread of smoke trailing off into the sky.

# Chapter 8

## 1

Talk of the old herdsman who had been buried up at Nishinoiri spread rapidly throughout Nezu. Exaggeration is always a temptation, not least with a story like this of death by goring, which awed the villagers, at least the more imaginative and curious among them, and provided the chief topic of conversation everywhere. The superstitious were convinced he must have committed some terrible wickedness in a previous life. All kinds of stories were told about what he had done before coming to Nezu: some said he had worked as a herdsman at Minamisaku, others that he was from Kai, others that he was an Aizu samurai who had come down in the world. No one knew that he had been the "chief" of the eta settlement in Komoro.

The morning after they held a party at his uncle's house for their neighbours who had helped with the funeral arrangements, Ushimatsu and his uncle went round to thank all those who had attended as mourners. Only his aunt stayed at home. By early afternoon, warm springlike sunshine was streaming across the onion patch in the back garden toward the veranda, where pumpkins were laid out in rows to dry. With no one to chase them from forbidden territory, the hens pecked at the flowers by the bamboo fence, or stood clucking in the sun, or hopped up onto the veranda to stalk unhindered over the floor of the living room. Ushimatsu's aunt was in front washing her cooking pots, bent double over the tiny stream that ran across the yard, when a man, a city gentleman to judge by his dress, appeared at the gate and asked with great politeness if this was where the Segawas lived.

Flustered—she had never seen him before—Mrs. Segawa took off her kerchief and bowed.

"I am Mrs. Segawa. But who might you be, sir?"

"Inoko is my name."

Ushimatsu would soon be back, she told him; so he decided to wait. Mrs. Segawa took him under the heavy overhanging thatched roof into the house. He looked up appreciatively at the smoke-blackened roof timbers. With his new interest in rural life, nothing gave him greater pleasure than the opportunity to sit and talk at the hearth of a peasant household. The usual open passageway to be found in such houses ran through from the yard in front to the garden behind; bales of charcoal, tubs for pickling vegetables, farming tools, and a huge heap of unwashed potatoes lined its walls in homely disorder. Just beyond the porch was the hearth, its wood fire giving off a delightful fragrance. Several old calendars and a faded colour print were stuck on the wall.

Mrs. Segawa explained to Rentaro the reason for Ushimatsu's absence and the manner of her brother-in-law's death. The fire was burning brightly in the hearth. The water in the old iron kettle hanging from the wooden pothook began to bubble. Mrs. Segawa got up to make tea for the visitor, when suddenly—memory plays strange tricks—the ancient custom she had so long forgotten came back to her: an eta household should never offer tea, or even a light for his cigarette, to a visitor who was not himself an outcast. Such was the usage prescribed by society long ago for the pariah class. Formerly the Segawas, like the rest, had obeyed this rule; not until they moved to Himekozawa had they dared to break it and associate with their fellow men as equals. Over the years, naturally, they had grown used to the new ways, to an easy friendship with neighbours, not merely serving them tea but exchanging spring and autumn gifts of food without themselves thinking anything of it or the neighbours suspecting that they were in any way different. With such a visitor, before whom she inevitably was constrained as she never was with the peasants of Himekozawa—he had come upon her so abruptly, too—it was not surprising that Mrs. Segawa found herself reacting in the old way, something she had not done for years. Her hand trembled, she noticed, as she poured out the tea. But Rentaro knew nothing of this. Gratefully he drank from the cup she offered, laughing at her tales of Ushimatsu's childhood before he outgrew his kite and top.

"Excuse my asking out of the blue," he said presently, in

a more serious mood, "but is it true there's someone by the name of Rokuzaemon, rather well off, who lives here in Nezu?"

"It is." She looked at him intently.

"You've heard about his daughter getting married, I expect?" Rentaro asked quite casually. Mukai, where Rokuzaemon lived, was an eta settlement on the outskirts of Nezu, less than a mile from Himekozawa. Rokuzaemon, an eta with a lot of money, was well known in the district.

"Getting married? No, I hadn't heard. Then they've found a boy for her, have they? She's been a long time waiting."

"Do you know the girl yourself?"

"She's very pretty. Fair-skinned and graceful, she is—too good-looking for an eta. That's what folk say. Twenty-three or -four, she must be, though the kimonos she wears make her look no more than eighteen or nineteen."

Something else seemed to have occurred to Rentaro as they were talking. Ushimatsu still not having come back, he said he would take a walk. Reminding Mrs. Segawa once again of how anxious he was to see Ushimatsu, he took the path leading to the rice fields, from where he could get a view of the mountains.

## 2

"Ushimatsu! Someone's called, asking for you. Inoko, his name is." Ushimatsu's aunt hurried to meet him as he came back.

"Inoko sensei?" Ushimatsu's eyes shone.

"He waited awhile, then he said he'd go for a walk till you came back. He's out there in the fields somewhere." Her tone changed. "Who is he, anyway?"

"My teacher."

"Your teacher?" She stared at him open-mouthed. "If I'd known, I'd have thanked him properly for coming. I thought he was just a friend. He talked like a friend, not like a teacher."

Ushimatsu was just going off to look for Rentaro when his

uncle came back, so he sat down with him to rest for a moment. Mr. Segawa looked very tired. He had no sooner set foot inside the house than he began repeating, "All over, thanks be, and nothing to be ashamed of!" Everything, to his great comfort, had gone through smoothly: the funeral, the party, the round of visits afterwards. "It's been a worry, seeing to everything." He sighed with relief. "Heaven has helped us, or we'd never have managed."

The peace of the Himekozawa cottage and the old-fashioned ways of his uncle and aunt, who knew so little of the changes in the world beyond their village, called up delightful memories for Ushimatsu. The tranquil clucking of the hens, sounding with such clarity through the dry afternoon air, accorded with his mood. To his aunt, so kindly, so strong and hard-working, yet with no children of her own, he was still a child. He could not help smiling at the way she treated him. "Look at the way he holds his cup—just like his father!" she said, laughing—and crying the next moment in spite of herself. His uncle laughed too. Ushimatsu savoured the strong tea his aunt had made—how good it tasted!—and the country cakes she had served him as if he were an honoured guest, with their hearts of bean jam made with black sugar, which had long been one of his favourites; they too brought reminders of his boyhood. *Home*—suddenly its meaning struck deeper than ever before.

He got up. "I'll go and look for him, then."

His uncle followed. Out in the garden he called to him urgently to stop. Ushimatsu looked round. Mr. Segawa was standing under the persimmon tree among the fallen leaves.

"About your visitor," he said in a low voice. "I remembered when I heard his name. There was a teacher called Inoko at the teachers' college. Is this Inoko the same one?"

"Yes, Inoko sensei."

"So it's him, is it?" Mr. Segawa looked around the garden to make sure they were alone. Then he held out a hand, with the thumb sticking up. "He's one of *them,* they say. Better be careful!"

Ushimatsu laughed. "Don't worry, uncle!"

He hurried off.

## 3

"Don't worry!" he had told his uncle; but he meant to tell Rentaro the truth. Just the two of them, alone together—such an opportunity might never come again. His heart began to race.

He came up with Rentaro on a bank of withered grass between two fields. Rentaro had reached Nezu earlier that morning with Ichimura, he explained; his wife had stayed behind at Ueda. As the lawyer was going to be busy canvassing, they parted at the inn and Rentaro came out to Himekozawa alone. It hadn't been possible to arrange a public meeting for Ichimura in Nezu, so they would not be able to hear him expound his views; but as a result, Rentaro was free to talk with Ushimatsu. Up here in the mountains, with the day so warm and springlike, it would be a joy to talk the whole afternoon through. The thrill of that day—it was not likely that such happiness would often come Ushimatsu's way again. To be near the man he had looked up to for so long, to hear his voice, to see his smile—to breathe with him the mountain air that to both of them meant home!

Ushimatsu did not enjoy their conversation only; silence too, in such company, was an exquisite pleasure. And Rentaro the man, as Ushimatsu talked with him, had a charm quite different from the tone of his writings. Stern though he looked at first, he proved to be warm and sympathetic, as approachable as any "ordinary" human being. Between himself and Ushimatsu, so much his junior, he allowed no barrier of reserve or ceremonious speech. Laughing or sighing freely as the mood took him, lying sprawled on a sunny spot on the bank, he spoke, among many other things, of his illness: of the terrible bouts of coughing that had come on when they took him to the hospital in a ricksha, of the haemorrhage he had thought must tear his chest apart. His chest gave him no distress now, nor did he have any pain elsewhere—for the moment, anyway, he was so fit he could forget his body and its troubles. It would be a different matter if there was any repetition of the haemorrhage; one or two more of those attacks and he would be finished.

As they talked, for all his delight in Rentaro's easy, open

manner, Ushimatsu could not forget himself. *When shall I tell him what I am?* Again and again, robbing him of all peace, the searing question returned. He is dying—what if he should infect me, he found himself thinking more than once, in horror at the disease—and mocked himself as often for his mean, cowardly, selfish fears. They talked of every aspect of Shinshu life—of the people of the Chikuma region, their lives and customs, of the relics of the middle ages that Buddhism and Bushido have here and there preserved, of the rise and fall of towns along the Shinetsu Railway, of the glorious heyday of the old Northern Highway and the decay of the towns that had once served it as post stations—killed by the railway. Before their eyes ranged the mountain peaks—Tateshina, Yatsugatake, Hofukuji, Misayama, Wada, Daimon, and the rest—and the panorama, from east to west, of the vast continuous slope that forms the base of the range. Far below, at the bottom of the valley, flowed the pale-gleaming waters of the Chikuma.

Out of a long familiarity with the place and a love of its beauty, which had inspired him since childhood, Ushimatsu pointed out and described each feature. Rentaro listened, his eyes following Ushimatsu's. He seemed especially interested in a cluster of houses on the plain of Yaebara, the other side of the Chikuma. The smoke of cooking-fires curled slowly from their roofs. Ushimatsu showed him the tiny hamlets of Yodakubo, Nagase, and Mariko, scattered along the river bank in a level, sunny stretch of the valley; farther up, in a shady ravine, the hot-spring villages of Reisenji, Tazawa, and Bessho, veiled in thick blue mist; the "pleasure ground" on a hilltop, where often the peasants would gather for merry-making, about the time the buckwheat flowers, to forget their labours for a while.

According to Rentaro, till recently this mountain landscape had meant little or nothing to him. A "panorama," yes, by virtue of its scale, but lacking distinction among the many pictures nature paints. Sheer size could not make up for the absence of a more profound appeal. Rising and falling like so many waves, these mountains called forth no response but feelings of confusion and unease. Such had been his view. But on this journey his eyes had been opened. Now, as for the first time, he saw in the slowly rising haze the breathing of the slopes, heard the voice of streams buried deep in distant ravines, sensed the rhythm of life in half-withered forests, gazed at the traffic of the clouds, white in a blue sky, or dark and heavy, or sunset red; and found new meaning in the words "Nature at rest on the plains, in movement in the hills."

Ushimatsu, with his own love of the mountains, was delighted with Rentaro's account of his awakening. No cloud or mist hung in the western sky that day, so even the Hida mountains stood out in the sharpest outline, a long white wall towering above the lesser ranges that rose, piled one above another, from the other side of the valley before them. Fresh snow must have fallen several times already this year. In the sunlight, under their canopy of blue, the mountains shone with an almost overpowering intensity; the dynamic contours of the huge mountain mass, the deep shadows of greyish purple marking the valleys, added to the grandeur of the prospect. There in the far distance soared the peaks, each as precipitous and inaccessible as its neighbour: Shirouma, Yakedake, Yarigatake, Norikura, Chogatake, and many others. There where no human being had ever penetrated were the hidden sources of the Azusa and Oshiro rivers; there above the giant glaciers the ptarmigan winged their lonely way. Exaltation came unbidden to Ushimatsu and Rentaro as they gazed at the lofty Hida range, nature's palace, in all its eternal, colossal grandeur. A faint yellowish tinge in the air that day mingled with the November sunlight to bathe the valley in a hardly perceptible haze. For a long while, their eyes riveted to the spectacle before them, the two men talked of the mountains.

## 4

Time and time again Ushimatsu was on the point of telling Rentaro his secret. The previous evening, thinking the matter over by lamplight, he had spent hours imagining all kinds of ways of broaching the subject, if by any chance he should find himself alone with Rentaro. Now here he was at his side, and he could speak only of the view, not a word of the one vital, momentous topic. . . . The more he talked, Ushimatsu felt, the further he seemed to be from saying anything.

At Rentaro's invitation, Ushimatsu went with him to the inn, where Rentaro had left orders for a meal to be ready when he returned. On the way Ushimatsu tried again to bring himself to speak. If only he could—Rentaro would understand him perfectly, and he himself would be so much closer to his friend. Several times he tried and failed. More than once he stopped in his tracks, sighing. This secret, this life-and-death secret: how *could* he give it away so lightly, even though the other was an eta like himself? Again he struggled to speak; again he hesitated, and the next instant reproached himself bitterly. Fear, doubt, and frustration assailed him once more.

Presently they came to Nishimachi, on the outskirts of Nezu. The stone Jizo[1] marked the beginning of the eta section; thatch-roofed eta dwellings stretched untidily down the sunny slope, among them a big house surrounded like a castle by high white walls gleaming in the sun—Rokuzaemon's, unmistakably. All the eta here lived by farming and making hemp-soled straw sandals. None traded in horse carcasses or worked with hides, as they did in the outcast section of Komoro, making shoes and samisen and drums. Here and there fine-quality straw, used in plaiting the upper side of the sandals that every household made, was laid out to dry. Ushimatsu remembered the old days at Komoro. His father and mother and his aunt had made many such sandals; he himself used to play with the *kawaso,* or special hemp, when he was small and had often sat at his father's side, imitating him as he plaited the straw.

They began to talk of Rokuzaemon. Though he did not know him, Ushimatsu did his best to answer Rentaro's many questions about the eta's character and way of life. Rokuzaemon had accumulated all his wealth himself. Some swore his money had been made dishonestly. He was greedy and vain, so it was said; determined, if money could buy the title, to have himself spoken of as a "gentleman." He had dreams, no doubt, of the figure he would cut in society—

[1] A Buddhist deity, protector of travellers and children.

that would explain the smart villa that Rokuzaemon, a crow masquerading as a peacock, had built himself in Tokyo. Hence too his extra-large contribution to the Red Cross, bringing him the title of Special Member, his patronage of other charities, his surrounding himself with paintings and antiques and even learned works—where else would you find a man, the neighbours were fond of saying, with so little learning and so many books.

They passed Rokuzaemon's house as they were still discussing its owner. The imposing white walls, almost incandescent in the full glare of the afternoon sun, enclosed several buildings. A group of eta children, the oldest a boy of six or seven, were playing dump outside the wall. Some of them had rosy-cheeked, engaging faces like any ordinary children; others looked brutish and stupid, their parentage stamped unmistakably on their features: evidence that even an outcast hamlet has its own class divisions. A man leading a horse came round a corner, shouting to the children as he passed—the father of some of them, obviously. A young girl—an elder sister?—her kimono tied roughly, with only a thin cloth belt in place of a sash, slipped like a shadow past Rentaro and Ushimatsu.

To breathe the air of this eta settlement, whose inhabitants lived in total unawareness of their ignorance and degradation, aroused in Ushimatsu an indescribable welter of pity, shame, and anger. He longed to get away.

"Sensei—shouldn't we be getting on?" he called to Rentaro, who was gazing at Rokuzaemon's house.

"See how everything about it reflects his character? By the way, I'm told there was a wedding here two or three days ago—did you hear about it?"

"A wedding?" Ushimatsu was incredulous.

"Not quite the ordinary kind, it's true—a political wedding, I suppose you'd call it." Rentaro laughed. "Politicians go about things differently from the rest of us, don't they?"

"I don't understand you, Sensei."

"Rokuzaemon's daughter was the bride, her bridegroom a Diet candidate. Interesting, don't you think?"

"A Diet candidate? Not the man who came up on the train with us?"

"That's the one, the fine gentleman—remember?"

Ushimatsu stared. "It sounds incredible—"

"I could hardly believe it myself. It's true, though."

"But how did you hear about it?"

"Wait till we get to the inn, and I'll tell you."

# Chapter 9

## 1

There was one family, in the section of Nezu known as Tsukakubo, that still had to be thanked for their attendance at the funeral. Ushimatsu promised to meet Rentaro at the inn after making this final call. He turned off the road onto a path across the fields. As he came to the foot of Tsukakubo Hill, a sweet-seller was standing outside a farmer's house blowing a merry tune on his flute to draw his young customers. Boys and girls ran up shouting and laughing from all directions. What delight the little wooden flute and its melodies gave their unspoilt ears, what childish dreams they summoned! And not only in the children who came to buy. Ushimatsu also stopped to listen in spite of himself.

Always, by some trick of memory, the sound of the sweet-seller's flute brought back his own childhood world. A childhood friend of his had married into the family he was on his way to visit at Tsukakubo. O-Tsuma, she was called. Her own family lived at Himekozawa, on the other side of an apple orchard from the Segawas, who were their nearest neighbours. They had often played together when he was eight or so, not long after the Segawas moved from Komoro. Her father, who was no stranger to hardship or to the difficulties of settling in a strange place—he had been adopted into the Himekozawa household, having come originally from a village near Ueda—had shown much kindness to the Segawas when they first arrived and had taken a special liking to Ushimatsu, invariably bringing him a present when he came back from a pilgrimage to the Grand Shrine of Ise or elsewhere. Not surprisingly, the children of these two neighbours quickly became playfellows. Besides, they were exactly the same age.

Happy memories revived. Though dimly, Ushimatsu could still remember what O-Tsuma looked like as a child, and how pretty she had seemed when he first set eyes on her; remembered too how at apple-blossom time they wandered among flower-laden branches exchanging the whispered secrets of their first childish love. Hardly fifteen years ago, that dreamlike, fairy-tale time; yet though so much else had faded, the innocent joy of those moments he recalled still. Needless to say, this boy-and-girl intimacy had not lasted. Soon Ushimatsu found a new friend, O-Tsuma's older brother, after which he played with O-Tsuma no longer.

O-Tsuma had come to Tsukakubo as a bride in the spring of her sixteenth year. Her husband too had been a school friend of Ushimatsu. The couple had married early, even by country standards, and had a brood of offspring while Ushimatsu was still deep in history and languages at the teachers' college. His pulse quickening with old emotions relived, Ushimatsu walked on up the hill. A stream on its way to join the Nezu River tumbled past the cottages, shallow, quick-flowing, and clean. Leaves drifted from the upper branches of the chestnut trees lining the track; the persimmons were already stripped bare. Only the water grasses showed a fresh green, their roots steeped in the brook, to delight the eye among the fading colours of autumn.

It was the time when farmers and their wives make their preparations for the long winter. A group of women were busily washing turnips in the stream, getting them ready for pickling. Ushimatsu spoke to one of them, a towel wound round her head for protection against the glare as she worked, her white arms showing where the sleeves were tucked back. To his astonishment, it was O-Tsuma. He marvelled at how she had changed, and she seemed no less surprised at the change in him.

Her husband and father-in-law were away that day, leaving only her mother-in-law and herself at home. She had five children now, Ushimatsu learnt. The two oldest had gone off to play somewhere. Three little girls, the oldest about five, clung to their mother, too shy even to bow properly; one stared wide-eyed at Ushimatsu, one hid behind O-Tsuma, and the youngest, a baby who could hardly walk, started to cry at the sight of the visitor's unfamiliar face.

"Funny girl!" O-Tsuma and her mother-in-law laughed. O-Tsuma gave the child her breast. It began to suck, still snivelling, but peeped at Ushimatsu every now and then in the most engaging way.

The gossipy mother-in-law chatted away. O-Tsuma served Ushimatsu tea. For her, too, his visit seemed to bring back memories.

"Ushimatsu! You've grown so!" she said, blushing a little.

When he had formally thanked them for coming to the funeral, Ushimatsu took his leave. O-Tsuma and her mother-in-law stood at the gate watching him go.

Once again, as he walked on up the hill to rejoin the road, Ushimatsu pondered on the changes in himself and others. This good-natured housewife with her graceful, womanly air bore no relation to the image of O-Tsuma he had kept intact through the years. The same age as himself, and with five children—could she be the little O-Tsuma, his first playmate at Himekozawa? The echoes of his childhood thus awakened brought heartache as well as sweetness. Compared with the man he was now, riddled with doubt and fear, how happy he had been as a boy! The days of innocence, of wandering with O-Tsuma among the apple trees, in ignorance of who or what he was, were gone forever. If he could but savour life once more as he had savoured it then, forget his outcast self. . . . Unendurable longings swept through him like the tides of spring . . . dreams of love and an outcast's despair mingling in a poignant vision of the splendour of youth. Ushimatsu thought also of O-Shio at Rengeji. In a fever of vivid, conflicting emotions, he hurried toward the inn where Rentaro awaited him.

## 2

A paper-covered lamp bearing the sign YOSHIDAYA

TRAVELLERS INN hung from the eaves, a reminder of the busy days the road had once known. Few merchants from other parts of the country travelled this way now. Most of the old tavern households along the road had reverted to farming; in Nezu, only two or three inns worth the name remained. The Yoshidaya was one of these, but nowadays business was so slack, after the changes the country had been through, that the proprietor had turned some of his rooms over to the breeding of silkworms. Yet for all their decay, these old country inns keep their special charm: so it was with the Yoshidaya—beans were laid out to dry on mats inside the gate, hens clucked in the garden, a picturesque old manservant bent under the weight of two buckets on a pole as he carried water from the well to fill the bath. Across the veranda, Ushimatsu could see a wood fire blazing in the hearth and children laughing and playing around it.

"Now I *will* tell him," he said to himself once more as he passed through the gate.

He was shown to a room at the back of the inn where Rentaro was sitting alone, the lawyer being still out. The paper on the sliding windows, the picture and its frame in the alcove—everything in the room was old-world and musty, but its quietness made it ideal for a talk between friends. To sit down at last opposite his friend, when Rentaro had given him a cushion and put fresh charcoal in the hibachi between them, still seemed to Ushimatsu a matter for wonder and delight; even the tea Rentaro served him with his own hand tasted different. He told Rentaro which of his books were his favourites, explained how the long *Modern Thought and the Depressed Classes* was the first he'd been able to buy, and spoke of the pleasure that *A Message to the Poor, Labour,* and *The Common Man,* each in its different way, had given him. He told of the thrill of seeing the advertisement of *Confessions,* of his walk home from the bookshop to his lodgings with a copy of it under his arm, imagining its riches, of the inspiration it had been as he read it far into the night—of the revelation it had given him of the oppressive power of "society," of the freshness and force of Rentaro's philosophy as he expounded it in *Confessions.*

Rentaro was delighted. When some moments later they went together to the bath, the maid having come to tell them it was ready, he still seemed to be turning over in his mind what Ushimatsu had said, surprised and heartened, maybe, by his enthusiasm, for if till now he had certainly thought of Ushimatsu as an understanding friend, he had never imagined he would have read, and with such sympathy, so many of his writings. His illness being what it was, there was an air about him all the time of constraint, of the fear, unknown to anyone in good health, of embarrassing others by his presence. This only deepened Ushimatsu's sympathy for him; his own horror of the disease vanished as they talked, and gradually even his sympathy began to give way to a genuine, unselfish fear for Rentaro's future.

Outside the bathroom window a stream tumbled over rocks, its music soothing them as they lay soaking in the limpid water of the big wooden bath. It was near evening. The dying sunlight filtered through the window, faintly outlining the room through the steam. Red all over and wrapped in steam, as if he were on fire, Rentaro got out of the bath to wash. For a moment, surrendering to the heat that brought the sweat pouring down his cheeks, Ushimatsu forgot his troubles.

"Sensei, let me wash your back." Ushimatsu climbed out of the bath, filled a small wooden pail with hot water, and knelt on the floor behind Rentaro.

"Kind of you—just a quick rub please," said Rentaro gratefully. Ushimatsu was overjoyed to be on such terms with the man he had admired for so long, to have the chance to learn at firsthand a little of his thinking, his speech, the way he lived from day to day. Both felt their friendship deepened.

"Your turn now." Rentaro ladled fresh hot water into his bucket. Ushimatsu refused several times. There was no need, he said; he'd taken a bath the day before.

Rentaro laughed. "Yesterday was one day, today's another. Come on, don't be so shy!"

"Thank you—but I'm troubling you, Sensei—"

"I'd make a fine bath-boy, don't you think, Segawa?" He started soaping Ushimatsu's back. "I remember going on a school trip to Joshu with some of the boys when I was still in Nagano. They voted me the champion eater of the whole party. That was before I fell ill, of course. So many things have happened since then. With this body of mine, I've really no right to have lived so long."

"That's enough now, thanks."

"What d'you mean—I've only just begun! Wait, we haven't got down to the dirt yet." Rentaro gave Ushimatsu's back a thorough rubbing, then rinsed it down with the hot water from the bucket; lather-white, soapy water meandered over the draining boards that covered the floor.

"I can't help feeling very depressed when I think of the people I come from, the people I belong to. I can talk to you freely about this, Segawa. The world of ideas, of the intellect, is still closed to us. It started to prey on me about the time I left the college at Nagano: life was pretty black then for months on end. That's what made me ill, really. But oddly enough, illness saved me. It was then I began to feel I must work, not just torment myself with thinking and worrying all the time. You said you read *Modern Thought and the Depressed Classes*—I was ill every single day I spent writing that book. Perhaps there'll be an eta or two of character who'll look at my books and think enough of them to say to himself, 'Inoko the eta wrote this, did he? Then I can do better still!' If that day ever comes, I'll be content. A springboard for others—that's what my life has been, that's what I want it to be."

## 3

Intending all the while to speak, but with something still inhibiting him, Ushimatsu left the bathroom with his secret still untold. The lawyer had not yet returned. Rentaro had asked the innkeeper to cook for the supper some dace caught a few hours before in the Chikuma, which he had bought on the way up from Ueda; he looked forward, he said, to sampling with Ushimatsu the freshness of these river fish, the first of the winter season. The cooking seemed to be under way. They heard someone mashing beans in a bowl in the kitchen, and the aroma of the dace being grilled over charcoal seeped into their room, mingling with wisps of smoke from sizzling fish oil.

Rentaro took some medicine from his bag, though his colour was not that of a sick man, especially after the bath, and inhaled the tiniest whiff of creosote from the bottle. Presently he returned to the subject of Takayanagi.

"Come to think of it, you and he must have left Iiyama at the same time."

"I thought it was odd, the way he seemed to want to avoid me," said Ushimatsu, smiling.

"That's proof he had something on his conscience."

"I can see him now, wrapping himself up in that overcoat, trying to hide his face."

Rentaro laughed. "Truth will out, eh?" He went on to tell Ushimatsu everything he had heard. The story of Takayanagi's secret had come from a surprising source—a relative of Rokuzaemon who was at the same time his bitter enemy, living in the village of Akiwa, the oldest eta settlement in Shinshu, which Rentaro had visited in the course of his study of eta problems. That morning, just as Rentaro and Ichimura arrived in Nezu, they had caught a glimpse of Takayanagi and his bride leaving, presumably on their honeymoon. Takayanagi had not seen them, but they recognized him from behind.

"Astonishing, isn't it?" Rentaro sighed. "What d'you think he means by it, Segawa? You watch him when you get back to Iiyama. He'll throw a big party to announce his marriage, I shouldn't wonder, and give it out as cool as you like that she's the daughter of a wealthy family from the other end of the country. He can't tell them she's an eta, that's certain."

The maid came in with their supper. A delicious smell rose from the freshly grilled dace. The fish, all plump and juicy-looking, were threaded on skewers of bamboo, the skin of their silver backs and white-and-yellow undersides done to a rich brown except for a few places where the thin beanpaste batter had come away, taking the skin with it, and the flesh showed through. Lured by the smell, a cat peeped through the sliding door behind the maid. They did not need her to wait on them, Rentaro told the girl, and she left the room, taking the cat with her.

"Let me serve you, Sensei." Ushimatsu filled Rentaro's bowl with steaming rice.

"Thank you. Why don't we serve ourselves from now on? Sitting down to a meal with you like this—it's like being back in the college dining room." Smiling, he began to eat, talking between mouthfuls. Ushimatsu picked up a fish by its skewer; the bones slid away easily from the flesh. He too talked eagerly, breathing in the delectable smell of the beanpaste batter.

"You know," said Rentaro, resting his right hand, still holding his chopsticks, on his knee, "I can't help admiring these modern gentlemen of ours, Segawa—they'll face *anything*, if only there's money in it. Look at the show Takayanagi puts on—it's all a sham: he has a job to make ends meet, I'm told. With a pile of debts, the moneylenders after him, and all kinds of obligations he couldn't meet, he hadn't a hope of contesting the election this year. But whatever troubles a man may have got himself into, to be willing to marry just for the money and nothing else—and anybody can see that's what he's after—it's too contemptible, don't you agree? Rokuzaemon's a respectable citizen, what's wrong with my marrying his daughter, I suppose he might say—or with a father giving his son-in-law a helping hand at election time, for that matter. And if he were to put it that way, I wouldn't quarrel with him, either. If he's simply had the guts to marry the girl he loves, at the cost of breaking society's taboo against the eta in the process, that's fine, but if so, why do it on the sly? Why does he have to come and go half-disguised, instead of openly like a man? And the rest of the time he's parading himself as a candidate for the Diet! Those are fine glib speeches he makes about 'setting the nation's affairs in order'—but what about his own affairs? Who was it who spoke of pygmy minds behind pompous masks? That's Takayanagi for you. It's horrifying, though. Money justifies everything nowadays, I know. Plenty of people are ready to sell themselves for life if only they can find a buyer, but what shocks me about him is that he can sell his soul and then pretend nothing has happened. And look at this marriage of his from *our* point of view, Segawa—the eta point of view. A crueller way of insulting us 'new commoners,' as they call us, would be hard to come by."

For a while they ate without talking. But Rentaro's feelings were too strong—all thought of his illness seemed to have vanished from his mind—for him to keep silent, and soon he began again.

"But Rokuzaemon isn't much better. What on earth's the good of giving his daughter to a man like Takayanagi? He likes the idea of bragging about his Dietman son-in-law when he goes up to Tokyo, I shouldn't wonder, but his conscience isn't going to give him an easy time. You'd think he might have given a bit more thought to the girl. She's his daughter, after all."

A deeper seriousness marked Rentaro's expression. Absorbed in thought, he said no more.

Listening to him, Ushimatsu had been as struck by the warmth of Rentaro's concern for his fellow eta as he had been astonished at the revelation of the politician's private life. There was a tragic grandeur to the spirit burning so intensely in Sensei's frail body—and the disturbing implication, perhaps, that only the sick are capable of such a depth of compassion.

## 4

Ushimatsu did not, after all, say what he had meant to say. It was well after dark when he left the Yoshidaya. Thinking it over as he walked home, he could have cried with vexation and wretchedness. *Why* hadn't he told him? Because of his father's commandment and the reminder from his uncle? Certainly it only needed one word from his own lips, and there was no telling whose ears the story would reach: Rentaro would tell his wife, and she being a woman wouldn't be likely to keep it to herself. There would be no escape then. But above all, he himself was afraid to *think* of himself as an eta . . . he had passed as an ordinary citizen so far, and of course he wanted to be accepted as such in the future; what could be more natural?

Ushimatsu found many excuses for his silence. But that was what they all were: excuses, thought up after the event in a futile attempt to justify his failure; he did not *really* believe they were what had prevented him from speaking. He had been deceiving himself, he saw now. To hide the truth even from Rentaro—no, his conscience would not allow it. What need was there to worry, anyway? What danger could there be in unburdening himself, not to a stranger but to a man he respected and loved, an eta like himself—and to him alone? What had he to fear? It would be absurd not to tell him, he said to himself sadly and in shame.

Nor was this all. The energies of youth were powerfully at work within him, like the stirrings of new grass beneath the snow. He yearned for spring, yet the life within him, walled in by suspicion and fear, could not expand and grow. Why should not the snow melt under the spring sun? Why should not a young man go forward fearlessly on his life's road, laying at his mentor's feet his offering of love and respect? The more he saw of him, the more he heard him speak, the more deeply he was influenced and the more desirable became the inner freedom Rentaro embodied. Yes, he must tell him—surely that was *his* way forward? So the tide of youth urged him on.

"Right—I'll see him tomorrow and tell him everything!" His mind made up, he hurried back to Himekozawa.

O-Tsuma's father came that evening and sat late, talking by the fire. Ushimatsu's uncle made no attempt to cross-examine him about Rentaro. One question, though, he did ask, just as Ushimatsu was going to bed.

"Ushimatsu—you didn't tell about yourself to that friend of yours today, did you?"

Ushimatsu stared at him. "Why should I, uncle?" But he did not speak from his heart.

For a long time after he got into bed he could not sleep. He was haunted by a strange waking dream, by a face that was now his father's as he had looked upon it for the last time at the funeral, now Rentaro's, pale and wasted by illness, now O-Tsuma's with her cool, bright eyes, gleaming teeth that showed with every word she spoke, and cheeks so quick to colour—so truly womanlike, her inmost feelings mirrored in every look and gesture—till suddenly the outlines shifted and the face was that of O-Shio. . . . Soon the vision faded. By dawn Ushimatsu had forgotten his dream.

# Chapter 10

## 1

The time to lay down his burden was near. Rentaro and the lawyer were going back to Ueda, and Ushimatsu had promised to accompany them. He and his uncle had to go to Ueda in any case, since the bull that had gored his father was being taken to the Ueda slaughterhouse that morning and they were required to attend the killing. A perfect opportunity to carry out his resolve of the night before—and there was no telling when they might meet again. It would not be hard to manage a moment alone with Rentaro on the road with his uncle and Ichimura out of earshot, and then. . . . Ushimatsu got ready to leave with his uncle.

Rentaro and Ichimura were waiting for them at the turning into the Ueda road. Ushimatsu introduced his uncle. Rubbing his broad, peasant hands, his uncle bowed.

"Thank you for the interest you have taken in my nephew, Sensei. And for calling on us yesterday. I was out, I'm afraid."

Rentaro answered courteously, with condolences on his brother's tragic death.

They had started out early. The road was still muddy from the dew, and cocks were crowing as they made their way through thick mist. But the day was mild, like early spring, even the dead grasses by the roadside seeming to revive in its gentle warmth. Through the low grey mist swirling about them even the treetops of the nearby forest looked remote and shadowy. Talking as they went, with now one pair in the lead, now the other—the lawyer's cheerful laughter echoing most often on the morning air—the four men hardly noticed the miles slip by.

As they were nearing East Ueda, Rentaro and Ushimatsu fell behind the other two. Slowly, patches of blue sky were beginning to appear through the mist, revealing the small white clouds of morning scudding not far above their heads. They could make out the village ahead of them, the smoke rising above thatched roofs: a landscape touched with magic by the fading mist.

Rentaro showed no sign of strain. Worrying constantly whether it was wise for him to be walking so far on this rough, stony road, Ushimatsu several times slowed his pace deliberately, letting his uncle and Ichimura go on ahead, but Rentaro did not seem to be short of breath. Ushimatsu was reassured. He glanced ahead at their companions, a hundred yards or more in front. Suddenly the sun broke through. Puddles gleamed on the road; a bland and genial light flooded the rolling expanse of Chiisagata Moor.

If he was to tell, now was the moment. He would not be breaking his father's commandment, he told himself. If he were to tell anyone else, a stranger, all the battles he had fought with himself till now would have been useless, chaff in the wind. But Rentaro—to tell *him* was to confide in an elder brother, a second father. . . . So he tried to justify what he meant to do. Ushimatsu was not rash or thoughtless by nature, nor so mad as to want to rush to his own destruction by ignoring the command his father had laid upon him with such rigour. *Do not tell!* echoed a solemn voice deep within him. A shudder ran through his whole body. He hesitated. "Sensei! Sensei!" The words were imprisoned on his lips; even as he struggled to speak them, some invisible power seemed to block his rebellious striving. . . . *Do not forget!* echoed the voice once more. . . .

## 2

"You're looking very thoughtful, Segawa," said Rentaro, glancing at Ushimatsu. "Look, we're lagging behind. Better walk a bit faster, hadn't we?"

Ushimatsu followed as Rentaro quickened his pace, and

soon they caught up with the other two. Ushimatsu's opportunity, elusive as a bird, had slipped from his grasp. But there would be other times, he consoled himself, when they could be alone together.

As the sun climbed higher, slowly the sky cleared to a deep, translucent blue, broken in the south by wisps of cloud. In the warm sunshine the air grew steamy; a vapour hung over the moors, the hills breathed a faint haze. The mud beneath their feet gave off a pleasant smell as it dried to a paler grey. Tiny green shoots, reminders of man's longing for spring, carpeted the wheat fields lining the road.

Each of the four men saw the landscape about him with different eyes. The lawyer spoke of disputes between landlord and tenant; Rentaro of the peasant's working life, its hardships and its joys; Ushimatsu's uncle of the trouble he had with weeds, of different kinds of soil and how they affected the harvest, of the careless ways of the hill folk compared with the farmers of the Kozuke plain—for these three, talk of the country was always talk of men's labour and livelihood, while for Ushimatsu, so much younger than the others, the landscape had so many other associations than those of work.

Their tiredness forgotten as each talked of what touched him most closely, the four men soon entered Ueda. The lawyer had a branch office in the town. He and Rentaro went to settle some business there, promising to rejoin Ushimatsu and his uncle later at the slaughterhouse to see the last of the bull. Rentaro's wife would be waiting for her husband at the office.

For Ushimatsu and his uncle, every step they took toward the slaughterhouse seemed to raise more poignant memories of the dead cowherd. They talked of nothing else. No need of reserve, no subject barred, now that they were by themselves.

"Six days already, Ushimatsu." Mr. Segawa sighed. "Six days since brother died and you came. The funeral's over, and the party for the mourners, and the calls on the neighbours. Six days, and tomorrow the seventh. They've gone so fast, I can't believe it wasn't yesterday I said goodbye to brother."

Deep in thought, Ushimatsu walked silently at his side.

"A man's life never goes the way he wants it. Brother struck sudden like that, just when he thought he might let up a bit. . . . He's left no money, no name. It wasn't for that he worked and struggled all his life, though—everything he did was for our sake, Ushimatsu, for your sake and mine. We quarrelled all right when we were boys. I remember the blows he gave me, and me blubbering more than once. But I know now there's nothing means more to a man than parents and brothers. The whole world can turn its back on him, but they won't give him up, never. That why I say, never forget your father, Ushimatsu." They walked on in silence for a while.

"Never forget how he cared for you and thought and worried about you," Mr. Segawa went on. "He said to me not long back, 'Now's the most dangerous time for Ushimatsu.' He was anxious for you, he said. Living out in the world like you do, it's different from up here on the mountain—out among the crowds, there's no place to run to for a man with something to hide. He hoped you would keep your head somehow and put your learning to good use, without stuffing your head with silly notions. But he couldn't be easy till you were thirty, he said. 'You needn't worry,' I told him. 'Ushimatsu won't let you down. I'll answer for him.' But brother shook his head. The trouble was, he said, a son inherited his father's faults. It was all right to be cautious, but being *too* cautious, as likely as not, would make folk suspect you all the more. I couldn't help smiling—'Start worrying about him being *too* careful and you'll never stop,' I told him." Ushimatsu's uncle laughed in his quiet way as he remembered.

"But you've done well to come so far," he went on, changing his tone. "You'll be safe now. Caution—it's part of you, you've proved that, and there's nothing you need more. You daren't ever be careless with anyone—it doesn't matter how great a teacher he is, or even if he's one of us himself: there's still all the difference between a stranger and your own flesh and blood. Whenever brother came down from the pasture, he'd look the two of us in the face long and steady and talk of you. Now that he's gone, talking of you'll be the only pleasure left us, your aunt and me. Remember, Ushimatsu—we've no children, no one to lean on. Only you."

## 3

The bull had already been delivered to the slaughterhouse. Its owner had come down earlier, to be ready for Ushimatsu and his uncle. The moment he saw them nearing the gate—they had found their way by following a butcher's boy pulling an empty cart—he hurried to greet them and thanked them effusively for coming. Sincere grief for the old cowherd's death showed in his face. Mr. Segawa cut him short, protesting that the tragedy had been entirely due to negligence on his brother's part and that they bore the bull's owner no ill will. To which the owner replied that grateful though he was for their attitude, he could hardly bear to look them in the face after what had happened and hoped that since it was an animal that had been the cause of death, they might be generous enough to regard it as an accident.

The slaughterhouse buildings consisted of five new single-storey sheds on the outskirts of the town, at the foot of Mount Taro. Several sharp-eyed dogs had congregated outside the gate. Now sniffing at Ushimatsu and his uncle, now growling sullenly, they seemed to be waiting for some provocation to set them yelping. The owner of the bull took Ushimatsu and Mr. Segawa through the black gate. A large yard separated the inspection shed and the slaughterhouse proper. A stout man of fifty or so was giving orders—the foreman butcher, clearly, and a veteran of the trade too, judging by the relaxed, genial tone in which he spoke. Working under him as slaughterers were ten young men, all of them obviously "new commoners," and poor, brutish specimens at that, marked out by the colour of their skin. "Outcast" might have been branded on each coarse red face. Some stared at the visitors with the glazed, half-wit expression common among the lowest of their kind. Some shrank away timidly after a furtive glance in their direction, which made Mr. Segawa, quick to notice such things, nudge Ushimatsu with his elbow. Ushimatsu shivered; his uncle's touch conveyed the secret message instantaneously, like an electric shock. If they had been recognized. . . . But it was soon obvious that the suspicion was groundless, and a moment later the two were talking again with the others.

Two bulls besides the one from Nishinoiri were confined in a pen, impatiently awaiting the death that was slowly closing in upon them, like condemned criminals in a prison cell. Ushimatsu stood with his uncle and the owner of the bull outside the stockade. He could feel no bitterness—it was an animal that was to blame, as the owner had pleaded with them to remember—but painful memories rose of his father's sad end, of his blood spilt over the grass of the pasture. The other two animals, Sado bulls both of them, one black, one brown, were poor creatures, too thin to serve any purpose now but the satisfaction of human appetite: a pitiful contrast with the well-filled frame and gleaming black hide of the splendid crossbreed from Nishinoiri. From outside the fence the owner stroked the bull's muzzle and throat.

"A terrible thing you did, wasn't it? I didn't want to bring you down here—it was your own doing. Remember that, and take your punishment calmly." He was like a parent exhorting his child to bow to his fate as he bids him a sad farewell. "Look, here's Mr. Segawa's son. Say you're sorry—tell him you're sorry! Even a beast like you has a soul: remember what I say now, and when you're born again, mind you come back as something sensible!"

Having thus admonished the bull, the owner told them something of the animal's history. Of all his herd, none came of finer stock. His sire had been imported from America, his mother's pedigree was such-and-such—but for the wild streak in him, he would have been the prize bull of all Nishinoiri. The owner sighed. Half of what the carcass fetched, he added, he would like to set aside for memorial services as some small comfort for the dead man's spirit.

Just then the veterinary surgeon arrived and greeted them

briefly, without removing his deerstalker hat. He was followed by the butcher who would be buying the carcasses. Soon afterwards, Rentaro and the lawyer joined Ushimatsu and his uncle in the main yard.

The slaughtermen were getting ready. They put on white coats, slipped off their rough straw sandals, and tucked up the skirts of their kimonos behind them in their sashes. A confusion of sounds filled the yards—the murmuring of human voices, laughter, the barking of dogs.

Time for the condemned bull to be led out of the pen. All eyes turned to watch him. The two Sado bulls, which had been quiet till now, suddenly grew restless, jerking their heads from side to side. Pressing his hand on the muzzle of the brown one, a slaughterman spoke to them, alternatively scolding and soothing. Animals though they were, some instinct warned them what was about to happen, urging them to escape if they could. The black one cantered round the wooden pillar to which he was tethered. But unlike the others, the Nishinoiri bull offered no futile attempt at resistance, not so much as a mournful bellow, as he was led away to die; with just a trace of breath showing white round his nostrils, his great eyes, dimmed with a faint purplish mist, seeming to glare at the bystanders, he marched with ponderous dignity to where the vet was waiting. This was the vicious beast that had savagely gored a man, yet the sight of it going so bravely to its death drew men's pity, too. Ushimatsu and his uncle were deeply moved. The vet walked round it pinching its hide, feeling its throat, tapping its horns, and finally lifting up its tail: the inspection was over. The slaughtermen surrounded the beast, and pushing and shooing, forced it into the shed nearby. Watching for his chance, the foreman threw a rope round its hind legs, and the beast toppled over onto the wooden floor. The owner stood outside half stupefied. Ushimatsu was deep in thought, his expression sombre.

One of the slaughtermen swung an axe, armed on one side with a piece of tubing four or five inches long in place of a blade, above his head. A single blow, and with a faint groan the huge bull breathed its last.

## 4

Sunlight poured into the shed, shining impartially on the dead beast and the white coats of the slaughtermen already busy around it. The foreman slit its throat, one man cut off its tail, another untied the rope; all climbed onto the carcass for the skinning. With so many vigorous young feet treading heavily on every part of it, a river of blood poured over the floor from the torn throat. From throat to stomach, from stomach to legs, they ripped off the black hide. The stench of blood and fat filled the shed.

Almost immediately the two Sado bulls were driven in and slaughtered in the same shed. As he witnessed the pitiful sight a second time, Ushimatsu's thoughts still turned about his father. Soon they finished skinning the Nishinoiri bull and struck off the horns; he watched the steamy breath rise from the flesh, encased in its wrapping of fat. The foreman, his hands and knife smeared with blood, walked from one carcass to another giving orders. One of his men swept up lumps of fat with a bamboo broom; another was sharpening knives on a grindstone. Then they split open the hip joints of the brown Sado bull and drove a wooden bar between them to hang it up by. "Hoist!" called one of the men, his eyes fixed on a wheel fastened to the ceiling. Slowly, in the centre of the shed, the great bulk of the carcass rose off the floor. Another man began to saw through the backbone.

The owner's eyes stayed riveted, as if in prayer, on what was left of his bull. By now its legs had been cut off, and the cleft hooves that had trampled the pastureland grasses tossed outside. A wet, limp mass of entrails covered with a layer of greyish purple tissue lay on the floor like a traveller's bundle. Three men were chopping flesh off the bones. Once again, for Ushimatsu, memory ousted thought. *Do not forget!* The dying man's last feverish breath, on which those words had been spoken, seared the very core of his living being; his father was reborn within him. . . . From the innermost depths of his consciousness a voice called in warning: *Ushimatsu, lad, will you turn your back on your father?* How poignant the rebuke! Will you turn your back on your father? Ushimatsu repeated to himself.

He had changed of course. He was no longer a child, to obey his father mechanically in everything. Others besides his father peopled his mind's world now. In a sense, the memory of his father's stern, austere character impelled him in the opposite direction, toward the notion of his freedom to enjoy and to suffer as he himself, and not his father, willed. How far apart the two men's attitudes—his father's teaching of submission to the world, and Rentaro's fierce anger at the world's heartlessness . . . Ushimatsu no longer saw his way ahead.

Coming to himself, he was aware of Rentaro standing beside him. A policeman had appeared and was watching the last stages of the butchering with the vet. The carcass of the Nishinoiri bull was being cut into four. The fleshy upper part of the right foreleg hung suspended from the roof; one of the slaughtermen was soaking the blood from it with a sponge. As the foreman began stamping each cut, the butcher's boy, who had been waiting outside, promptly loaded his cart with the rush-lined boxes provided and pulled it noisily into the shed.

"Twelve *kan* five hundred! . . . Eleven *kan* seven hundred!" One by one, great chunks of meat from the dead bull were lifted onto enormous scales. One of the slaughtermen called out the reading; licking his pencil, the butcher recorded it in a notebook.

Their duty as witnesses to the bull's end completed, they said goodbye to the bull's owner and started across the yard to the gate. Ushimatsu looked back once more at the shed. Some of the young slaughtermen were still sweeping up the entrails, others steeping their feet in buckets of water to wash off the blood. Sunlight caught the thigh and foreleg swinging from the roof, picking out the gleaming white fat and yellowish suet around the groin—for Ushimatsu it was no longer the relic of a hideous tragedy: only a huge lump of meat.

# Chapter 11

## 1

"Well, we got through that all right, I'm thankful to say," said Mr. Segawa as they came through the gate, his hand on Ushimatsu's shoulder. "The worst of the danger's over now."

"Uncle, don't speak so loud—your voice will carry!" warned Ushimatsu. He glanced at Rentaro and the lawyer, who were some paces ahead of them.

"My voice carry?" His uncle laughed. "Who can hear it, d'you think—a croak like mine? I'm easier now, I tell you. Now we've come so far, we'll be all right, I know we shall. I've been so worried. But tonight the three of us can sleep in peace."

The butcher's cart passed them laden with meat; the clatter of its wheels echoed through the parched mulberry fields. Dogs ran after it barking excitedly. The simple Mr. Segawa was so relieved, a broad smile seemed to have settled permanently on his faintly pockmarked face. Of the potent ideas that were exciting the country's youth he had no conception. To his old-fashioned mind, it was enough that his family was safe, as the weather was fair around them. Quickening his step and calling to Ushimatsu, who was lagging behind lost in thought, he began to look out for somewhere for a meal.

After they had eaten, Ushimatsu left his uncle and went to the lawyer's office, where Rentaro was waiting for him, together with his wife. They had only three hours left to enjoy each other's company. Rentaro's wife was returning to their home in Tokyo, while Rentaro and the lawyer were bound for an inn at Komoro; they would all be leaving Ueda by train just after four o'clock. His wife began to urge Rentaro to go back with her to Tokyo, but he cut her short. With him, his friends and any younger men he might be able to help came first, and members of his family second; it was for the lawyer's sake that he had decided to stay on in Shinshu. His wife knew this very well. Given the kind of man he was, it was natural enough, but he was still not wholly recovered from his illness, and what if he should have a relapse up here in the mountains? Anxiety showed in her face.

"Don't worry, I'll take good care of him!" promised the lawyer. Thus reassured, she did not persist.

He would miss her as well as her husband, thought Ushimatsu with deepening regret. Her quiet grace and charm had struck him when they first met on the train, but there was more to her than charm—she showed herself neither ingratiating nor proud but straightforward, frank, and generous-minded. Dress evidently interested her little. She made no attempt to smarten herself for the journey back to Tokyo, merely combing her hair once or twice in their presence, and wasted little time on their packing. There was something about her in *Confessions*, Ushimatsu remembered. He tried to picture to himself their history—Rentaro, his teacher, as he now regarded him, and the girl of good family who had chosen to marry an outcast.

The hours slipped by, and soon it was time to leave for the station. The lawyer, as much in demand as men of his profession always are, was caught just as he was setting out with the others, and had to discuss a case, watch in hand, on the doorstep. Rentaro and his wife went on ahead. Ushimatsu followed, wondering aloud when he would see his beloved sensei again. With pleasure and with sorrow too, he carried Rentaro's bag, the last small service he could do for him.

The three were almost dazzled by the brightness of the early winter sunshine in which the town lay bathed. As they began to descend the hill past the ruined castle, Ushimatsu listened to Rentaro and his wife—he was walking just behind them with his friend's suitcase.

"I shall be perfectly all right, I tell you. There's no need for you to worry," Rentaro was insisting a little testily.

"But you're *not* well, that's just the trouble." She sighed. "You don't take the slightest bit of care of yourself, and heaven knows what risks you take when I'm not with you. And the winter weather up here in the mountains—it frightens me even to think of it."

"It's not like being at the seaside, that's true." He laughed. "Still, it's been pretty warm so far this year, much warmer than usual for Shinshu. This kind of air isn't going to do me any harm. Look, I haven't had a single cold since we came up here—that proves it, doesn't it?"

"You're better, certainly. But I'm saying that's all the more reason for being extra careful: suppose you were to have another attack now, just when you've begun to get well?"

"If I were as careful as you want me to be, I'd never get any work done."

"Work? You can work as much as you like when you're fit again. I do wish you'd come back to Tokyo with me, though."

"There you go again—you don't see the point! Why is it that women never seem to understand these things? Surely you realize how much Ichimura's done for me. Nobody with a head on their shoulders would keep telling me to go back to Tokyo when I owe him so much, least of all in front of him: it puts my sincerity in doubt. Also there are some things I want to look into up here on my own account. I've got to see for myself how the people live in the mountain villages if I'm to work my ideas up into another book. It's an ideal opportunity." His voice lightened. "Ideal weather, too! A spring day come out of turn. I'm going to enjoy this trip. You go home and wait for me. I'll be back soon, and I'll bring you some presents to remember Shinshu by."

The two walked in silence for a while. Behind them, Ushimatsu shifted the case from his right hand to his left. They came to the great white-walled storehouse, the only one of the castle buildings still standing.

"I haven't told you another reason why I've been asking you to come back with me," said Rentaro's wife dispiritedly.

"Anything special?"

"A dream I had last night upset me." Her voice trembled. "I lay awake all night afterwards. Rentaro, I'm so worried about you. . . . It's so strange. It was more than a dream, somehow—"

"And that's why you're so keen on my coming home

with you? What nonsense!" Rentaro laughed cheerily.

"Maybe it's not such nonsense as you think. People often dream about what's going to happen to them. It's made me so nervous I can't get it out of my mind."

"Dreams are nothing to go by."

"Queer things do happen, though. . . . Rentaro, I dreamt you were dead."

"Bah—superstitious chatter!"

## 2

A strange conversation, certainly, thought Ushimatsu, but he did not take it too seriously. Surprising that a woman of her straightforward, outgoing temperament should be upset by such things. Dreams were like a child's imaginary world, displays of fantastic images detached from time and place. Rentaro's death, though—could anything so absurd have found its way into his wife's dream, particularly now that he was so much better? It was like a woman, of course, to brood over such insubstantial things. As he pondered thus on the springs of thought and feeling in the opposite sex, their ways seemed to Ushimatsu stranger than ever. Most women are the same, he told himself tentatively; he found himself thinking of his superstitious landlady at Rengeji—and then of the girl, O-Shio.

They crossed the bridge near the station. Mrs. Inoko fell behind a little. Changing the case back to his right hand, Ushimatsu walked at Rentaro's side.

"How long will you be staying in Shinshu, Sensei?" he asked wistfully.

Rentaro smiled. "At least until Ichimura's got through the election. To tell you the truth, with my wife feeling as she does, I did think of going back to Tokyo. If there were nothing special about the election to keep me, I'd do as she says without a murmur. Not that I can be all that much use to Ichimura by staying. If you look at it from his point of view, he's got his own good reasons for standing, and if he's going to fight an election, one opponent's much the same as another as far as he's concerned. But for us eta, the fact that it's a fight between Ichimura and Takayanagi makes the election just that bit more interesting." Rentaro stopped suddenly, and glanced back at his wife before walking on. "Just look at what Takayanagi's done. However low and dirty and ignorant we eta may be, there's a limit to the trampling we can take. . . . We've got to get Ichimura elected somehow: a man like Takayanagi *can't* be allowed to win. It would be a different matter if I hadn't heard about him. But for me as an eta, knowing what I know about Takayanagi, to go home without saying a word—it'd be too cowardly."

"Then what do you mean to do, Sensei?"

"To do?"

"When you say you can't go back without saying a word."

"I mean to strike the one small blow I'm capable of, that's all." Rentaro laughed. "With Rokuzaemon's money behind him, he'll be buying votes, that's for certain, and hiring thugs to browbeat anyone who stands up to him. As for me—my weapons are one pair of straw sandals and one tongue. That's what makes it so interesting. Fascinating, really. He's relying on money to fight for him—money, and nothing else at all." He chuckled again.

"I hope everything works out well."

With Rentaro still laughing at the prospect before him, they reached the station.

There was still a little time before the train for Komoro and Tokyo was due. A crowd of passengers filled the waiting room. Rentaro's wife caught up with them; together they waited for the lawyer. Rentaro offered Ushimatsu a cigarette, and lit up himself.

"Shinshu's a remarkable place," he said after taking a puff or two. "No other part of the country treats us eta like they do here." He looked at Ushimatsu, then at his wife, then at the crowd around them. "I'm as human as anybody else, as you know, Segawa, with the same feelings as the next man. This being Ichimura's election campaign, not just an ordinary trip, I didn't think it was for me to go with him—who knows how my presence might upset the voters, I thought. I might well do more harm than good. I decided against making any speeches, anyway. But these Shinshu folk are different. Do you know, they've been *asking* me to speak! At Komoro, for instance, this evening, on the same platform with Ichimura—" He broke off with a laugh. "Why, seven hundred turned up when we spoke at a meeting here in Ueda. And what's more, they listened. There's nowhere like Shinshu for practising speech making, the newspaper chaps in Nagano say, and they're absolutely right. Maybe the people who live up here in these mountain provinces have a special thirst for knowledge. Nobody would have any dealings with anybody of my kind anywhere else, but here in Shinshu, would you believe it, it's 'Sensei! Sensei!'—they won't let me go." Again he laughed. His wife listened, smiling wryly.

The sale of tickets began, and the crowd pressed toward the booking-office window. Just then the lawyer dashed up, beaming broadly, his huge frame shaking as he ran; at once, hardly pausing even for a word of greeting, he joined Rentaro and his wife in the queue at the gate. Ushimatsu followed them, clutching a platform ticket.

The Tokyo-bound train was twenty minutes late, so the passengers were congregated on the platform. Rentaro's wife sat on a bench under the clock, gazing abstractedly around her; the lawyer walked about among the crowd; Ushimatsu stayed at Rentaro's side, hoping wistfully, right up to the last moment of their parting, that his friend would somehow sense his true feelings. With his clog he began to trace a picture on the parched ground. Rentaro, leaning against a pillar, watched the queer shape, neither ideograph nor any other recognizable symbol, forming under Ushimatsu's foot.

"The train's pretty late, isn't it?"

Ushimatsu started at Rentaro's words. He rubbed out the lines on the ground. A schoolboy who had been watching turned away, smiling inanely.

"By the way, Segawa, I nearly forgot—would you let me have your address in Iiyama?"

"I've moved to Rengeji since I saw you last."

"Rengeji?"

"Rengeji temple, Atago Street, Iiyama, is the address."

"Thank you. I can't be sure, but it's just possible I may be going up in your direction before I finish."

"You'll be coming to Iiyama?" Ushimatsu's eyes brightened suddenly.

"Yes, I may be, but first of all there's this tour of Chiisagata, then we'll be calling at Nagano again. So I can't be certain yet. If we do get as far as Iiyama, I promise I'll look you up."

A steam whistle blew. A long train belching black smoke was approaching the station from the Naoetsu direction. Porters, their faces as grimy as their uniforms, bustled to and fro; in a moment the stationmaster himself appeared. The train drew up, its many passengers lining the windows. Rentaro's wife and the lawyer hurried on board.

"Goodbye then, Segawa." Rentaro followed them into the same compartment. A porter slammed the door. The stationmaster, who was standing beside Ushimatsu, raised his hand and blew on his whistle, and in the same instant the train began to move. From an open window, Rentaro's wife—paler even than usual, her face stamped itself on his memory—called another goodbye to Ushimatsu. Gathering speed, the passengers slid past him like shadows. Ushimatsu stood rooted to the spot as if in a stupor. *Sensei has gone.* . . . When at last his consciousness registered the fact of their parting, the train itself was already out of sight, leaving little puffs of smoke that drifted for a moment, hugging the ground, till caught in a gust of wind they disintegrated and vanished into the winter sky.

## 3

Why, when a man wills above all else to speak of his deepest feelings, should he find it so difficult? That day of all days, Ushimatsu had been clear that he would tell Sensei; more than once he had braced himself to speak—and now had parted from his friend and teacher, his silence still unbroken. How bitter the conflict within him between fear and the ache of unfulfilled longing—how dark his loneliness that evening as he walked the road back to Nezu!

The first seventh-day from his father's death passed without any untoward incident. They visited his grave, a service was read for the repose of the dead man's spirit, and with the special shojin meal that Ushimatsu's aunt prepared for their neighbours, the period of special observances finally came to an end. Tired out with all they had had to see to, Mr. Segawa and his wife sighed with relief that everything had gone so smoothly. Only Ushimatsu knew no peace. Meeting and talking with Rentaro had been an even more painful goad to his self-questioning than the reading of Sensei's books. More than once, intending to think out more clearly the pattern of his life, he went out to wander on the slopes of Chiisagata. Time and again, as he walked on Nezu Hill or down Himekozawa Valley, or trod the withered grasses by rice fields where the birds still sang, he stopped to gaze at the light-filled landscape and felt afresh the tides of youth surging in his veins. Power from that source he did possess; of this he was certain, but the power was blocked within him, and how to set it free he did not know. He walked the ridges, his thoughts repeating themselves in unvarying, endless sequence. Nature brought comfort, inspiration: but which turning to take at the crossroads—this she could tell no man. To Ushimatsu's question, the fields, the hills, the valleys gave no answer.

That afternoon two letters came for him, both from Iiyama. One was from his friend Ginnosuke. Always a good correspondent, Ginnosuke wrote freely and at length, just as if he were talking. After many condolences on his bereavement came the news from Iiyama, together with the latest gossip about the principal, rude remarks about Bunpei—"a pity *I* haven't got the district inspector for an uncle!"—and a lot more, poured out in a long, chaotic scrawl just as the fancy took him. Ginnosuke inveighed against the poor status and treatment of teachers in primary schools. No young man of spirit and sensibility could possibly stay in general education as it was at present, he declared. For his own part, thanks to a recommendation from a lecturer in the natural history department of the college at Nagano, his appointment to an assistantship at the Agricultural College had been confirmed, and before long he would be leaving Iiyama to devote himself entirely to his botanical studies.

The will to advancement and distinction flared strongly

in Ushimatsu as he read his friend's letter. Like most of his fellow students, he had entered the teachers' college simply to provide himself with a means of earning a living—all those who offer themselves for training as primary school teachers come from pretty much the same background—but he was certainly not content with his present position. Yet apart from going to the Higher Teachers' College in Tokyo to train as a secondary teacher—Ginnosuke's case was exceptional—there was no way at all for a primary teacher to advance. He would have to work out his term,[1] a virtual prisoner, till the end. He had thought of taking the secondary training at the time of his graduation from Nagano, and if only he had applied, there was not much doubt he would have been selected. Yet in the sad awareness of his eta birth, he had felt no urge to apply, either then or since. Suppose he did qualify at the Higher Teachers' College, and took a job at a middle school or a primary teachers' college, what if he were to meet the same fate as Rentaro? *Nowhere* would he be safe. Better to stick out the ten years at Iiyama, buried in the country; he could use the time to study, to prepare himself for a career in some other field. Had he not been an eta, though, he would never have let any friend overtake him in the race. . . . Ushimatsu sighed. How he envied Ginnosuke!

The other letter had "From Class 1, fourth year, written by its chosen representative" on the back of the envelope. The "chosen representative" was Shogo. The style was precarious, a reproduction, almost word for word in places, of the form for a "letter of greeting and inquiry after the recipient's health" that Ushimatsu had taught them in a composition lesson. Below the signature, "To Segawa sensei, presently at Nezu, from Kazama Shogo," right at the end of the page, a postscript had been added in smaller script: "Elder sister at Rengeji sends her greetings too."

"Elder sister sends her greetings," Ushimatsu repeated wistfully. To think about O-Shio undisturbed, he went

[1] Teachers trained at government expense were required to work in government schools for ten years. See pp. 124, 164.

into the yard behind the house. Beyond the yard was the apple orchard, rich in memories. Trees he knew as young saplings had grown thick trunks; some, worm-eaten and rotten, were all but dead. From all the healthy trees long, thin, leafless branches hung in profusion, twining with their neighbours to left and right as they had grown and spread at will: the very picture of early winter. From the base of its trunk, up past each fork, the secret cradle of next season's shoots, to the last leaf or two hanging limply here and there on an outer twig, each tree in turn, as Ushimatsu walked by, lay shadowed at his feet. Under some of the trees chickens wallowed in dust baths, trying, he supposed, to shake off bird lice. A thatched roof rose above the trees, the other side of the orchard—the house where O-Tsuma was born. He had often been there to play. The thin blue smoke escaping from between the thatch and the earthen walls brought back such delightful memories. *Elder sister sends her greetings.* . . . It was just here, among these same trees, that he had played with his little friend O-Tsuma long ago. Here they had often run, shy of the crowd, to hide among the gleaming leaves; here exchanged their whispered vows and wandered in a trance of innocent love.

As he recalled these things, the faces of O-Tsuma and O-Shio appeared in turn among the procession of images from the past. The two were not particularly alike—indeed they were distinctly unlike in age, in looks, in character—yet whenever he thought of the one, he found himself thinking also of the other. Surely, but for the curse of his eta birth, neither image would have had such power to move him. But for that curse, he would never have felt this poignant sense of waste, of youth unfulfilled; never have suffered so acutely this desperate longing, a doubling and trebling of the ordinary pains of youth, for the world's simple joys. The closer the fetters of his destiny as an eta tightened about him, the more acute these longings became . . . he saw now it was only because she had not known what he was that O-Tsuma and he had once been able to wander among the apple trees exchanging those honey-sweet words. Whose red lips, if their owner had known, would ever have smiled for him? And supposing the truth *did* become known—the mere thought itself bred new pain, new resentment.

Bewildered by confused images of misery and tenderness, Ushimatsu walked as before among the trees. Suddenly a hen cackled, the sound echoing through the silent air of the orchard. *Elder sister sends her greetings.* Repeating Shogo's message to himself once more, Ushimatsu turned back to the house. O-Shio was much in his thoughts as he went to bed that night, and again the next night, and the next. True, by morning he had all but forgotten her and spent the days brooding over his future life and work. Half the period of mourning for his father had slipped by in tormented self-questioning, yet when it came to what practical steps he should take, no new way opened. For five days he had thought harder than ever before about his life's direction—or so it had seemed at the time—but in retrospect, all his "thought" had been only vague and wishful dreaming. There was no alternative but to go back to Iiyama and continue as before. Young, inexperienced, poor, chained to teaching by the ten-year rule—as he looked to the dark future, Ushimatsu trembled with bitterness and with fear.

# Chapter 12

## 1

Once the service to mark the end of the second week of mourning was over, Ushimatsu decided to leave Himekozawa without delay. In their anxious concern for their nephew's welfare, Mr. and Mrs. Segawa busied themselves in all kinds of ways, looking up the calendar to see if the day was propitious for travel, preparing new sandals, making five big rice balls when three would have been ample and wrapping them up in bamboo sheaths, with pickled melon in a separate packet. O-Tsuma's father came over to see him and sat awhile by the fire talking of old times. There was no end to the talk of the dead cowherd, reminded of him as they were by each glance at the old haversack hanging on the grimy wall. As his aunt served him strong and fragrant farewell tea, Ushimatsu felt the kindly, consoling warmth of family ties.

His uncle went with him as far as the statue of the guardian god of travellers at the village boundary. Under the massed grey clouds hanging low overhead, the bleak Chiisagata valley looked even darker and wilder than usual. The Eboshi mountains were invisible. Maybe the snow had already come to Nishinoiri, where his father lay. Down here the cold wind had stripped many of the trees, leaving even their topmost branches bare and bringing a forlorn, wintry air to the upland scene. The long harsh Shinshu winter, the very thought of which makes one shiver, had come at last. The mountain folk had already started to wear their winter caps of rough yellow-dyed silk. Loaded packhorses passed him, their steamy white breath telling of the merciless speed with which the weather in these parts can change. Inhaling the icy air, Ushimatsu made his way down the stony track. By the time he reached the edge of Araya village, his fingertips were red and swollen and numb.

It was a little after midday when the train he had boarded at Tanaka reached Toyono. He sat down in the little tea house in front of the station and took out the rice balls his aunt had given him. Hungry he certainly was, but *five!* He could hardly throw away the ones he didn't want, and they were too good to give to the dogs in the street, so he wrapped them in the bamboo sheaths again and pushed them into the pocket of his cloak.

Having eaten his fill, Ushimatsu tightened his sandals and set out along the road to Kanizawa, the riverboat terminal. It was nearly three miles to walk, but distances shorten on the return journey, and before he had gone very far—as he thought—along the level stretch of the Northern Highway, it brought him once more to the bank of the Chikuma, here flowing wide and slow. He hurried to the landing stage, only to be told that the Iiyama boat had left a few minutes before. Nothing for it, then, but to wait for the next one. Even so, that was better than walking all the way, he decided, and sat down in the nearby tea house.

Sleet began to fall. The clouds grew darker still, till a

leaden pall covered the sky from end to end. An hour went by. With his thoughts in turmoil, the long wait was torture foı Ushimatsu, besides which there was the physical discomfort—he had walked so fast from Toyono that his hair lay unpleasantly damp on his forehead, and his vest was sticking, hot and sweat-sodden, to his back.

Presently, as he was relaxing with his kimono open at the chest and moistening his parched throat with the strong Shinshu tea, passengers began to arrive in ones and twos for the next boat. One went through to sit by the charcoal foot-warmer[1] in the inner tea room; some tried to dry their coats at the stove; others sat listlessly about the room, hands in pockets, listening to the talk around them. The proprietress, in a thick padded coat that stuck out behind like a tortoise's shell and with a kerchief wound round her head, even indoors, bustled about providing cushions for her customers and serving them with tea and sweets on well-worn lacquer plates.

Suddenly two rickshas drew up with a clatter outside. They seemed to have been hurrying, despite the sleet, so as not to miss the next boat. All eyes turned to the entrance. The ricksha men set to work briskly—spurred on, no doubt, by the prospect of a good tip—removing the rain covers and carrying in several pieces of baggage.

Behind them came their passengers.

## 2

To Ushimatsu's astonishment, the first of the new arrivals was Takayanagi. A queer thing indeed, that after their meeting on the way to Nezu he should run into him again on the way back—the two of them waiting for the very same boat! On the way out, Takayanagi had been alone; now he had a young woman with him, presumably his wife. The woman walked past where Ushimatsu was sitting, a hood of light-coloured crêpe pulled down over her forehead. Glancing after the slender figure wrapped in a

[1] The *kotatsu,* a small charcoal heater placed under a table covered with a quilt. In winter the Japanese sit at the table with their feet, and if necessary their hands, kept warm under the quilt.

sleek new coat of serge, Ushimatsu recognized her instantly. He recalled the story Rentaro had heard about Takayanagi, and realized with fresh amazement that it must all have been true.

The couple were shown through to the room with the foot warmer. The only other occupant of the room, a priest in his fifties, spoke to Takayanagi at once in the most familiar way; obviously they were old friends. Soon laughter could be heard from the inner room. Ushimatsu turned away and was staring out at the dreary, sleeting sky when something he heard from behind him caught his attention and made him listen in spite of himself.

"So that's what it was—I was wondering why I hadn't seen you all this time," the priest was saying knowingly. "And I thought you were busy canvassing! Well, well, so that's what you've been up to. I'd no idea it was anything so auspicious."

"I've *felt* pretty busy, I can tell you," said Takayanagi with a complacent laugh.

"Excellent! But your wife—excuse me—is she from Tokyo too?"

"Yes, indeed."

That "indeed" made Ushimatsu smile. From what he could overhear, Takayanagi and his wife were on their way back to Iiyama after a tour of some of the beauty spots near Tokyo. A shrewd and devious man, Takayanagi had obviously made the long detour on purpose, so as to avoid returning direct from Nezu. With the priest as captive listener, he began boasting in the most ridiculous way. Ushimatsu saw through his lies so clearly, he could no longer bear to sit there listening. How terrifying the world and its ways, he thought, comparing the Takayanagis' dark secret with his own. Simulating indifference to the talk around him, he got up and sauntered outside the tea house to look at the weather.

The sleet was still pelting down, a foretaste, if the sky was any guide, of the snowstorms that sweep down every year from Echigo to Iiyama. Through it he could make out the broad expanse of the river, faint and faraway-seeming in the mist, and the grey clouds drifting low along the opposite bank. Higher up, mountain peaks peeped momentarily through gaps in a pall of snow-laden clouds and disappeared. Ushimatsu stood staring at the river. But before he was conscious of it, his mind had reverted to the couple in the tea house behind him. Several times, against his better judgement, he turned to look at them. Then the sale of tickets for the boat began on the landing stage, and the tea house quickly emptied. The boat was due to leave in two or three minutes. The Takayanagis, mingling now with the crowd, glanced more than once in his direction, furtively almost—or was it his imagination? So at least it seemed to him. Whether the girl knew him or not he had no idea, but he certainly knew *her;* her hair might be different—it was done up in the style proper for a newly married woman—but she was Rokuzaemon's daughter all right, beyond a shadow of doubt. Keeping close beside her ambitious husband, her shyness hidden under a layer of powder and showy makeup, she walked down the path to the landing stage. Wondering what they were thinking, Ushimatsu followed.

## 3

The boat was of unusual design, like a houseboat. It had windows and was painted white, with two red lines running round below the gunwale. The baggage was stowed in the after half of the saloon, which was partitioned off by a makeshift wooden door; the other half made a long narrow room for the passengers. The ceiling was too low to allow standing. Into this confined space the travellers who had been waiting in the tea house now crowded, to sit crammed together on the mat-covered floor.

A moment later they heard a pole being dropped with a splash into the water. The boat began to slide off the sand; the two oarsmen eased it away from the bank.

Ushimatsu sat forlornly by himself in a corner with his legs outstretched, smoking a cigarette and thinking. He glanced through the window. It was quite bright outside, with the light reflected from the water lending beauty even to the driving sleet. The murmur of the river lapping against the side, the sleepy rhythm of the oars astern, heard only when the mind pictured the oarsmen at their work: the stillness of a river journey. Willow trees here and there on the desolate banks, now seen from a distance, like shadows, now looming over them as they glided below drooping, withered branches. What was going to become of his life, Ushimatsu asked himself. Who could know? He stuck his head out of the window and looked at the sky ahead, above Iiyama. The wall of snow clouds, ashen, massive, impenetrable, chilled the heart of the lonely young outcast. Indescribable feelings racked him, chequered visions of horror and of remembered happiness.

How were they at Iiyama—his friend Ginnosuke, the hapless, worn-out Keinoshin? And the priest's wife at Rengeji, and O-Shio? Suddenly he remembered Shogo's letter. To meet her again—this at least he could look forward to. The mere thought of the fusty walls of Rengeji, so long as *she* was there, was like life flowering in the desert. . . . *Ren-geji! Ren-geji!* The very sound of the oars in their even, rhythmic plashing seemed to spell out the name.

The sleet changed to snow. Gossip was the only means of whiling away the boredom of the journey. The priest in particular, who had stayed with the Takayanagis, soon had everyone smiling sardonically at his unpriestlike flow of political small talk and the bantering tone in which he delivered it. According to him, an election was a game, a play with the politicians as actors: "All the rest of us are required to do is enjoy the spectacle." There was laughter at this, and some shouts of protest, which soon developed into an argument, some standing up for the politicians, others deriding them like the priest.

"Ichimura's coming in a few days—you'll see something then, I promise you," said somebody.

"You wouldn't be saying that if you hadn't fallen for their tricks!" retorted another. The lawyer's name came up repeatedly, to Takayanagi's evident disgust. At each mention of his opponent he smiled sarcastically, his lips curling in a sneer.

While others joined in the argument, Takayanagi's wife listened at her husband's side, trying to keep him in a good mood. She was a pretty girl and attracted many glances, the more so because of her finery as a newly married woman. Everything about her—her *marumage* hairstyle with a gay ribbon of crimson, her smooth and full complexion, and the winsome, girlish way she put her hand up to hide her charming mouth each time she laughed—showed how little she knew as yet of domestic cares. Yet feelings always give themselves away, and there was a hint of unease in those bright eyes, a preoccupied air in their too-steady gaze. Once or twice she put her lips to Takayanagi's ear and whispered something. Once Ushimatsu caught her glancing hesitantly in his direction, as if she was beginning to realize she had seen him somewhere before.

Pity for a fellow outcast filled Ushimatsu each time he looked on the beautiful eta girl. Had she not been of a different race, her beauty and her father's money would have assured her a husband of worth and substance—no need then to have served as a bait for the pompous adventurer sitting beside her. Poor girl! Yet the secret of her birth was *his* secret—and suppose she did recognize him! But if she remembered him simply as someone she had seen in Nezu or Himekozawa, and no more, he had nothing whatever to fear; if anything, the fear would be on her side. . . . For one thing, he had been home so little in the last four or five years. Once when he graduated, and now this trip, after nearly three years. Even so, when in Nezu he had deliberately kept clear of the eta settlement at Mukai, and when he *had* been that way, nobody was likely to have taken any special notice of him, or if they had, they couldn't have known who he was or where he came from. No, he was safe. It was his own knowledge of the sordid secret the Takayanagis were hiding that had made him—paradoxically—afraid for himself. That whispering in Takayanagi's ear—it could have been nothing to do with him. What had seemed a wish to avoid him, that expression on her face—just shyness probably.

And yet all the time at the bottom of his mind the misgivings remained, undispelled. Ushimatsu tried not to look at the Takayanagis.

# 4

It was twelve miles downstream to Iiyama. What with putting in at several little jetties on the way, and weaving slowly through makeshift pontoon bridges of the kind that get swept away in every flood, the journey took three hours. When the boat reached its destination, it was nearly five o'clock. All the passengers were put off at Upper Iiyama, since the boat was going no farther. Ushimatsu followed the others up the bank. Snow lay on the stony beach and on the pontoon bridge. Night and a snowfall had come together, and the buildings of the town gleamed faintly white in the gloom. Here and there lights were being lit. Suddenly through the darkness came the long-drawn-out boom of a temple bell—the bell of Rengeji. Simple Sho, that would be: he had climbed the bell tower as he did every evening at this hour, and was swinging the great wooden beam to toll the passing of this winter day. The sound filled Ushimatsu with an indescribable happiness. Now at last, he felt, he was really back in Iiyama.

During the fortnight he was away, people had made the customary preparations for winter: the rough reed screens that would help keep off the snow had been fixed in place in front of each house, right up to the eaves. A true snow-country scene confronted Ushimatsu, such as one sees in the towns and villages of Echigo. Men and women were walking busily up and down the snow-covered road, in the centre of which a narrow strip had been trodden nearly black. Everyone was in a hurry. Stepping aside constantly to let them pass but in no less haste to get home himself, Ushimatsu was nearing Atago Street when he met a boy coming from the opposite direction. As they drew closer, he saw that it was Shogo, carrying what looked like a bottle of saké. The boy was shivering.

"Segawa sensei!" Shogo shouted delightedly, running toward him. "I couldn't believe it! You've been quick, Sensei—we never thought you'd get back so soon."

How good to be welcomed like that! As he watched the expression of sheer delight on the boy's innocent face, it was like meeting O-Shio already.

"Out on an errand, are you?"

"Yes." Smiling, Shogo showed him the dark-coloured bottle. He had been sent to buy saké for his father.

"Thank you for your letter, Shogo." He questioned him about school and about who had been teaching him while he was away. Then he asked after Keinoshin.

"Father?" Shogo smiled sadly. "He's—he's at home," he replied, obviously finding it difficult to know what to say. That in his childish way he too pitied his father showed in his expression. Ushimatsu noticed he was not wearing any socks. It was easy for Ushimatsu, watching the small, forlorn figure standing there clutching the bottle, to imagine how his father was spending his days since he had lost his job.

"Give your father my greetings when you get home."

A quick, boyish bow by way of an answer, and Shogo ran off. Ushimatsu went on his way through the snow.

## 5

He entered the Rengeji gate just as the young acolyte was sounding the gong to mark the end of the evening sutra-readings. Snow clung to his coat in patches. The priest's wife had seen him coming and ran out to welcome him home as if he were her own son. The others followed. Kesaji, the servant girl, dusted the snow off his back and shoulders; Simple Sho brought hot water for his feet. Ushimatsu sat in the porch, pulled off his snow-caked sandals, and soaked his feet, tired out in mind and body—and wondering vaguely why there was no sign of O-Shio. Gratefully aware as he was of the warmth and kindliness with which he had been received, her absence somehow left a void.

A figure in a white robe and stole appeared from an inner room, and Ushimatsu was introduced for the first time to the priest of Rengeji. He had returned from a visit to Kyoto while Ushimatsu was away. This evening, he explained, he had a memorial service to conduct at the home of one of his parishioners; so after exchanging brief greetings with Ushimatsu he left, attended by the acolyte.

The evening meal was served downstairs in the priest's

living quarters. Sitting round Ushimatsu, the priest's wife, Sho, and Kesaji commiserated with him on the long, tiring journey and plied him with questions about how things were at home. Some youthful-looking clothes had been left hanging on a clothes rack that stood up against the grimy wall—O-Shio's. She had been invited that evening to an old schoolfriend's wedding, Ushimatsu was told. Of course—he recognized the clothes as her everyday things: a long haori coat with a crisscross pattern, and underneath it a kimono of striped taffeta, the sleeves folded together, with a beautiful coloured under-kimono peeping like plum blossom from the slits beneath the shoulders. To Ushimatsu, these clothes that she wore from morning till night, as motionless as the solid wall behind them, made her seem yet more alluring. The oil lamp played its part too; in its soft light, gleaming through the incense-laden air, all colours and surfaces shone with a subtle, elusive charm.

They talked of many things. To sympathetic hearers, as shocked as he had been by the suddenness of the tragedy, Ushimatsu described the events at Nezu—his father's last hours after being gored by the bull, the night-long vigil in the hut, the service by the pastureland grave. He told them too of the herds of cattle that roam the slopes of Mount Eboshi, chewing the cud, licking the salt scattered by the cowherds, drinking from the mountain streams, and of his visit to the slaughterhouse at Ueda and the bull's blood running on the wooden floor. Of his meeting with Rentaro and of his having travelled back in the same boat with the Takayanagis—of the sad story of the beautiful young eta girl, in particular—of these things he told them nothing.

Gradually, as he was speaking, Ushimatsu was aware of a strange feeling. Believing his audience would listen carefully to what he had to say, he threw himself into his story, taking trouble to make it as vivid as he could; but the priest's wife made irrelevant comments, and now and then asked him suddenly to repeat something when she could not possibly have misheard or misunderstood—as if she were thinking all the time of something else—and responded to what she heard only in a mechanical, dreamlike way. Finally he realized she was not listening at all. Taken aback, he watched her intently.

Her eyelids, he saw now, were swollen with weeping. Impatient by nature, she seemed more excitable and sensitive than usual. Now and again a dark shadow crossed her face, as of some anxiety too deep for words. What could it mean? Nothing special had happened during his absence, it seemed: Ginnosuke had been "kind enough to call"; Bunpei had dropped in several times for a chat. On the temple side, the priest had returned—but there had been nothing else, nothing new. Then why this queer change in the atmosphere?

Kesaji went upstairs to light his lamp. O-Shio still had not come back. Still wondering why the priest's wife should have acted so strangely, Ushimatsu climbed the dark staircase to his room.

He did not sleep till late that night, kept awake by overtiredness. As was almost habitual with him now, the moment his head was on the pillow he started thinking of O-Shio. Yet her image was never clear. Often he would confuse her with O-Tsuma and would vainly try to trace her picture in his mind—her eyes, her cheeks, her hair; but no matter how hard he tried, no matter how close imagination brought her, the details refused to fall into place, the parts to become a whole. Sometimes it was the quiet, modest tone of her voice, sometimes the girlish smile on her lips—but nothing is less sure than memory: remembered one moment, they faded as quickly. O-Shio eluded him still.

# Chapter 13

## 1

"Is there anyone at home, please?"

A man of some substance was standing at the door of the priest's quarters at Rengeji. It was the morning after Ushimatsu's return. Downstairs they had finished breakfast some time ago, but Ushimatsu had not yet come down to wash.

"Is there anyone at home?" came the voice again.

Kesaji ran out to the porch from the kitchen.

"May I ask"—the visitor spoke with extreme politeness—"May I ask whether a Mr. Segawa lodges here—Mr. Segawa, of the primary school?"

"Yes, sir," replied Kesaji, letting her sleeves down and bowing.

"Is he in, by any chance?"

"Yes, sir."

"Then would you give him this, and tell him, please, that I should like very much to see him?" The gentleman handed her his visiting card. Asking him to wait, Kesaji hurried upstairs.

Ushimatsu was still in bed. Kesaji knelt by his pillow and told him of the caller. Half-asleep still, he grunted and stretched his arms. When finally, after rubbing his drowsy eyes, he glanced at the visiting card, he sat up abruptly.

"Him? What does he want?"

"He wants to see you, he says."

"He can't have come to see *me*." Incredulous, he read again from the card: "Takayanagi Risaburo. . . ."

Impatience for an answer to the caller showed in Kesaji's face and in the fidgeting of her plump body as she sat by his bed, sleeve-cord in her hand.

"Must be a mistake, I should think," he said at last. "There's no reason why he—he, of all people—should call on me."

"But it's you he's asking for. Mr. Segawa of the primary school, he says."

"It's so strange . . . Takayanagi asking for me—what on earth can he want? All right, tell him I'll see him, will you?"

"What about your breakfast?"

"Breakfast?"

"You've only just got up, haven't you? Will you have it downstairs? I've kept the soup hot."

"No, I won't have anything, thanks. I'm not hungry this morning. Show him into the living room downstairs and ask him to wait. It won't take me long to get this room ready."

Kesaji went downstairs. Ushimatsu glanced round the room. He must change, clear away the bedding, put his scattered belongings in the closet. Among the row of books in the alcove were some of Rentaro's. Hurriedly he slipped them under his desk—then took them out again and hid them at the back of the closet. There was nothing of Rentaro's to be seen now in the room. A little easier in his mind, he ran downstairs to wash. But what business could this man have with him, who on the two journeys when chance threw them together had not merely not spoken to him but had deliberately avoided him? Even before he took Takayanagi up to his room, Ushimatsu was trembling with suspicion and fear.

## 2

Takayanagi introduced himself. "I know your name well, Mr. Segawa, though I have not had the privilege of making your acquaintance."

"It is good of you to call." Ushimatsu took him upstairs to his room. Unable to fathom Takayanagi's intention, he felt constrained and tense even before they sat down facing each other. Not for a moment, he told himself, dare he relax. Yet he managed an air of unconcern as he set out his own cushion and a white blanket folded in four for Takayanagi.

"Please sit down," he said cheerfully. "I am sorry I kept you waiting. I was so late going to bed last night, I'm afraid I overslept."

"On the contrary, I must apologize for disturbing you when you were still resting," Takayanagi answered smoothly. "I thought of speaking to you yesterday on the boat. No doubt it was rude of me not to, when I first noticed we were fellow travellers. But it would have been even more discourteous, I decided, to introduce myself to you out of the blue in such an inappropriate place."

He might have been mouthing the hollow phrases that precede a business deal. Yet there was an undeniable magnetism in his crisp, affable tone. His appearance, smart and expensive, reflected the vanity that burned within this would-be politician: a watch chain of the kind affected by the very rich hung ostentatiously from his sash; two rings, both of pure gold, gleamed on his fingers. Why should he have come? Ushimatsu asked himself again and again. But when he compared Takayanagi's secret with his own, he could not look him in the eyes for long.

Takayanagi edged a little closer. "I understand you have suffered a bereavement, Mr. Segawa. A great loss for you, I am sure."

"Thank you," Ushimatsu answered, staring down at the floor. "My father met with a tragic accident."

"A sad business, indeed." Takayanagi changed his tone. "Let me see—we met at Toyono Station two weeks ago, did we not? I got off at Tanaka, and so did you, Mr. Segawa, I believe? I thought so. You were on your way home that day, no doubt. We shared both journeys, it seems." He laughed. "One might suppose there was some karmic connection between us, don't you think?"

Ushimatsu did not answer.

"Which brings me to the point." Takayanagi spoke slowly and with emphasis. "It's because I see just such a connection that I'm here talking with you. The fact is, it is not difficult for me to guess at something that must often lie heavy on your mind, Mr. Segawa—"

"What do you mean?" Ushimatsu interrupted.

"It is not difficult for me to guess, I said, and if I have taken the liberty of calling on you at this inconvenient hour, it is because from my point of view there is something that I should like you to understand—"

"I do not follow you."

"Listen, then, if you please—"

"I have been listening, very carefully, but I don't see your point."

"My point? As I said, I should like you to try and understand—something quite simple." Takayanagi lowered his voice. "You may perhaps have heard—I have recently taken a wife, thanks to the good offices of friends of mine and of the lady's family. Strangely enough, my wife says she knows you well."

"Your wife knows *me?*" Ushimatsu laughed. "But what if she does?" he added in a different tone.

"It's precisely because she says she knows you that I've come here to have this talk, Mr. Segawa."

"By which you mean—"

"One can never be sure with women's talk, of course, it's so hard to pin them down. But it seems that a distant relative of hers, a good many years ago, was very friendly with your father." Takayanagi watched Ushimatsu closely. "But leaving that aside, if my wife claims she knows you, I imagine you can hardly be indifferent to what she says. And I myself, no less than you, have cause to feel uneasy—so much so, in fact, that all last night I lay awake thinking about it."

For a while there was silence between them, as the eyes of each probed the other's intentions.

Takayanagi sighed. "I hope you will understand, Mr. Segawa, that it was only after very careful deliberation that I came to see you. No one but you knows about my wife and myself, and we are the only ones who know your secret. We should understand each other, don't you think?" Takayanagi changed his tone. "As you know, it's not long till the election. Just now, particularly, it is absolutely essential that I have your cooperation. If you refuse to do as I say, I shall kill you—we'll die together. I don't say I'm threatening murder, but I'm ready for it, if need be, or I wouldn't have come."

## 3

Takayanagi stopped abruptly as footsteps sounded on the staircase.

"Another visitor for you, Segawa sensei," Kesaji called from outside. Ushimatsu got up and slid back the door; the "visitor" was standing there already, smiling broadly.

"Tsuchiya!" Ushimatsu could not repress a sigh of relief.

Ginnosuke nodded to Takayanagi; assuming, in his usual confident way, that the other caller must have dropped in on some more or less trivial business, he all but ignored him.

"You came home last night, I gather," he said easily, the same old Ginnosuke, gay and lively as always but with a new light now in his plump, rosy face, born of the hopes he had of the college assistantship he would soon be leaving school to take up. His close-cropped head, paradoxically, gave him something of the weight and dignified air of a young scholar. Ushimatsu felt a new sense of esteem for the friend he had known so long, and his expression said as much. Ginnosuke spoke briefly of his sympathy for Ushimatsu in his loss. Takayanagi, puffing at a cigarette, listened in silence to the two friends.

"Thanks for all you did while I was away," said Ushimatsu, pulling himself together. "You took care of everything at school, they were telling me downstairs."

"I got by. It's not all easy going, of course, when one's teaching two classes at the same time." Ginnosuke smiled ruefully. "But tell me, what'll you be doing the rest of the time?"

"The rest of the time?"

"The mourning period for your father. You're entitled to four weeks' leave, you know."

"No, it would be unfair to the school—and to you especially."

"I don't mind, not in the least."

"It's Monday tomorrow, isn't it? I'll start tomorrow, anyway. But tell me about yourself. Your dream's come true, hasn't it? I was really glad when I got your letter—I never thought they'd make up their minds so quickly."

Ginnosuke could not hide his pleasure at the prospect before him. "It's what I wanted, certainly. I've been lucky."

"You have indeed." A shadow fell across Ushimatsu's delight at his friend's success. "Has the prefectural office sent you word in writing yet?"

"No, not yet. There's the question of what to do about my compulsory teaching period, you see. I can't just walk out any time I like. Still, the prefecture's been very good about the financial side of it. They want less than a hundred yen back from me."

"As little as that?"

"I'd have had no right to complain if they had demanded I pay back the full cost of my training. It's wonderful they've let me off so lightly. Father was quite excited when I wrote to ask him for the money. He'll meet me in Nagano, he says, and we'll go together to the prefectural office and settle the whole thing. They're sure to let me know officially before long. I don't suppose I'll be staying here with you in Iiyama much beyond the end of the month." Ginnosuke glanced again at his friend as he spoke. Ushimatsu sighed.

"By the way," Ginnosuke went on, "Inoko sensei, the one whose books you're so fond of—he's up here in Shinshu, isn't he? It was in the paper yesterday."

"In the paper, was it?" Ushimatsu flushed.

"Yes, the *Shinano Daily*. He's consumptive, they say, but he seems to have plenty of fight in him still."

Takayanagi turned his sharp eyes on Ginnosuke at the mention of Inoko. Ushimatsu was silent.

"Even the eta have some good in them, I suppose," said Ginnosuke nonchalantly. "His ideas are a bit neurotic maybe, but one can't help admiring his courage in choosing to fight for them the way he does. Maybe it's something to do with his being consumptive, I wonder. His speeches are really impressive, the paper says. You'd better not go and hear him, though, Segawa—it'd make you ill again."

"Nonsense!"

Ginnosuke burst out laughing, his head thrown back. Once again Ushimatsu relapsed into silence. A sudden stupor seemed to have swept over him, as if every organ in his body were momentarily paralysed.

What's the matter with him? Ginnosuke asked himself. Must be his health again, I suppose.

For a while the three men sat without speaking.

"I'll be going then, Segawa." When Ginnosuke broke the silence, Ushimatsu was already himself again.

"Stay a bit longer," he urged Ginnosuke several times.

"Not now, I'll call again."

Ginnosuke left the room.

## 4

"This Inoko he was speaking of," said Takayanagi, tapping the ash off his cigarette, "he's a friend of yours?"

"No." Ushimatsu hesitated. "No, not a friend."

"But you are connected with him in some way?"

"No."

"I see."

"How could I have any connection with him, when I've told you already the man is not a friend of mine?"

"I suppose not, if you put it that way. He spends so much time with Ichimura, I thought I'd ask you if you knew what there is between those two."

"I haven't any idea."

"He's a crafty one, that lawyer. No matter what nice things he says about Inoko, he's got hold of him somehow, and he's using him for his own selfish ends. Those high-sounding phrases of his make me want to laugh. He's in politics for what he can get out of it, like the rest of us. But nobody who isn't in the same line of business can be expected to understand how ugly it is behind the scenes." Takayanagi sighed. "Even I don't mean to spend all my days swimming in the political sea like I am now, Mr. Segawa. As far as I'm concerned, the sooner I get clear of it, the better. But what am I to do? With no special training, without the formal education that you and your like have had, what chance does a man have in the struggle to survive that society faces him with if he sticks to the ordinary kind of career? A politician's life seems all glitter and show to you, I daresay, and so it is, but only on the surface. There can't be any life that's so grand outside, and so mean and mercenary backstage, as ours. It's all right for a man of property who dabbles in politics just to amuse himself, but for people like me, who got bitten with a passion for politics when they weren't much more than boys, there's literally nothing else we can go in for. How many politicians are there today, d'you think, who make their living by nothing but political discussion and argument? The truth about us politicians doesn't bear telling, Mr. Segawa. Perhaps you won't believe me when I tell you frankly that if we don't get ourselves elected to the Diet, many of us, we're not going to have enough to eat." He laughed. "But facts are facts, after all. If I don't win this election, I'll be in deep water. I *have* to get myself elected, and I'm pleading with you to help me—by telling no one about my wife. . . . In return, I'll keep your secret. We both promise to keep our mouths shut, in fact. For mercy's sake I beg you to agree. Remember, my life is at stake, Mr. Segawa, and you can save it!" Takayanagi suddenly moved from the blanket he had been sitting on and bowed his head to the floor before Ushimatsu, like a dog pleading with an angry master.

Ushimatsu paled slightly. "You seem to have decided everything for yourself, Mr. Takayanagi, but—"

"Don't destroy me, Mr. Segawa!"

"—but listen to me for a moment. I don't altogether see what you are driving at. After all, what reason is there why I should tell anyone about you and your wife, when I have absolutely no connection whatever with either of you?"

"No immediate reason maybe, but—"

"No, it doesn't make sense. There's no reason for me to help you in the way you ask, and no reason either for you to help me."

"But—"

"But what?"

"In that case what do you mean to do, Mr. Segawa?"

"Nothing—what should I do? We are strangers, you and I. There's nothing more to be said."

"Strangers, are we?"

"As far as I can remember, I have never spoken about you or your affairs to anyone, nor will there be any cause for me to do so in the future. I don't like gossip. And apart from anything else, Mr. Takayanagi, I have never met you before today."

"Maybe you won't ever have occasion to speak about me, nor I about you. But 'maybe' isn't quite good enough for me. Now that I have been as frank with you as I have, I want to hear your reaction more fully, and having heard it, to do what I can to be of service to you. I think rather more frankness on your part would be to your advantage, Mr. Segawa."

"I am grateful to you for the kind thought, but I do not deserve it."

"I think you cannot be altogether unaware of what is implied by this visit of mine."

"That is your misunderstanding, Mr. Takayanagi."

"My misunderstanding, is it? Can you call it that?"

"I don't know what you mean."

"If that is your attitude, I shan't say any more. But there's still room for talk between us, I think. What I'm proposing is only for our benefit, yours and mine. Nobody else stands to gain in any way. Think it over, Mr. Segawa. I'll call again."

# Chapter 14

## 1

On Monday morning the principal came to school early as usual. Every morning before lessons began it was his habit to shut himself up in his private office, next to the visitors' room, partly to look over his schedule for the day, partly to avoid the grousing and tobacco smoke in the staff room. Ushimatsu had returned that morning after his two weeks' absence. Meeting him in the corridor, the principal greeted him briefly before disappearing into his office.

He had hardly sat down when there was a knock on the door. The principal recognized it as Bunpei's. It was a regular arrangement, by which the principal would receive at frequent intervals a report on all kinds of confidential matters from his favourite teacher. The secret resentments of the men teachers, which they would never have expressed in his presence, the current gossip among the women, festering jealousies over the timetable or differences in salary —all these things he could learn of in detail in this way, without stirring from his office. Anticipating some such titbits of information from Bunpei this morning, the principal let him in. Before long they began to speak of Ushimatsu.

"That was a queer thing you said just now, Katsuno," said the principal in a low voice. "You say you've discovered something new about Segawa?"

Bunpei smiled. "That's right, Principal."

"You don't make yourself very clear with all these vague hints. Can't you come to the point?"

"One can hardly speak lightly—I think you will agree, Principal—of what might affect a man's good name for the rest of his life."

"For the rest of his life? What d'you mean?"

"Supposing what I have heard is true, if it were to get known in the town, I don't think Segawa would be able to stay in the school. More than that, it's as likely as not society would disown him altogether. There'd be no second chance for him anywhere then."

"He'd have to leave the school—society would disown him, you say? That would be like a sentence of death."

"That's just about how serious it would be. Of course I haven't confronted him with it myself, but from all I've heard—" Bunpei grinned.

"You still haven't told me anything. What is it you've discovered?"

"But if it gets about that I told you, Principal, I could be in trouble myself."

"Why?"

"They'd think I was trying to discredit him so that I could take his place. Of course I need hardly say, Principal, I haven't any such intention. It's not out of any desire to blacken Segawa that I'm telling you this."

"Of course, of course, who could suggest such a thing? You don't need to worry, Katsuno. After all, you've got your evidence from other people, haven't you? You haven't started anything on your own." Bunpei's mysterious, knowing smile whetted the principal's curiosity still further. "Just to make sure, suppose I say it wasn't from you I heard it—how would that be, Katsuno? Out with it, then—no one else can hear."

The principal leaned forward. Bunpei started to whisper something in his ear; as he listened, the principal visibly changed colour.

A sudden knock on the door. Bunpei jumped up and walked over to the window. The door opened; Ushimatsu walked in—recoiling a step in spite of himself as he saw who the principal had with him. He stared at them distrustfully, wondering what they could have been discussing.

"Excuse me, Principal," he said in a matter-of-fact tone.

"Should we start classes a little late this morning?"

"Aren't they all here yet?" said the principal, taking out his watch.

"Quite a number are late, I'm afraid—the snow, no doubt."

"That may be, but it's time, and we must stick to the rules. Rules come first, whether the children are here or not. Get the janitor to ring the bell, will you?"

## 2

Ushimatsu had never felt his mind so numbed and lifeless as he did that morning. At the start of the day he had got up and dressed in a kind of coma; it was the same on his way to school, as he trudged once more along the snow-deep road with the lunchbox the priest's wife had prepared; even when receiving the condolences of his fellow teachers or surrounded by his class and responding to their barrage of questions, he spoke as if still half-asleep. In class the scene before him would fade; he would find himself explaining the textbook and answering questions like an automaton. It was his turn for supervisory duty during playbreaks that day. Every time the bell rang for a break, boys and girls rushed to him from all directions, clinging to him and shouting, "Sensei! Sensei!" What he said to them in reply he hardly knew, walking among them like a man in a dream.

Ginnosuke ran up. "Segawa—you don't look well!" So much, and no more, Ushimatsu remembered; whatever else Ginnosuke had said passed unheard.

One thing he did not forget—the present he had brought for Shogo. During the lunch hour older and younger students alike played in and out of nearly every room in the school, chasing each other and singing and shouting. Some went on the playground to play snowballs. Ushimatsu's classroom was empty, as it happened. Finding Shogo, he took him in from the corridor and produced something wrapped in newspaper.

"This is for you, Shogo. There's a notebook inside—you're to open it when you get home, not at school. Do you understand? It's a present from Sensei." He wanted to see the boy's face shine with surprise and delight. But Shogo seemed strangely reluctant to accept the present. Wide-eyed, he stared in turn at Ushimatsu and at the packet he was holding out. Why should Sensei, of all people, want to give him a present?

"I don't want it," he murmured.

"But, Shogo—" Ushimatsu said, looking him in the face, "when someone offers you something you have to accept it, you know."

"Thank you, but I don't want it."

"But what shall I do with it, Shogo? I brought it specially for you."

"Mother'll be angry with me."

"Mother? Don't be silly! Tell her it's a present from me, and she won't scold you. I'm a friend of your father, you see, and your sister helps look after me at the temple. I've been wanting to give you something for quite a while. You know those Western-style notebooks, Shogo, with lines across the pages—it's one of those. You take it home, and do your writing in it—compositions, anything you like."

As he put it in the boy's hands, footsteps sounded outside in the corridor. Ushimatsu hurried out of the room, leaving Shogo behind.

## 3

The end of the east corridor, where the staircase led up to the first-floor classrooms, was one of the quieter places during the midday recess. Here, while Ushimatsu was supervising the play outside, the principal and Bunpei were talking, leaning side by side against the grey wall.

"This story about Segawa—who did you hear it from?"

"A very strange source." Bunpei smiled. "A very strange source indeed."

"Can't imagine who you mean."

"I can't tell you his name. He was willing to tell me what he knew, but the information being what it is, he wouldn't let himself be quoted as the source. He's standing for the

Diet, I may say. Not the kind to say anything irresponsible."

"For the Diet, eh?"

"You follow me, Principal?"

"The man that's just brought a new wife back with him?"

"Not far out."

"I see: maybe he heard something on his trip round the villages. Evil can't be hidden, Katsuno. It's frightening almost, how it's bound to come out sooner or later." The principal sighed. "It's a shock, though. I'd never have dreamt Segawa could be an eta."

"I could hardly believe it myself."

"He doesn't look like one, certainly. His complexion's no different from the rest of us, nor his build."

"That's why we've all been deceived."

"I suppose so. I should never have guessed. There's nothing at all that gives him away—"

"Appearances are deceptive, Principal. What about his character, though?"

"Nothing unusual, as far as I've noticed."

"But the way he behaves, the things he says—don't they strike you as odd? Watch him carefully, Principal, and tell me what you make of that wary, furtive look of his."

"A wary look doesn't prove he's an eta."

"Maybe not, but listen. He was living in that lodging house in Takajo Street, remember, and when that rich eta who came into town for a cure was turned out of the house, Segawa suddenly moved to Rengeji. A little odd, wasn't it?"

"It was rather, I suppose."

"Then there's the connection with Inoko Rentaro. Why should Segawa be so attracted to a man with such twisted ideas, when there are so many other writers to choose from? Why make such a to-do about an eta writer's books? There's more to his craze for Inoko than just a reader's admiration for his favourite author."

"True."

"And there's something else I haven't told you yet, Principal. An uncle of mine lives in Komoro, in a district called Yora, which is bounded by a little river. The other side of the river is Mukai, the eta section. According to uncle, every family in this eta section has the same surname —Segawa."

"Aha, that's interesting."

"The people in Mukai still don't use this surname, though. They always call each other by their given names. In fact, I daresay none of them had any surname at all before Meiji,[1] and then when families had to register under the new system, the whole community registered under the one name."

"Wait a moment. Segawa comes from Nezu, up in Chiisagata, not from Komoro."

"That doesn't prove anything. Uncle says Segawa and Takahashi are some of the commonest eta names, anyway."

"Now you mention it, I think I've heard something like that myself. But supposing it were true about Segawa, surely he'd have been found out long before now—when he was at college, for instance?"

"You'd think so. But that's reckoning without Segawa himself, Principal. He's quite clever enough to have hoodwinked everybody so far. Nobody could have managed it who hadn't a bigger than usual share of cunning."

The principal sighed. "Even so, it's still a wonder he's never been found out. I've noticed there's *something* queer about him, certainly—he can't be always brooding like he is without some good reason."

Suddenly the bell rang for the beginning of afternoon classes. Straightening, the two men began to walk down the long corridor, the other end of which was quickly jammed with boys and girls hurrying to their classrooms, their indoor slippers clap-clapping on the wooden floor. Ushimatsu, caught in the crowd, glanced down the corridor at the principal and Bunpei.

"You're right, Katsuno," said the principal as he noticed Ushimatsu. "It would ruin his entire career. We'd better look a little closer into this secret of his."

"But please be sure to tell no one, Principal"—Bunpei stressed his words—"that your information comes from the gentleman who is standing for the Diet. It would make my position very difficult."

"Of course."

[1] That is, before the Meiji Restoration of 1868.

# 4

For Ushimatsu's class, the last lesson on the timetable that afternoon was singing. The music teacher came to Ushimatsu's room to take over the class and marched the children off to his own room. Till three o'clock Ushimatsu was free. Recalling suddenly what Ginnosuke had said the day before about there being an article in the paper on Rentaro's Shinshu trip, he hurried to the visitors' room, where papers were laid out each day on the table, and found a crumpled copy of the *Shinano Daily* of two days before, still unfiled. His heart leapt in surprise and joy when he found the article. But where should he read it? Someone might disturb him if he stayed in the visitors' room. In his classroom? In the janitor's room? He couldn't be sure of being alone there either. Still undecided, he stuffed the paper in his kimono pocket and went out into the corridor. Perhaps in the big hall on the first floor. . . . As noiselessly as he could, he climbed the stairs.

The hall, a huge room with nothing in it but rows of long benches, was used only for special occasions, such as the celebration of the Emperor's birthday; on ordinary days it was quiet and deserted—far safer than a classroom. Sitting on a bench, Ushimatsu took out the paper. But no sooner had he begun to read than he found himself going over his conversation with Takayanagi. Not once but three times he had lied about his association with Rentaro and Rentaro's relationship with Ichimura . . . three times denied the man to whom he owed so much, whom he revered as his teacher and guide, as if he were no more to him than any stranger. "Sensei! Forgive me!" he murmured as he took up the paper again.

A vague terror pulsed suddenly through his mind. Even while he read of his teacher, he was thinking all the time of his own life, tracing its stages—a crisis was upon him now, he saw, and until he could work out how to meet this crisis he was paralysed, incapable of action. . . . *What should he do?* The question was easily asked, but his numbed, bewildered mind refused to answer.

"Hallo, Segawa! What are you reading, I wonder," said

a voice from behind him. Ushimatsu paled. It was the principal; spying, to judge from the queer expression on his face. He was standing by one of the benches. Ushimatsu had not heard him come in.

He tried to sound casual. "Only the paper, Principal."

"The paper? Anything interesting?"

"Nothing special."

For a moment neither spoke. The principal walked over to the window and looked out at the snow.

"What d'you think of this weather, Segawa?"

"It looks like winter's really here, doesn't it?" Ushimatsu murmured.

They left the hall together. As they walked down the stairs side by side, Ushimatsu was conscious of a strange feeling of discomfort. Perhaps he was too mistrustful, but the principal's attitude toward him seemed to have changed. There was a new coldness in his manner, and behind it, Ushimatsu somehow sensed, an insistent probing, as if the principal were bent on nosing out his secret. Goaded thus by his suspicions, for Ushimatsu even to walk beside him was an ordeal. Once or twice, as step by step they came down the stairs, their shoulders touched; each time a cold shiver ran down his limbs.

The janitor was ringing the bell for the end of lessons. Ushimatsu left the principal and mingled with the children pouring from their classrooms. Before long they would be on their way home down the snowy roads, with the excitement of school still on every eager face. Some swung their empty lunchboxes; some carried schoolbooks tied in a cloth wrapper on their heads, slippers in hand, and abacus tucked under one arm: a clamour of whistling, singing, chattering, and shouting voices, mingling with the barking of dogs, echoed through the stillness of the winter afternoon. Uncertain and afraid, Ushimatsu followed the children out of the gate. To watch them in their innocence only reminded him of his own unbearable wretchedness.

"Going home, Shogo?"

The boy nodded, smiling. "I'll be going to the temple later. Elder sister said I could."

"Oh yes, there's to be a sermon tonight, isn't there?"

said Ushimatsu, remembering. He stopped for a moment, looking after Shogo as he scampered down the broad main street. Suddenly his head swam; he nearly fell. Someone was bearing down on him from behind, he felt sure—to arrest him. . . . A shout of *"Outcast! Dirty outcast!"* He turned in terror.

No one there. How could there have been? Grasping for comfort, Ushimatsu laughed in mockery at his own weakness.

# Chapter 15

## 1

Destiny seemed to be closing slowly in upon him with all its overwhelming, obdurate power. Back in his upstairs room at Rengeji, Ushimatsu dropped his bundle, tossed aside his hakama and haori, and threw himself on the floor, sunk in despair. Incapable alike of sleep and thought, he lay as if unconscious.

After a long while he sat up and looked around the room. Snatches of laughter reached his ears from the living room downstairs. Bunpei had called again, by the sound of it; it was he that was causing the merriment. And that innocent, bubbling laughter—Shogo must have come already. Once or twice Ushimatsu caught a girl's voice—O-Shio's—among the others. Listening intently, he paced the room.

"Sensei!" Shogo burst in. They—the priest's wife, O-Shio, Simple Sho—were having tea downstairs, he said, and he had been sent to ask Ushimatsu to join them. Everyone was in fits of laughter; somebody had been in tears already, the talk was so funny.

"Katsuno sensei's here too," he added.

"Katsuno?" said Ushimatsu with a smile. A sudden flicker of hatred crossed his face, to vanish instantly.

"Come down with me, Sensei!"

"I'll be down in a minute." But he did not want to go. With a final "Don't be long, Sensei!" Shogo scurried off down the stairs.

The laughter again. . . . He could visualize the scene perfectly without going down. The priest's wife, determined to forget some private worry, joking with the others in that masculine voice of hers; O-Shio, sitting by the priest's wife after serving the tea and listening with a quiet smile to the others; the nauseating spectacle of Bunpei, contemptuous of his audience of two women, an old man, and a boy yet showing off before them as if he were the only true specimen of manhood—and spreading who could tell what gossip . . . who, if he had not been born an eta, could possibly envy such a man, whatever his position or connections?

"Why aren't you coming, Sensei?" Shogo had come up again to fetch him.

Unwilling to disappoint him altogether, Ushimatsu proposed they should go together to look at the temple hall, where the service was to be held later that day.

From the bottom of the stairs two separate corridors led from the priest's quarters to the hall. If they took the back one, alongside the garden, they would have to pass the living room, where Bunpei was holding forth. Ushimatsu took the front way.

## 2

A row of what had once been priests' rooms opened off the righthand side of the corridor. From one or two of them Ushimatsu heard voices—lodgers perhaps: with all its outbuildings, the temple was so large and complex that he had no idea how many others besides himself it accommodated. Several of the rooms, though, were unoccupied. Dark and cheerless, they were evidently little used for any purpose. Even in the long corridor, as Ushimatsu walked down it with Shogo, there was an oppressive, musty air of monastic decay about the dark, discoloured walls, the grime on the pillars, the paint flaking off the decorated panels.

As they reached the corner just before the entrance to the hall, they heard footsteps behind them. They both turned. It was O-Shio, running toward them and blushing even before she spoke.

"Mr. Segawa!" Her bright eyes shone. "I wanted to thank you," she said, a smile on her lips. "My brother told me of the present you gave him."

Just then a voice called her—the priest's wife. O-Shio turned at once to listen.

Shogo looked up at her. "You're wanted, sister!"

The voice called again. Ushimatsu watched her as she hurried back, as if startled at her recall, down the corridor. Then he opened the door to the temple.

A great stillness filled the hall, like that of some long-deserted ruin. Apart from the ticking of the clock hanging from a lacquered pillar, there was nothing under the high dark ceiling to make the smallest noise; silence penetrated into every corner. Everything the eye could see—the golden shrine pockmarked with rust, the lifeless man-made lotus flowers, the angelic figures painted on the walls, inviting the imagination to dwell on the spiritual world—all these things testified to the glory of a former age, and to its passing. With Shogo, Ushimatsu stepped up into the shrine and walked past the portraits of the saints hanging in its shadows.

Ushimatsu studied the boy's profile. "Shogo, who do you like best in your family?"

Shogo did not answer.

"I'll guess, shall I?" He smiled. "Your father, isn't it?"

"No."

"It's not him?"

"No. He does nothing but drink all the time."

"Who is it you like most, then?"

"Elder sister."

"O-Shio?"

"I can tell her anything I like. Even things I can't tell father."

In the "north room," a recess off the north side of the hall, there was an old painting of the Buddha's death and entry into nirvana. Most religious pictures of this kind found in temples are commonplace imitations, more sensational than artistic, with colours used haphazardly and a background that bears no relation whatever to nature as it really is in the tropics. The Rengeji picture was no exception, but some small spark of creativity in the painter had made it a little more vivid than most, and even if there was little feeling about it of religious passion, it did have a compelling seriousness. Not for Shogo, though. He inspected the weeping animals and birds without surprise or wonder, as if they were something out of a fairy story, and laughed in his childish innocence at the death of the Buddha.

Ushimatsu sighed. "You've never thought anything about death, I suppose, Shogo."

"Me?" Shogo looked up.

"Yes, you."

"Death? No, never."

"Of course not. Nobody would at your age."

Shogo laughed. "Elder sister talks about it, though."

"Your sister?" Ushimatsu stared at him.

"She's funny sometimes. Wishes she were dead, she says, all blubbering. Wonder why she gets like that?" Shogo cocked his head, whistled for a moment, then ran out of the hall.

Ushimatsu was left alone. The images around him sank back into a deeper silence. The brass censers, the vases, the altar lamps—even these inanimate, never-changing shapes seemed like so many monks withdrawn into solitary contemplation; the statue of Kannon above the altar, an incarnation of silence rather than of mercy. Standing in the remote stillness of this place, he thought of *her:* a flower among the ruins. . . . His blood quickening, he walked to and fro among the rounded pillars, murmuring her name: *O-Shio! O-Shio!*

It was growing dark. In the pale twilight filtering through the paper-covered doors at the front of the hall, the pillars cast their long shadows on the tatami floor. Wearily, painfully, the winter day retreated.

Two men in white robes came into the hall—the priest and his assistant. Lamps were lit within the shrine, and in the hall, six candles. The priest, his palms joined in prayer, sat by a gilded pillar beside the shrine, at the corner of the sanctuary; the assistant priest was opposite him on the other side, but in a lower position, in the outer sanctuary. To the solemn note of the sutra bell, the two men started chanting: "Namu kara kanno, toraya, ya. . . ."[1] The evening service had begun.

How lonely, how desolate the evening! Ushimatsu leaned against a pillar in the little room off the hall, his eyes closed. *Supposing O-Shio were to find out?* The brittle hollowness of his existence as an eta struck home more bitterly than ever. Enigmatic images of death and of human friendship and love took shape in his brain and faded in restless succession. That he should have to face such misery *now,* endure a burden he had never known before, never sought. . . . The smell of incense drifting on the cold evening air conveyed an indescribable sadness.

Suddenly the two voices stopped. The priest and the assistant priest had finished their chanting of the sutras and were murmuring nenbutsu. After a moment the priest, rosary in hand, moved away from the pillar. The assistant priest did not stir. Ushimatsu watched them both till the older man had finished intoning from the book of the Founder's Last Precepts and the younger had received the text, hands raised reverently to his forehead, and stood up to leave the hall. One by one the candles were blown out. Only the lamp before the shrine still gave out its dim light.

## 3

After supper, preparations began for the public sermon. Following an old custom for such occasions, huge paper lanterns bearing the temple crest were brought out of storage; Simple Sho and the assistant priest hurried back and forth along the long corridor between the priest's quarters and the hall to hang them in position.

Gradually a crowd began to collect in the hall—Rengeji parishioners, of course, and others who had heard that a sermon was to be given came along with their friends. Watching so many people gather, eager to listen to a sermon, not only old men and women, their working lives

[1] A Japanese corruption of the Sanskrit mantra *Namo Ratnatrayāya,* "Homage to the Three Treasures" (the Buddha, the Law, and the Priesthood).

already behind them, but active, busy men from every walk of life, a bystander would have been reminded how tenaciously the ancient faith still survives in Iiyama. In this town, indeed, it is nothing unusual even now for ordinary folk to quote in their conversation famous phrases and sayings from the scriptures. Young girls too, as eager as the rest, each with her rosary in a beautiful embroidered bag tucked in her kimono, made their way to Rengeji.

For Ushimatsu, that evening was the most delightful, and the saddest, of any since he had come to live in the temple. How he looked forward to listening to the sermon with O-Shio! Yet to be so piercingly aware, tonight of all nights, that he was an outcast—nothing had ever been so hard to bear.

The priest's wife, O-Shio, and Shogo had come to the hall already and were sitting together in a corner of the "north room" In the "middle room" and the "south room" too, men and women parishioners were greeting each other and chatting in twos and threes, a note of excitement in their voices, however reverent they tried to keep them. Simple Sho made a comical figure, threading his way with conscious pride through the crowd in the formal haori coat it was his special joy to wear on such occasions; the priest's wife and O-Shio smiled at his show of dignity. Ushimatsu sat by the wall where the names of parishioners who had paid for masses to be read in perpetuity for their dead relatives were posted, with the amount each had contributed. O-Shio was close by; he could breathe the scent of her hair. In profile, under the festive light of the lanterns, she looked younger than ever. She was sitting with Shogo in front of her, her arms around him—how perfect a picture of sisterly love, thought Ushimatsu, every glance in her direction an inexpressible delight.

There was still a little time before the sermon was due to begin. Bunpei arrived; he greeted the priest's wife, then O-Shio and Shogo, then Ushimatsu. The mere appearance of the colleague he disliked shattered Ushimatsu's dreams, jerking him back to reality, and to bitterness and anger as he watched Bunpei talking so familiarly with the priest's wife and making O-Shio laugh at his jokes. Bunpei came into his own in the company of women and children. Stimulated by their presence, he could make the most trivial remarks sound interesting and important—and then there was his adroit, ingratiating manner, which appealed to women particularly, suggesting there was far more to him than was really the case. Compared with Ushimatsu, who was so taciturn as to seem secretive, Bunpei gave the impression of being the kinder of the two. Ushimatsu made no attempt to please. Gentle and friendly though he was with Shogo, no one would have thought his behaviour to O-Shio anything but indifferent.

"What d'you think of that piece in the *Nagano News,* Segawa?" Bunpei would not leave him alone.

"What piece?" Ushimatsu stared at him, on his guard. "I haven't seen today's papers."

"That's odd—very odd."

"Why?"

"I'd have thought anybody who worships Inoko sensei the way you do would have looked at the report of that speech of his already. You read it and see. It's interesting what the paper has to say about him, too. 'The Lion of the New Commoners,' they call him. Some clever[2] reporters about, aren't there?"

What was he really thinking, behind the casual words, Ushimatsu wondered. O-Shio was still listening, looking at each of them in turn.

"I don't know about his arguments—they're another matter—but I certainly admire his spirit," Bunpei went on. "The report of his speech made me want to read his books. Tell me, you're the one to ask, obviously—which is supposed to be the best of them?"

"I couldn't say."

"You're joking, surely. I'm beginning to get interested in the eta, Segawa. If they can produce a man like Inoko, they must be worth studying, that's for certain. That's how you came to read his *Confessions,* I imagine?" There was a sneer in his voice.

[2] The reporters' cleverness consisted in an untranslatable pun on two words that are pronounced alike but written with different ideographs: *shishi,* lion, and *shishi,* man of public spirit.

Ushimatsu smiled but did not answer. Hearing the word *eta* spoken in O-Shio's presence, he had turned pale in spite of himself. Anger and terror rose to his lips in turn. Bunpei's sharp eyes were on him, watching for the subtlest change in his expression: "Too bad, Segawa—it's futile trying to hide it!" they seemed to be saying.

"You've got *some* of his books, surely. Lend me one, there's a good fellow. Any one will do."

"I haven't got any of his books."

"Haven't got any—don't be absurd, of course you have! Don't try to pretend you haven't. Why shouldn't you lend me one, anyway?"

"I'm not pretending. I haven't got any of his books, that's all."

Just then the priest of Rengeji took his place to begin the sermon. Bunpei and Ushimatsu fell silent; the congregation straightened up, ready to listen.

## 4

The priest was the same age as his wife, Ushimatsu had been told. But being a man, he still looked quite young. When he appeared on the preaching platform in the outer sanctuary in his black robes and gold-bordered surplice, he gave the impression of having lived a far loftier, more truly religious life than the worldly priests Ushimatsu had known in Chiisagata. Besides his distinguished appearance, with broad forehead, prominent nose, and rather formidable eyebrows, his expression clearly revealed a nature at once mild, upright, and wise.

The first part of his discourse began with the fable of the clever monkey, who knew everything there was to be known. By studying hard, remembering what he had read, and memorizing in particular a great many sutras and other religious writings, he amassed enough learning to qualify him to become all men's teacher. Being an animal, though, he lacked one thing: the capacity for faith. We human beings may know far less than this monkey, but by faith—and by faith alone—even the most commonplace of men can achieve Buddhahood. "Be thankful, therefore, that your karma has permitted you to be born into the world of humankind, and do not neglect to call in faith on the name of the Buddha, night and morning, every day of your lives!" So the priest launched upon his sermon.

"Namu Amida Bu . . . Namu Amida Bu. . . ." The murmur of praying voices filled the hall. Men and women took out their purses and placed their offerings on the tatami in front of them.

For the second part of his sermon the priest took as his theme the merits of Matsudaira Totomi-no-kami, a former lord of Iiyama. It was from his time that the town had become noted as a centre of the Buddhist faith. Already in his youth the quest for religious truth had burned in Lord Matsudaira's heart. When he had to go to Edo for the four-month period that the provincial lords were required to spend in the shogun's capital every other year, he put to those whom he met the question that had oppressed him for so long—what becomes of a man after death? None of the shogun's courtiers or learned Confucian scholars, or even Hayashi Hiko himself, rector of the Shogunal Academy, could give him any answer. So he resolved to enter religion: took lessons in the Way from a priest in Shibuya, handed over his domain to his nephew, and five years later took the tonsure, to become the great pioneer of the faith in Iiyama. What inspiration this story of religious awakening could offer! The riddle that had defeated the world's scholars, none but the man of faith could answer.

"Namu Amida Bu . . . Namu Amida Bu. . . ." Once again the voices of the congregation rose in unison, sweeping through the hall like a gust of wind. Offerings were laid a second time upon the floor.

Once or twice even while the priest was speaking, Ushimatsu found himself staring at O-Shio's profile, though he had been consciously trying not to look at her so as not to attract attention. How fresh and youthful she looked! Yet inexplicably he saw a tear trickle down her cheek, and now and then she sniffed or blew her nose unobtrusively. A shadow of melancholy appeared and reappeared in her expression, mingling with its girlish charm. What thought or pang of feeling had caused it, Ushimatsu wondered. It was hardly likely that the sermon could have moved a young girl like her so much. Not to mince matters, the priest's way of preaching was old-fashioned in the extreme and had an alien sound to the ears of one born in the new era of Meiji; to listen to its stereotyped phrases and ill-assorted fragments of philosophy against the backdrop of gleaming gilded images was like watching a historical drama. No, it was inconceivable that it could have had any emotional effect upon her, or upon anyone of her years.

Shogo was getting very sleepy, he could see. The boy leaned back against his sister, his head drooping. O-Shio tried hard to keep him awake, shaking him gently and whispering in his ear, but he was already past responding.

"Try and stay awake a little longer, Sho—people will laugh at you!" she said finally in exasperation.

"Put him down on the floor if he wants to sleep." The priest's wife came to her rescue. "It's natural: he's still a child, after all."

"He's such a baby sometimes, I don't know what to do with him." O-Shio put her arms round her brother's shoulders so as to lay him down. He was apparently fast asleep by now. As she did so, Ushimatsu leaned toward her a little; she looked round at Bunpei, at the priest's wife, at Ushimatsu, her cheeks reddening.

## 5

The third part of the sermon consisted mainly of stories from the life of Hakuin. Long ago there lived in Iiyama a well-known priest of the Zen sect, Etan by name. While he was still seeking the Way, Hakuin came to Iiyama to see this priest, hoping to practise *zazen* under him and to profit by his teaching. As he neared the town, he met a man trudging up the valley with a load of leaves on his back. The man's hair was close-cropped, but he wore a long thick beard. Guessing who it must be, Hakuin launched his request there and then, like a samurai sword thrust, with the Zen word *somosan*— "will you teach me the Way?" When he had begged the master a second and a third time to take him,

Etan at last recognized his fervour, and Hakuin went to live with him as his disciple.

After some time, however, even Hakuin found himself in difficulty with the *koan* the master gave him—or rather in despair: he began to think Etan must be mad to set him such questions, till finally, unable to bear it any longer, he ran away. In deep distress, he made his way through the outskirts of Iiyama. It was harvest time, and toward evening he threw himself down to rest by a great heap of fresh-cut rice ears. Not long afterwards, a farmer who had come to hull the rice, not seeing him in the shadow of the heap, accidentally struck the seeker unconscious with his mallet. In due time, as the night dew moistened his lips, Hakuin revived—and in thatinstant attained enlightenment. Another version of the story has it that the moment of enlightenment came when he stumbled into a pedlar of lamp oil on the road and slipped on the oil that was spilt. Whichever it may have been, the spot is marked to this day by the little hermitage of Jokan-an,[3] which was built to commemorate Hakuin's sudden attainment of spiritual vision.

To the younger members of the congregation, at least, this story was unfamiliar. The priest's peroration—his own comments on the Hakuin episodes—fell into a fixed pattern, as did the conclusion of every sermon he preached. Even for a man as outstanding as Hakuin, to enter the Way by one's own efforts was far from easy; for the parishioners and congregation of Rengeji, members of a sect that preached salvation not by man's own effort but by faith in Amida, the call was to place their trust in him, to believe in him alone, to let him lead them in the Way. Given faith, the commonest, the most ordinary of mortal men would attain the goal. Indeed, for them there was no other way but to abandon self and entrust their lives humbly to Amida, the Buddha of Boundless Light.

The sermon was over. "Namu Amida Bu . . . Namu Amida Bu. . . ." The chanting continued for some moments. More coins were added to the offerings already made. Demurely, her palms placed together in prayer, O-Shio re-

[3] Jokan-an: Hermitage of Calm Vision.

peated the nenbutsu along with the priest's wife, but even as she did so the tears trickled unchecked down her youthful cheeks.

Presently, clasping their rosaries, the congregation began to leave. The priest's wife and O-Shio got up from where they had been sitting and stood by a pillar, bowing to the parishioners as they went out. A crowd formed round the doors leading out of the hall; it had started snowing again. The groups of young women were the last to leave. The style and patterns of their kimonos, reflecting at the same time each girl's individual taste and her eagerness to keep up with the latest fashions in the town, fascinated O-Shio; she watched them closely, as if dwelling on the contrast they represented with her own quiet, cloistered life in the temple household.

"That sermon gave us something to think about," Bunpei was saying to the priest. "I was very impressed by what you told us about Hakuin—I hadn't heard all of it before. The bit about his meeting a man coming up the valley with a load of leaves on his back, and asking him point-blank, 'Will you teach me the Way?'—there's a lesson for all of us in that, don't you think?"

The priest, and everybody who overheard, could not help laughing at Bunpei's chatter and the elaborate gestures with which he mimed Hakuin's meeting with Etan.

Soon everybody had gone home, and the great hall was deserted once more. The assistant priest and the acolyte began clearing up, while Simple Sho went round collecting the offerings. Ushimatsu was no longer to be seen in the hall. Taking Shogo with him, he had gone back to the house. While Bunpei had been scattering the sparks of his wit for the benefit of the priest's wife and O-Shio, Ushimatsu, his quiet thoughtfulness unnoticed, had looked after the boy.

# Chapter 16

## 1

Ushimatsu found it more and more of a strain to go to school. One day, unable to face the ordeal, he sent a message to say he would not be going in. He had slept late that morning. Eight o'clock struck; nine, ten—and still he was asleep, even the sun, shining through the paper-covered windows directly onto his pillow, failing to wake him. Kesaji had cleaned all the other rooms and had even finished swabbing the stairs and the wooden floor of the corridor. Whenever she went upstairs to look, Ushimatsu was still lying sprawled on his bed like a drunkard after an orgy, looking pale and utterly exhausted. With the bedclothes in disorder, books lying scattered over the floor in one corner, an unopened cloth-wrapped package in another, the chaotic state of the room—as if every object in it, suddenly endowed with a life of its own, had flung itself down after cavorting in some wild dance of its own devising—reflected perfectly the turmoil in the mind of its inmate.

When Kesaji came in with his hot water, Ushimatsu was at last sitting up on his bed, dazed and half-asleep still, his face haggard from strain and from overlong, unhealthy sleep. "Shall I bring your breakfast?" Kesaji asked; but Ushimatsu did not want to eat. "You aren't well, that's plain," she murmured as if to herself, and left the room.

It was cold, a real northern winter's day. A single tiny winter fly flew round the ceiling looking for the window. Ushimatsu remembered the flies in his room in Takajo Street, before he moved to Rengeji; it was only a few weeks ago, yet there were so many of them then, they were quite a nuisance. Appearing from nowhere, like the dust, they would congregate suddenly over the lintel, then scatter as suddenly all round the room in a frenzy of buzzing, as if they sensed the autumn wind and were determined to live their short lives to the full. Now it was the season when one noticed even this lone survivor. Staring at it, Ushimatsu realized it was nearly December.

For someone in his position, perfectly able to work, it was hard to lie idle like this and be always thinking, thinking. The government had paid for his education, and in return he was bound to teach, to teach for ten long years whether he liked it or not. It was fair, of course; he recognized that. Yet he had lost the will to work. The bed on which he had slept so far into the morning lay beneath him like a grave for one in whom hope had died. Ushimatsu fell back upon it once more. Soon he was fast asleep.

## 2

"Segawa sensei! Visitors for you!"

Roused by Kesaji, Ushimatsu saw Ginnosuke at the door and with him the young probationary teacher, both of them still in formal school dress. Afternoon classes had been cancelled, Ginnosuke explained, so that a retired army captain, on a lecture tour of the provinces to promote the "military spirit," could address all the pupils together. Otherwise they wouldn't have been able to get away. Sitting up in bed, Ushimatsu stared at his friend.

"Don't get up!" said Ginnosuke at once, his genuine concern evident in his expression.

Ushimatsu pulled the white blanket off his bed and wrapped it round himself like a dressing gown.

"Sorry to be in such a state. I'm not really so bad."

"A cold, is it?" The probationer looked closely at Ushimatsu's pale face.

"I suppose so. My head's been throbbing all night—I just couldn't get up this morning."

"No wonder you look so pale," said Ginnosuke. "You'd better be careful—there's a lot of flu about. Why not take something for it? A bowl or two of well-grilled *miso*[1] in hot water will cure most colds." He changed his tone. "Oh yes, I nearly forgot—I've brought you a present." Undoing his cloth wrapper, Ginnosuke took out Ushimatsu's salary envelope for November. "As you didn't come in today, I got

[1] A paste made from soybeans and fermented rice, much used in Japanese cooking.

it for you. I think it's all there—better check it over, though."

"Many thanks." Ushimatsu took the envelope from him. "Yes, it's all here. So it must be the twenty-eighth today, after all. I was so sure it was the twenty-seventh."

Ginnosuke threw back his head and laughed. "Forgetting payday—you *must* be in a bad way!"

"It's true, I've been in such a fog since yesterday." Ushimatsu pulled himself together. "Only two more days of November left, and not much longer till the end of the year. Think of it, another year gone and nothing to show for it, not in my case, anyway."

"It's the same with all of us."

"You've nothing to regret, now you've got the job at the agricultural college. You'll be free there, free to do what really interests you."

"Which reminds me: the children say they want to have my farewell party tomorrow."

"Tomorrow?"

"But not if you're going to be in bed—"

"Don't be silly, I'm all right now. I'll be back at school tomorrow."

Ginnosuke laughed. "You get better the same way as you fall ill—in a rush. It's a bit odd, you know—moaning in bed one minute as if you were at death's door, and swearing you're fit and well the next. Never mind, it's your way, I suppose. What's more important, it's not much longer that we'll be able to spout our nonsense at each other. We'll have to say goodbye soon."

"You're really going, then?"

The two were deeply moved. Suddenly the probationer, who till then had been puffing at his cigarette and listening quietly to their conversation, spoke up.

"I heard a curious thing today. It seems people in the town are saying there's a 'new commoner' on the school staff. An eta masquerading as one of us."

# 3

"Who says so?" Ginnosuke turned to face him.

"I don't know," said the other with a trace of embarrassment. "It's probably only a rumour."

"Some rumours are worse than others. One thing's certain—it'll be damaging to us at school if that kind of story gets about. The townspeople spread all kinds of nonsense about us teachers. What makes them do it, I wonder. Look at our staff, though: is there any one of us who looks the least bit like an eta? It's ridiculous as well as insulting. Don't you think so, Segawa?"

Sitting wrapped in his white blanket, Ushimatsu did not answer.

Ginnosuke laughed. "There's the principal, of course. He's unpleasant enough, with his everlasting insistence on discipline, but still, nobody would take him for an eta. The same goes for the other teachers. Wait a minute, though, what about Katsuno? With that revoltingly superior air he puts on, he's the only one of us anybody could possibly suspect."

"That's ridiculous." The probationer laughed in turn.

"Who do you suppose it is, then?" said Ginnosuke in a bantering tone. "You, maybe?"

"Stop fooling!" retorted the probationer.

"You lose your temper so easily, that's your trouble. I didn't say it *was* you, did I? Even a joke's not safe with a fellow like you."

"All the same," said the probationer seriously, "suppose it were true?"

"Impossible," said Ginnosuke decisively. "Just think for a moment. We know all our teachers' backgrounds. There are a few like you who've come here straight from the special training course, some like Bunpei who've taken the teacher's certificate exam, and some like Segawa and myself, who've been through training college, and that's all. If your eta was one of the training college people, he'd have been found out at college. Living with all the others in a dormitory, he'd never have been able to keep it secret all the way through to graduation day. Anyone who takes the certificate exam has already been teaching a long while. Everything would have been known about them already, so that rules them out. The same goes for you and the other probationers. See what I mean? To start spreading this story now —it just doesn't make sense."

"I never said it *was* true," insisted the probationer. "I only said, supposing it *were*—"

"Supposing, are you?" Ginnosuke laughed. "But there isn't any call to suppose anything."

"Maybe not. But if by some remote chance what they say *did* turn out to be true, what d'you think would be the upshot? It frightens me just to think of it."

Ginnosuke did not reply, and neither of them referred to the subject again.

When they got up to go a few minutes later, Ushimatsu's face was lifeless, as white as the blanket he was clutching around him.

"Segawa's still bad," Ginnosuke muttered half to himself as he and the probationer went down the stairs.

For some moments Ushimatsu stared dully at the room around him. Then suddenly he got up, changed quickly, and took out of the closet some books and pamphlets he had hidden away in a corner. They were Rentaro's, all of them: *Modern Thought and the Depressed Classes,* into which the eta writer had poured every drop of vitality and passion he possessed; the pamphlets *The Common Man, Labour,* and *A Message for the Poor; Confessions;* and other writings besides. Ushimatsu looked through them one by one. Then he blocked out his name where he had stamped it with his seal on every flyleaf, took five or six language reference books he had no further use for from the alcove, and was wrapping them with the others in a furoshiki when Kesaji came in.

"Are you going out?" the maid asked him.

Flushed, Ushimatsu did not answer.

"Going out in this cold?" she exclaimed, shaking her head as she saw how pale he was. "How can you, when you've been feeling too bad to get up, even?"

"I'm all right now."

"You'll be feeling hungry, then. Have some breakfast

before you go. It's halfway through the morning, and you haven't had a bite."

Ushimatsu shook his head. "I don't want anything."

Mechanically, hardly aware of what he was doing, he took down his overcoat from the wall and put it on, together with his hat. Some of his salary that Ginnosuke had brought from school he locked away in the drawer of his desk; the rest, still in its envelope, he dropped into his sleeve, with only the vaguest idea of how much he was taking with him and how much he had left in the desk. With the bundle of books under one arm, hiding them as best he could with the sleeve of his overcoat, Ushimatsu walked unhurriedly through the gate as if for a stroll.

## 4

Snow lay deep on the roads and on the roofs of the houses. Labourers in straw snow-hats and leggings of plaited rushes, travellers with their heads and shoulders wrapped in blankets, plodded up and down the street. Several sledges, some drawn by men, some by horses, slid past Ushimatsu. The long overhanging eaves that served to keep off the snow, known locally as *gangi,* and the cloisterlike passageway beneath them had come into full use already. A start had been made on piling the snow in a massive ridge all down the middle of the street—the famous Iiyama "snow mountain" of so many poems—serving as yet another reminder of how hard and bleak life in these parts could be in winter. The sky threatened still more snow. One glance at the faint, listless sun was enough to make Ushimatsu shiver as he walked.

There was a secondhand bookshop in the upper part of the town where he had once managed to get rid of some old magazines. Fortunately no one was browsing over the trays outside when he arrived; taking off his hat, he went in and casually produced his bundle. The bookseller was sitting in his living room, which opened on to the back of the shop.

"I've brought a few books and oddments—I'd be glad if you'd take them off my hands."

The bookseller gave him a shrewd glance. Then with a tradesman's smile he drew the bundle toward him.

"Anything you like to give me will do," Ushimatsu added.

After undoing the bundle and looking at the covers of the books, the bookseller separated them into two piles. Each of the language books he opened and looked through; Rentaro's he pushed carelessly to one side.

"How much are you expecting for them?"

"Tell me what you think they're worth."

"Let me see . . . business is rather sluggish just now. There's very little demand for this kind of thing. I'll take them if you wish. I can't give you much of a price for them, though. Even so, to be frank, it'll be for the English books. These others I'd be taking as a favour—they're worth nothing to me." After a moment's thought he went on. "Maybe you'd better take them back?"

"I'd be grateful if you could take them, now that I've brought them all this way."

"Very well then. Shall I price the two lots separately or together?"

"Together please."

"Shall we say—fifty-five sen? That's as far as I can go."

"Fifty-five sen?" Ushimatsu smiled cheerlessly. He was ready to accept any offer, however low, and the transaction was over in a moment. One should never sell books, he felt as strongly as anyone; yet these were a special case. . . . Entering his name and address in the bookseller's account book, he picked up his fifty-five sen—but before leaving, checked once again the places where he had erased his name. One book, he found, he had missed. Borrowing a writing brush, he drew thick black strokes over the red characters of his name. This done, he would be safe. So he told himself. But in his mind there was only darkness and confusion; of what his next move should be he had no idea. As he left the bookshop and walked down the passageway under the eaves, thinking over what he had just done, he was already near to tears.

*"Sensei, Sensei—forgive me!"* he mumbled repeatedly. He remembered his denial when Takayanagi had suggested he was a friend of Rentaro. Conscience, unblunted, struggled with excuses—surely, if he was to protect himself at all, he

had no alternative? The agony struck deeper. In shame and in fear, not knowing where he was going, Ushimatsu walked on.

## 5

Unbidden, Ushimatsu's feet led him to the same dingy eating house where he had spent that evening drinking with Keinoshin. He pushed open the sliding door. Two or three men were eating or drinking; the woman of the place, the skirt of her kimono tucked in her sash, was busy at the sink.

"Anything to eat?" he asked her.

She paused to wipe her hands. "Sorry, nothing much today. Boiled fish and beancurd soup, that's all."

"I'll have both. And some saké please."

A pedlar who was winding a towel round his sweating head turned to stare at Ushimatsu from his seat on a saké barrel; a peasant still in his snowshoes, leaning against a pillar, looked round at him; a labourer, a sledge puller by the look of him, who was drinking standing up from a cup the woman had just filled to the brim with brownish, frothing saké, raised his eyes over the cup to gaze like the others at the unfamiliar figure whose entry had checked their conversation in midflow. The inquisitive silence did not last; in a moment voices were raised again in talk and laughter. The fire crackled in the hearth. As Ushimatsu pulled closer the little table the woman had set before him and began to eat, breathing the scent of woodsmoke from the pile of burning brushwood, the pedlar got up to go and another customer came in carrying a fishing rod.

"Well—another surprise!" exclaimed the new arrival as he noticed Ushimatsu. It was Keinoshin. He propped his rod against the wall.

"Kazama! You've been fishing?"

"Talk about the cold!" He sat down opposite Ushimatsu. "It's so freezing down by the river, I gave up."

"Manage to catch anything?"

"Not a single thing," Keinoshin replied, sticking his tongue out by way of emphasis. "Standing there shivering all morning and never getting a bite—really, Segawa, it's more than a man can bear."

There was something oddly comic in the way he spoke. The peasant and the sledge puller burst out laughing.

"Have a drink." Ushimatsu emptied his cup, refilled it, and pushed it across the table.

"For me?" Keinoshin stared at him. "Bless me, that's something I wasn't expecting. It's a day of surprises—that explains why I didn't catch anything, I suppose."

The woman brought another bottle of hot saké. Trembling with cold and the lust for drink, Keinoshin greedily savoured the aroma from the bottle.

"Seems quite a while since I saw you, Segawa. This fishing—since I stopped teaching, there's just been nothing to do: that's why I took it up. I had to do something—"

"Can anybody catch anything in this weather?" Ushimatsu stopped eating and stared at him, chopsticks in hand.

"I'm a novice, that's the trouble. A man of my age a novice, how d'you like that?" He laughed. "The people who do it for the trade get a kick out of the game even in winter—they have the knack, you see, not like the rest of us. If it wasn't for the wind, though, it wouldn't be so bad." He swallowed another cupful of saké. "But listen, Segawa—there's nothing so cruel to bear as a life that's useless. I can't stand by and watch when my wife's working for all she's worth. Even so, it's not so bad on days when I can go fishing, but when the weather keeps me in, there's just nothing, nothing. . . . As a matter of fact, I sleep a lot of the time. What else is there, I tell myself—"

This last confession, made with such pathetic earnestness, moved Ushimatsu deeply.

"By the way, Segawa," Keinoshin went on as he raised the cup to his lips with the gloating gesture habitual to the confirmed drinker. "About Shogo. You've had him in your class a long time now, and he's come on a lot. But things being what they are at home, I can't do as well for him as I'd like, so—well, what it comes to is, I'm thinking of taking him out of school. What d'you think of the idea, Segawa?"

# 6

"Not that I *want* him to give up, mind you," he continued. "Every father wants his boy to finish primary school, even if he goes no further. It'd be such a pity to make him stop now, when he's only got till next April before he's due to graduate. But I've no choice, that's the misery of it. He may not be quick off the mark, but he doesn't altogether dislike learning, as far as I can see. As soon as he gets back from school, he sits down at his desk and starts working on something or other all by himself. I wish his arithmetic wasn't so weak. Composition's his strong point, though. You should see the joy on his face when he comes home with an 'excellent' from you in his book! And the thrill it was for him the other day when you gave him a new exercise book and told him to write whatever he liked in it . . . he put it away carefully in the bookcase but kept on getting it out again, I don't know how many times, to have another look. He even talked about it in his sleep that night. Yes, it'll be a pity to take him away. But what's a man to do when he's as many children as I have? Children—they may be small, but they take some looking after. A row of mouths waiting to be fed morning, noon, and night, and up to all kinds of mischief the rest of the time." He laughed again. "I can tell you these things, Segawa, because I know you understand.

"But I'm a father, after all. I can't say to them, 'Don't eat so much—no seconds of rice even if you *are* hungry!' How could any father be so mean?"

Ushimatsu couldn't help smiling at this effusion. Keinoshin too managed a forlorn smile.

"Then again, if it wasn't for his stepmother . . . to tell the truth, it's because my second wife and I don't get on so well that I've been thinking of putting him out to service somewhere. I could cry, Segawa, every time I think of O-Shio and the boy, and the unhappiness my marrying again has meant for those two. Why should stepmothers be so suspicious? Only the other day we had trouble, the day they had the sermon at the temple. Shogo came back late that evening. My wife was mad at him—the sparks flew then, I can tell you! 'Go on, out you get! Been telling tales at the temple, I suppose, like you always do, and having your head stuffed with wickedness by that sister of yours. That's why you don't listen to *me,* I know!' Oh, she let him have it all right. And the boy himself is so timid, he just crept into bed without a word and lay there blubbering. It was then I said to myself, I'd better send him away—with one mouth fewer to feed and one thing less for my wife and me to fight over, maybe we could make a better go of it at home. Or perhaps I'll leave myself and take him with me. The family'll have to break up. It's got so bad, there's no other way left now." Keinoshin's weak, querulous side was taking over. By now the saké had taken effect: his cheeks, his ears, even his hands were flushed. Ushimatsu's colour did not change—if anything, the more he drank, the paler he became.

"But surely things aren't that desperate, Kazama." Ushimatsu tried to comfort him. "I'll be glad to help you in any way I can. Drink up that saké and pour me a cup, will you?"

"Eh?" Keinoshin stared at him. "Here's a wonder now. Pour *you* a cup, you said? You're quite a drinker then, Segawa—and I thought you couldn't touch the stuff!" He filled the cup and held it out to Ushimatsu, who drained it at one gulp.

"My, but you're in a hurry!" exclaimed Keinoshin, still more astonished. "Anything the matter, Segawa? Sure it's all right to pour it down like that? Better slow down a bit. There's nothing odd about *my* drinking, but when *you* start, it's enough to get anybody worried."

"Why?"

"Why, you say? Obvious, isn't it? Our lives are so different, yours and mine."

Ushimatsu laughed, a harsh laugh of despair.

## 7

Keinoshin sighed deeply, as though there was something else on his mind of which he could not bring himself to speak. The peasant and the sledge puller had left. Apart from the woman, who was busy washing dishes, and a child standing idly by the back door, there was no one to disturb the two men in their talk. Everything in the room was dingy from ancient smoke and soot, recalling the long history of the Northern Highway; the straw sandals and bunches of dried gourd-shavings[2] hanging from the wooden pillars of the room and the row of yellow pumpkins up against the wall were typical of the old-style saké shop or tea house to be found so often on the fringe of these small mountain towns. In a patch of sunlight on the spacious earthen floor a kitten lay asleep. There was even a hen squatting in a corner, its eyes shut and head sunk into its feathers against the cold.

The smoke curling up from the fire to find its way out under the eaves showed bluish white in the weak sunlight from the doorway. Lost in thought, Ushimatsu stared at the fire. There was solace in the bright flames, and the warmth generated by the saké he had forced down his throat made him tremble once again with the urge to weep, regardless of who was with him—if only he *could* weep, aloud and freely . . . yet no tears came. Instead, he laughed aloud.

Keinoshin sighed again. "There are some people one can know for ten years and still feel each time you meet them that you're no closer than when you first met. Then there's the other kind—the people you may not be terribly close friends with, but somehow you just feel you want to tell them everything that's on your mind. Like you, for instance. As a matter of fact, you're the only one, for me. . . . There's something else I'd like to tell you about, Segawa—" He hesitated. "I—I went to see my daughter the other day. I hadn't been for some time."

"O-Shio?" Ushimatsu's pulse quickened.

"She sent a message asking me to go, you see. Rengeji being Rengeji, if you follow me, and with my wife being the way she is, I've made a point of visiting her as little as possible. But this time, she said, there was something she wanted to talk over, so off I went—it was a while since my last visit, as I said before. How they shoot up, don't they, the young ones. I hardly recognized her. Anyway, when I asked what was troubling her, she said she couldn't bear to live at Rengeji a day longer, and would I please, please take her back home right away. Well! And no wonder, either,

[2] Used in Japanese cooking.

when she told me why. I found out for the first time what sort of man that priest is."

Keinoshin shook the china saké bottle to see how much was left. Pouring out what there was—not quite enough to fill his cup—he took a sip, wiped the corners of his mouth with his fingers, and went on. "Here's how it is. Listen, Segawa. You'll agree, I think, there are plenty of men around with a fine reputation for character and integrity who have a streak of weakness in them where women are concerned. The priest of Rengeji is one of them, it seems to me. He's got plenty of learning, he's a fine speaker, he's a good man, with all the qualifications you can think of, and above all he's had a strict religious training—why is it that he, of all people, should go astray? When she first told me, I just couldn't believe it. It *can't* be true, I told myself. One can never tell, can one, Segawa? He was away for a long time in Kyoto, you remember. When he came back, you had just gone home. It was then it started. He began acting strangely toward her, she said, not at all like an adoptive father. . . . He's supposed to be a servant of the Buddha, isn't he? He's supposed to preach the Law, isn't he, in those robes of his? I'd have thought he'd have a bit more respect for his job as a priest than to carry on the way he has. It's a sordid, stupid story—I can't tell you. . . . And his wife, she's more jealous by nature than most, which makes it worse. The girl's so miserable and frightened she can't sleep anymore at night, she says. I was so shocked when she told me. I can understand her wanting to come home all right. I don't want to leave her in a place like that, and she could come home tomorrow as far as I'm concerned. If only my wife were a bit more understanding, we'd manage somehow, with all of us together. But with the way things are, even Shogo is one too many, and if O-Shio were to come back, I just couldn't face my wife anymore. How would the eight of us eat, for one thing?

"So you see, Segawa, I couldn't just tell my daughter, All right, come home then! You'll have to stick it out, I said—anyone can endure what's not beyond his power. Enduring what's *un*endurable, that's real endurance! That's what I told her. If you can keep your courage up, I said, and stay as close as you can to his wife, you'll get by. Even if he's not exactly behaving as a father should, you owe him something for bringing you up, and in any case, you've been adopted, don't forget: you're *his* daughter now, and whatever trials you have to face at Rengeji, you can't come home anymore. Rengeji is where your duty lies—your duty to your parents. . . . I made her agree to stay in the end. It's so terribly hard on her, though. If only my first wife were still alive—" Anguish showed undisguised in Keinoshin's face; his eyes shone with tears.

So that's what it is, thought Ushimatsu. Keinoshin's story explained what even he had noticed—the feeling of a dark cloud lurking in the shadowy corners at Rengeji, a constant threat to the peace of the household, the source of wordless tension between the priest and his wife; as though even when on one side the sun was shining and voices were raised in happy laughter, in another quarter of the sky a storm was always looming. Every day it was the same. He had imagined, though, that the cause was ordinary domestic bickering, only on a more elevated level than in other households perhaps, both the husband and the wife being in this case disciples of the Buddha. That the ominous cloud might somehow be associated with O-Shio had never occurred to him. This would also explain the wife's artificially free-and-easy manner, her jokes, her overloud, mannish laughter; and the tears he had noticed more than once on O-Shio's cheeks. Keinoshin's story had solved the riddles.

For a long while the two men sat opposite each other in despondent silence.

# Chapter 17

## 1

When at last the time came to pay the bill and leave the Sasaya, Ushimatsu remembered for the first time that he had put some of his salary money in his sleeve before he came out—fifty sen in silver coins and one five-yen note. While his father was alive, he had sent money home every month. That was no longer necessary, but he had to be careful even so, he had spent so much on the trip home. Any expenditure that was not strictly necessary he could not afford. But now something else worried him. He felt less sorry for himself than for Keinoshin and his family, and was eager to help—until Shogo graduated, anyway; perhaps he could pay the boy's fees. It would be for O-Shio's sake really, of course.

Keinoshin having drunk so much, Ushimatsu decided to see him home. Together they walked down the snow-covered street. Simultaneously with the wave of physical energy that filled his whole body in resistance to the freezing wind, Ushimatsu recovered some of his courage. Keinoshin reeled, rather than walked, beside him—he was not so drunk as to have forgotten his fishing rod, but his feet were shaky in the extreme, barely managing to carry him in a shambling zigzag. He looked ready to collapse at any moment in the snow.

"Mind how you go, Kazama!" Ushimatsu warned him.

Keinoshin steadied himself. "Afraid I'll fall? I *like* the snow—better than the floor at home!"

To this Ushimatsu had no answer. He shuddered; supposing Keinoshin were to fall asleep in the snow. . . . He kept close beside him, his mind full of the old teacher's pitiful decline and of the stresses confronting his unhappy daughter.

Keinoshin's home was an old, tumbledown thatched cottage. Originally he had lived in a samurai house in one of the narrow lanes near the castle, but that was long ago; he had moved to the cottage when he came back to Iiyama from Shimotakai. A Shinto prayer, with a picture of a flock of crows, was pasted on the doorpost as a kind of charm. Bunches of dried radish leaves and red peppers hung from the clay wall; a rough screen of woven reeds, hanging from the eaves, gave some protection from the snow. It was the day for paying the rice rent, it seemed; a huge pile of unhulled rice lay on the earthen floor inside the entrance, and outside, a mat had been spread for the measuring. Holding Keinoshin by the arm, Ushimatsu went in with him. Otosaku saw them from where he was working by the back door, and came running over to bow and greet Keinoshin with the humble politeness he never forgot to show, even now, to one who in former times had been his master and patron.

"The mistress gave orders for the rent to be paid today as usual, Mr. Kazama. I brought my brother with me to help."

Oblivious to what Otosaku was saying, Keinoshin fell to the floor. From another room came the sound of a child crying and of his wife's voice, tense with anger.

"Look what you've done now—will you never stop being naughty, you—"

Otosaku listened for a moment. Then he turned to Keinoshin. "Taken too much again, have you, master," he murmured in sympathy. He and Ushimatsu carried Keinoshin across the room and laid him in the shadow under the sliding window, where he would be out of the way and less conspicuous. Just then Shogo came in whistling.

"Shogo!" Otosaku called to him. "Go to the landlord's, will you, and ask him to step over as soon as he can."

## 2

Before long Keinoshin's wife appeared, to discover that her drunken husband had been brought home once again by Ushimatsu. The children looked at each other, cowering in anticipation of their mother's reaction. But she merely glanced contemptuously at her husband—restrained, no doubt, by Ushimatsu's presence and by that of Otosaku and his brother—and gave a weary sigh. Then, sitting down one moment and jumping up the next to scold one or other of the children, she began to thank Ushimatsu for his repeated kindness to her man and for his present to Shogo. Ushimatsu saw only too easily how impatient and prickly and short-tempered she was—the common faults of a woman in her forties, displayed now without any attempt at concealment.

Another child came in and stood gaping, without so much as a bow.

"O-Saku! Can't you bow? It's rude to stand like that in front of guests, stupid. Why do my children have to be so naughty. . . ."

O-Saku, a wild, graceless tomboy of a girl, ignored her mother. Ushimatsu found it impossible to think of her as O-Shio's stepsister.

"This one's the worst of the lot. I wish she could find it in her now and then to do what she's told—"

But O-Saku paid no more attention than before. Suddenly she darted out.

A ray of afternoon sunlight penetrated into the cottage, brightening the dirty paper-covered sliding window through which it came but showing up too the brownish, sooty stains on the paper, which looked as if it had not been changed for years.

"There's a bit of sun again," Otosaku said cheerfully. "We're lucky—it looked more like snow a few minutes back." With his brother, he began to get things ready for the payment of the rice rent.

The winter sun shed its pale, yellowish light on the signs of poverty and decline. Anyone who has been inside a peasant cottage will be able to visualize the boarded hearth where Ushimatsu was sitting—the "room" used by the family alike for its own meals and for receiving guests. An earthen-floored area, occupying at least a third of the whole area of the house and serving as kitchen, workroom, and storage space, stretched from the entrance across to the back door. On shelves to one side were stacked plates, bowls, an oil lamp or two, and a quantity of odds and ends; from the wall opposite hung a sickle and bags of seeds; sacks of charcoal jostled in a corner with tubs of pickled vegetables, next to a jumble of kitchen utensils and farming tools. An improvised chicken roost hung from the roof, but it was empty, like a deserted birds' nest; evidently the family kept no poultry to speak of.

Ushimatsu could not get away from the thought that though O-Shio had not been born here, it was within these earthen walls, according to Keinoshin, that she had been brought up till her adoption into the temple family. The cottage contained three "rooms," all of them dimly lit because of the high ceilings and the deep overhanging eaves outside. Coarse brown paper covered the walls, unrelieved by any decoration except for several out-of-date calendars and a few cheap prints. O-Shio's childish eyes, as she stood before these decaying walls, would have looked on the men and women pictured so crudely in these prints as her friends. Wistfully, Ushimatsu visualized other such scenes from an irrecoverable past.

A man of fifty or so wearing a formal haori coat and a dark green hat, both of silk, appeared in the doorway.

"The landlord's come," Shogo announced as he came in with the visitor.

## 3

The landlord was a member of the town council. A grim-faced, taciturn man, after a nod to Ushimatsu he went and warmed himself by the fire. Men of his sort are common in northern Shinshu; they wear an angry look on their faces all the time for no apparent reason, but in fact the expression is misleading—they are not necessarily angry about anything. Knowing this, Ushimatsu paid no special heed to his brusque entry but went on watching the preparations for the handing over of the rent. Still he could see before him, as vividly as ever, Otosaku and his wife and Keinoshin's wife getting in the harvest on that autumn day when he had watched them in the fields outside the town. More than half the great mound of rice heaped up in the unfloored area in the middle of the cottage, the fruit of a whole year's labour, was now to be handed over as rental for the land they worked.

A girl of sixteen or seventeen—Otosaku's niece—came in from somewhere, threw a three-pint measure on the straw mat beside the rice, and ran out again. Keinoshin's wife stood in a corner surveying the scene, one hand on her hip and a sour expression on her face. Her youngest girl ran in crying—the four-year-old, O-Sue. Otosaku spoke to her, trying to calm her down; she only shivered and sobbed, her whole body shaking violently with each burst of tears. What she was saying it was impossible to catch.

"Stop crying, and mother'll give you something nice!" Keinoshin's wife called to her. Still sobbing, O-Sue went over to her mother.

"My hands are cold!"

"Cold, are you? Better get in the foot warmer, then. Clutching O-Sue's hand in her own, she took her through to a room at the back.

The landlord left the hearth. Hunched against the cold, his hat pulled down, his sleeves folded round him like a bird's wings, and his head sunk on his shoulders, he stood waiting for Otosaku to begin measuring out the rice that was due him.

"Well, sir, what do you think of this year's crop?" said Otosaku, looking up at him.

The landlord's reply was barely audible. Scooping up some ears with his white hands, he put one in his mouth, then scrutinized the little heap on his palm.

"Some empty husks, by the look of it."

"No, there's no husks, sir—or maybe the sparrows have had a peck or two, but you'll find the weight's all there, good solid grain. I'll make up a bagful to weigh."

Six new straw sacks were brought out. Otosaku filled a winnowing basket with rice, then shook out the contents into a 30-pint measure. When the landlord had smoothed off the overflow with the levelling rod and tested the weight of the measure by the feel, Otosaku poured it into one of the waiting sacks, leaving his brother to pack it down tight. But his brother's silence as he worked irritated Otosaku.

"You take this, then." He tossed the winnowing basket to his brother. "Someone's got to give the cries, or it doesn't seem like we're paying the rent the proper way."

"*In* you go, *down* you go . . . once round, *in* you go, *down* you go," he began to chant. Six times the big measure was emptied into every sack, and the smaller measure—the one the girl had brought—three times, making over three bushels in all.

"Six sacks—that'll be your full share, sir," said Otosaku as he fastened the mouth of the last sack.

The landlord did not reply. He stood in silence, his eyes narrowed in concentration as if he were checking his calculations on an invisible abacus.

Otosaku's brother brought a large pair of scales to weigh the sacks. Between them, flushing with the effort, they hoisted a sack onto one side. The landlord, after making sure the balance was level, steadied the chain holding the weights as he added up the total.

"What does it come to?" Otosaku peered down at the weights. "Huh, there's enough and to spare."

"A hundred and fifty-five and a half pounds—well, I'll be—" put in his brother.

"Nothing but pure grain there, all through," said Otosaku, straightening up.

"You haven't allowed for the weight of the sack." The landlord still wasn't satisfied.

"You're right, sir, but a straw sack don't make much difference."

"A hundred and fifty-five pound'd be plenty for me," muttered his brother.

"It's all pure grain and no waste," Otosaku repeated, his eyes fixed on the obdurate expression on the face of the landlord.

## 4

Watching this scene, Ushimatsu felt the pathos of the tenant farmer's lot. No matter how hard Otosaku worked to help his former master in his decline, never forgetting, honest peasant that he was, the debt he owed the family from long ago, Keinoshin's wife must find it all but impossible, out of her own meagre resources, to support such a large household. "Eight of us—how could we eat?" her husband had whined over his saké when telling Ushimatsu of O-Shio's plea to be allowed to come home. It was true. How *could* she come back—to *this?* Ushimatsu shuddered to think of it.

"Won't you stay for a cup of tea, sir?"

In response to Otosaku's invitation, the landlord promptly sat down again by the hearth. Still standing, Otosaku took out his pipe.

"Six sacks and one bushel extra, I make it," he said, puffing away.

"One bushel—what d'you mean?" said the landlord

contemptuously. "Two bushels, two bushels and a quarter, it should be."

"Two bushels, then."

"Two and a quarter—no, two and a half. Two and a half, that's it."

Keinoshin's wife had been listening in silence to this dialogue. Suddenly she could bear it no longer.

"Oto! Let him have it, and don't argue. I'll do without, that's all."

"Mrs. Kazama, you needn't have—" Disconcerted, Otosaku stared at her.

She sighed. "What's the good of my slaving and struggling when the man of the house never does a thing but drink? I tell you, I've no spirit to work anymore, with such a swarm of children on top of everything else, and so stupid and disobedient, the lot of them—"

"Don't talk like that, Mrs. Kazama! Leave it to me, I won't let you down." The faithful Otosaku did his best to comfort her. Wiping her eyes with her sleeves, she started to prepare a meal. Otosaku's brother, who had gone out earlier, came back with a newly bought bottle of saké. Big rice bowls and small plates were laid out; it looked as though every morsel of food in the house was to be offered to the landlord to go with his drink. How pitiful that they even had to entertain so exacting a landlord, thought Ushimatsu. Otosaku took charge, setting out a dish of *konnyaku*[1] and fried beancurd, cooked in soy sauce, with pickled vegetables to go with it. Presently he poured out a cup of saké for the landlord.

"You'd like a drop of this, I think, sir? It's cold, the way you like it."

For the first time the landlord allowed himself a smile.

Ushimatsu had something he wanted to say to Keinoshin's wife. Till now he had been waiting, uncertain when he would have a chance to speak to her. Now that the landlord had started on the saké, there was no telling when he would leave. He got up from the hearth, refusing Otosaku's invitation to drink, and called Shogo over to the front door.

[1] A stiff paste made from the plant called "devil's tongue."

Standing in the shadows, he took his salary envelope from his sleeve. Shogo was to give the money to his father, Ushimatsu explained. It was to be used to help pay Shogo's fees so that Keinoshin would not have to take him out of school as he had been thinking of doing.

"All right? You know what you've got to do?" Ushimatsu pressed the envelope into the boy's hand. "How cold your hand is!" He squeezed the hand in his own. Looking down at the innocent, childish face, he found himself recalling O-Shio's cool, tear-moistened eyes.

## 5

Ushimatsu walked home consoling himself with the thought that at least he had done what he could for the family, for O-Shio's sake. By the time he was nearing the great gate of Rengeji, the grey clouds had sunk lower, as if more snow were on the way. To Ushimatsu's already joyless mood the sombre evening added a deeper sense of loneliness, of foreboding. Faintly, in one far corner of the sky, a streak of crimson lingered from the vanished sun.

The priest's bell—it was the hour of the evening scripture-readings—fell strangely on Ushimatsu's ears. It was no longer the pure music of the cloister, unworldly, remote. The note of sublime grace had faded from the cadences of the sutras; in the voice of the chanter Ushimatsu heard only an echo of the passions of common men. Contempt for the priest, or rather fear, welled up within him as he went over Keinoshin's story. Yet what had happened had shown too how fragrant a flower she was, how compelling her womanly charm—which thought inclined him rather to pity than to condemn. Even he could see clearly now how things really were in the temple household. In the light of what he had heard from Keinoshin, the canker showed even in apparently unconnected, trivial things. Slowly, he realized now, the warmth he had sensed in the family when he first moved in had faded.

In the corridor on the way to his room he met O-Shio. Even in the waning light of early evening he caught at once her pale, lifeless expression, the sadness that filled her black eyes. She looked him in the face for a moment, surprised, it seemed, at his gloomy, dispirited air. Their eyes met; each bowed and passed on in silence.

Back in his room, the last of the light had all but gone. But Ushimatsu did not light his lamp. For a long time he sat as if in a stupor, alone in the darkness.

## 6

"Mr. Segawa! Are you studying?"

It was nearly two hours later when the priest's wife slid back his door. Some notebooks, including the one in which he entered his lesson plans along with any ideas or impressions he wanted to record, lay open on the desk before him. Ushimatsu sat deep in thought, his shadow thrown onto the faded wall by the yellow light of the oil lamp, which shone forlornly on the night air. A thin haze of tobacco smoke was diffused throughout the room.

"Could I trouble you—would you please write a letter for me, Mr. Segawa?" Paper and envelope in hand, she waited for his reply. Ushimatsu was struck by something unusually serious in her manner.

"A letter?" he repeated.

"I want to write to my sister in Nagano. She's married to a priest in a temple there." She hesitated. "I started writing myself, but women ramble on so—once we begin, we don't seem to be able to come to the point, to get down in so many words what made us want to write in the first place. That's why I thought I'd ask you to write it for me, to keep it short and to the point. Women's letters are so unbusinesslike. I've wasted several sheets already. It doesn't have to be anything elaborate, either—if I could trouble you to put it simply, so that she gets the message—"

"Of course," Ushimatsu said simply. "I'll be glad to write it for you."

Encouraged by this reply, she explained what the letter was to be about. A "personal matter" had arisen which she was anxious to talk over with her sister; would she please come to Iiyama immediately on receipt of the letter . . . from Kanizawa there was a regular boat service to Iiyama, but if she didn't like the boat, she should come as far as she could by ricksha and then take a sledge. This time, the priest's wife concluded, she had finally made up her mind: a divorce was the only way.

"I can ask you to write this kind of letter for me, Mr. Segawa, when I couldn't ask anyone else—" Tears began to show in her eyes. "I haven't told you the reason. You'll find it hard to believe, I shouldn't wonder—"

"No." Ushimatsu interrupted her. "I did hear something already from Mr. Kazama."

"Keinoshin told you, did he?" There was a new concern in her expression.

"I don't know any of the details, of course."

"The whole affair is so ridiculous, it's humiliating to talk about it even to you," she said with a deep sigh. "It's a sickness, behaving the way he does at his age—how else can you explain it? Don't you agree? Except for this disease of his, he's a good, gentle man, as fine a husband as you could wish for: I still believe in him, even now."

## 7

"I don't know why I should be so easily upset," she went on through her tears. "When this kind of thing happens, I can't settle to anything. It's not as though it was the first time he's had this sickness. He was only sixteen, you know, when the last priest, his father, died, and he had to take over. Two years after I came here as a bride, he went off to our parent temple in Kyoto for training. There were young priests there from all over the country, and he was reckoned one of the ablest of them all, I've been told. His mother and I and his assistant, the father of the assistant he has now, looked after the temple while he was away—for five years altogether. It was then that his trouble started. The girl was the eldest daughter of a man who kept a little inn off Fishmonger Street. When we found out what was happening, the assistant priest was very concerned and went off to Kyoto at once to see him. I can't tell you what I went through then, left all on my own as I was and trying desperately to make sure his mother and the parishioners didn't get to hear of it. Eventually we persuaded him to break with the girl. She was given some money, of course. After that he should have learned his lesson once and for all, you might think, but there's no telling with a disease that's congenital. Three years later, when he went to teach in a True Pure Land school in Tokyo, he had another bout."

Forgetting the letter she had come to ask him to write, she poured out the whole sad story. For all her usual air of cheerful detachment, her woman's nature drove her now to seek a listener.

"Of course," she continued, "that second time he went away we couldn't let him go alone. The school was going to pay him a salary, and his assistant was willing to take charge of the temple, besides which his mother wanted to see Tokyo, so the three of us took a room together in a temple in Takanawa. The school was quite close: he used to walk to work, down what they call the Street of the Two Nettle Trees. There was a young widow living in one of the houses along the street, an educated woman and very devout. She asked my husband to go and talk to her about religion. I can see her now—a slender, graceful girl with beautiful white hands. I met her when she came to the temple cemetery to visit her husband's grave. Once when her name cropped up in conversation, my husband was quite contemptuous. Her mind's twisted, he said, sneering almost—twisted beyond redemption. What do you think, Mr. Segawa—even then he was having an affair with her. It wasn't long before she was pregnant, though, and then he changed his tune. 'I'm very sorry,' he says, on his knees before me.

"Well, he's honest at heart, as I said before. The moment he sees he's really done wrong, he repents so sincerely you can't help feeling sorry for him, and when he begged me to help, I just couldn't abandon him, and wrote off to the assistant priest asking him to come to Tokyo to help me straighten things out a second time. I thought to myself then, it's because I haven't given him a child. Maybe if he had children of his own, he wouldn't be so wayward. Maybe I should adopt *her* baby and bring it up as mine. Sometimes, though, when I thought of the shame of it—his making her pregnant under my very eyes, you might say—I felt so humiliated I decided I'd just have to leave him. But women are so weak, Mr. Segawa. One kind word, and they forget everything that's gone before. Before long, the only thought in my mind was how hard life would be for him without me. Then the child was born. It was premature, and to make matters worse the mother couldn't feed it, and it didn't live two months. I suffered a good deal, I can tell you, till he gave up teaching and we came back to Iiyama. . . .

"Ten years ago, that was. Since then he's settled down. He never misses his sermons, three times a month, and visits all the parishioners to read masses on their death days, including the families who are out in the country. He stays the night if he can't get back the same day. They've grown to have such trust in him, all of them, and showed it a few years ago when we had to get the roof of the great hall repaired. If only he'd gone on like that till now! Popularity seems to bore him, though, and when he gets bored his sickness breaks out again. That's the way he's made. Men are strange creatures. . . . Take my husband, he's so sensible usually, but once the sickness is on him, he can't tell right from wrong any more than a baby. Do you know, he's fifty, Mr. Segawa? Fifty, and still getting infatuated. Pitiful, isn't it?

"I know there aren't many priests in Iiyama nowadays who don't meddle with women in one way or another, but having an affair with a tea-house waitress is one thing—or even getting themselves a regular mistress—but to run after O-Shio . . . I just don't know what to say. I can't see how a man like him can get that sort of obsession in his head, when he's such a good man in other ways. There must be something wrong with him—a streak of madness maybe. O-Shio tells me everything. I'm not to worry, she says: she won't let him have his way, whatever happens. The girl's got plenty of spirit, and I trust her because of it. We had a good cry together, she and I. Be strong, I told her—he's sensible and considerate at heart, and once he really understands how the two of us feel, he'll change, but whether or not he comes to his senses depends entirely on our sincerity. I *can't* think too badly of him. It's only for his own sake that I've made up my mind to leave him, in the hope that it'll make him see sense at last."

# 8

Ushimatsu wrote the letter in the way she wanted it written. Again and again, obviously very worried about what the future might hold, she murmured the name of the Buddha.

When finally she left him, Ushimatsu lay down by his desk thinking, but before long he was asleep. He had got into the habit these days, once he lay down, of sleeping on and on like a corpse, as if he could never sleep enough. It was a strange kind of sleep, too, like a fall into some deep, dark pit, so that even when he woke up his head was always heavy. It was the same that night. Waking after a while, he lay for a time in a dull stupor. When his mind finally cleared, it was very late. There had been a heavy snowfall, and no sound was to be heard now save an occasional thud as a lump of snow disintegrated and fell from the window. The night was sunk in a profound, torpid silence. Downstairs, everyone had gone to bed.

Suddenly a faint sound caught his ear—a youthful voice quietly sobbing . . . where from, he couldn't make out . . . somewhere downstairs, in the dark corridor. . . . Who was it, trying so hard to stifle tears? He listened: someone was opening the shutters of the north corridor, it seemed—looking out into the night. It *was* O-Shio—he recognized the sobbing voice as hers. A shock of fear and pity assailed Ushimatsu. True, he had been listening in a kind of trance, and when he got up and began to walk about the room, the voice was no longer to be heard. Puzzled, he stopped and listened again, his head to the wall. Finally he began to doubt his own ears. Maybe it had been a dream, that voice—he couldn't be certain he had really heard it. He stood with folded arms, staring dully at the dying flame of the oil lamp. It was halfway through the night, and he was tired, so tired in mind and body that when he took his bedding out of the closet he scarcely knew what he was doing.

Drowsiness seized him. Half-asleep already, he put on his nightclothes and slipped once more into forgetfulness.

# Chapter 18

## 1

The massive snowfalls the district experienced every year came at last, blanketing every house and street in the town. More than four feet had fallen in the night, and abruptly Iiyama changed its aspect, presenting everywhere scenes truly characteristic of the harsh northern winter. There being no longer any place left to pile the snow where it would be out of the way, it was heaped up in the middle of every street in a continuous "snow mountain," both sides of which were scraped smooth and beaten firm, so that if you stood back a little, the "mountain" looked exactly like a long white wall. More snow was then heaped on the top and trampled flat, then more, and so on, till it reached the level of the eaves. Iiyama might have been a town dug out of the snow.

When Takayanagi Risaburo and a member of the town council ran into each other on Iiyama's main street, groups of men and women were hard at work clearing snow. The two men exchanged the seasonal greeting, "A heavy fall it's been!" and were going on their ways when the councillor called Takayanagi back.

"By the way, have you heard about that teacher, Segawa?"

"No." Takayanagi was emphatic. "I've heard nothing."

"They say he's an eta."

"An eta?" said the other with every sign of astonishment.

"Scandalous, isn't it?" The councillor grimaced. "Mind you, several people have been passing the story round, and who originated it I don't know. But there's somebody who has proof, he says—"

"*Who* says he's got proof?"

"That I can't reveal. He insisted his name mustn't be mentioned," the councillor said with a confidential expression, as if he had already given away more than he should have. "Keep it dark, will you? I've told you as a friend, but don't pass it on."

Takayanagi's lips twisted in a derisive, knowing smile. They parted, the councillor staring after Takayanagi as the latter hurried off. Going on his own way in the other direction, the gossipy councillor had hardly gone a hundred yards when he met someone else he knew, a younger man this time. The more confidential he told himself his information was, the harder it became not to share it in a conspiratorial whisper.

"That Segawa, the teacher—he's one of these—" He held up four fingers, but the young man looked blank.

"You know what that means, surely." Smiling, the councillor brandished the four fingers again.

"Sorry, I've no idea," the young fellow said, still puzzled.

"Slow on the uptake, aren't you? 'Four legs'[1] means eta—outcast . . . I've told you in confidence, remember: don't pass it on, whatever you do!" With this emphatic injunction, the councillor left him and continued on his way.

Just then the probationary teacher who had called on Ushimatsu with Ginnosuke passed by on his way to school. The young man ran up to him. The usual "snow greeting" followed, and a moment later they were already talking of Ushimatsu.

"This is confidential, between you and me, but that teacher in your school, Segawa—they say he's an eta . . . I still can't quite believe it, though."

"I've heard somebody else say that." The probationer stared at his friend. "Maybe it's true then, after all?"

"I met a friend just now. He stuck four fingers in front of me, like this, and said, 'Segawa sensei's one of these'—which made no sense to me. I asked him what it meant, and he said 'four legs.' "

"Four legs? Another name for an eta, isn't it?"

"Apparently. Gave me a shock, though, it did. A sly one, he must be. I can't imagine how he kept it dark all this time. One of those dirty, loathsome fellows *teaching* at your school . . . it's disgusting—"

[1] That is, animal, subhuman.

"Ssh!" The other checked him, glancing back suddenly the way he had come. Ushimatsu, also on his way to school, was approaching along the snowbound passageway that was all that remained of the street. Huddled in his overcoat, he walked unseeing, as if in a dream, yet deep in thought too if his sombre expression was any guide. Turning momentarily to look the two men in the face as he drew level with them, he strode on toward the school.

## 2

Not many children came to school on time, because of the snow on the roads. Unable to start their classes, the teachers gathered in groups to chat, some in the staff room, some in the janitor's office, some in the music room, as if to celebrate the holiday that heaven had granted them this snowbound day.

In a corner of the staff room four or five teachers were sitting round a big hibachi. The probationer went over and joined them, and before long, though without anyone having raised the subject directly, they were talking of Ushimatsu. Occasional bursts of laughter from one or another of their number brought others over to see what was so amusing, and finally Ginnosuke and Bunpei joined them.

"Which side are you on, Tsuchiya?" said the probationer, glancing at Ginnosuke. "It's about Segawa. We're divided into two parties, it seems. You've been his closest friend ever since you were at college together. Let's hear what you think."

"What d'you mean, two parties?"

"Well, some of us say that the rumours going around about him are true and some are convinced there's nothing whatever in them."

"Wait a moment," said another of the group coolly, a teacher of one of the fourth-year classes, with the beginnings of a beard. " 'Two parties' isn't quite accurate. Some of us aren't committing ourselves either way."

"It's nonsense, I'm certain of it." The gymnastics teacher was emphatic.

"You see how it is, Tsuchiya." The probationer looked at the faces of the little crowd that had gathered round the hibachi. "As to how the idea of Segawa being an eta got about in the first place—well, there's been a lot of argument, but what it boils down to really is Segawa's own attitude being so queer. That's what started all the talk. Any teacher would be furious to hear it rumoured that there was an outcast among his colleagues—it's only what you'd expect: to have that sort of talk going about is an insult to all of us. So if Segawa's conscience is clear, shouldn't he be as angry as the rest of us? He ought to have *something* to say on the subject, surely. But no, he doesn't, not a word, and the only explanation of his perpetual silence is that he's hiding something. That's the line some of us took, anyway. But then somebody else—" He stopped in mid-sentence. "Maybe we'd better drop it, though."

"Don't be absurd—you can't leave it in the air like that," cut in a tall, first-year teacher.

"Go on—better finish, now you've started!" The voice, faintly derisive, was Bunpei's. He was standing behind the probationer smoking a cigarette.

"It's not a joking matter." The fire had kindled in Ginnosuke's eyes. "I know all about Segawa. He and I have been friends ever since we started at the teachers' college together. To say he's an eta—it's utterly ridiculous, impossible. I don't know who invented the story, but if there *is* such a rumour going about, he'll have to reckon with me. It's deadly serious, this—not just teatime gossip."

"Of course," replied the probationer. "That's why we're so concerned about it. Here's another thing someone said, though: whenever anyone starts talking about the eta, Segawa changes the subject—and not only that, but he puts on a queer look, as if he's embarrassed or upset in some way, which makes one wonder all the more. Something odd somewhere, isn't there? If only he could get out a word or two—'Eta? So what, who cares about *them?*' or something of the kind, like the rest of us—no one would suspect him."

Ginnosuke shrugged his shoulders defiantly. "All right then—is there anything of the eta about him, anything at all? Let's start from that."

"He's been looking pretty down lately, that's a fact," said the fourth-year teacher, fingering what there was of his beard.

"Down? That's no evidence—it's just his temperament," Ginnosuke objected. "He's not the only one. You don't have to be an eta to look a bit serious, you know."

"They say the eta have a special smell, don't they? Maybe we could take a sniff and see?" put in the first-year teacher, smiling.

"We needn't go that far," said Ginnosuke, smiling in turn. "I've seen plenty of eta. Their skin's darker than ours—you can tell them at a glance, and being shut out from society has made them terribly warped inside too. There's no chance of a solid, manly character developing out of such a background, and how could one of them possibly take any interest in learning and study? Isn't it obvious from all this what the truth is about Segawa?"

"How do you explain about Inoko sensei, then?" said Bunpei with a sneer.

"Inoko Rentaro?" Ginnosuke hesitated. "He—he's an exception."

"All right then, Segawa could be an exception too," the probationer retorted, clapping his hands and laughing. The others joined in the laughter.

Just then the door of the staff room opened, and Ushimatsu came in. Suddenly silent, all the teachers gathered round the hibachi turned to face him.

"Segawa! How's your illness?" Bunpei asked, weighting the last word with undisguised sarcasm. The probationer glanced at the first-year teacher, who was standing beside him; they smiled knowingly at each other.

"Thanks," Ushimatsu answered at once. "I'm much better now."

"A cold, was it?" inquired the fourth-year teacher drily.

"Something of the kind—nothing much, anyway." Ushimatsu changed his tone. "It's a pity the attendance is so poor this morning, Katsuno. If no more come, it looks as though we'll have to cancel Tsuchiya's farewell party. The ones who have turned up are looking so disappointed, when they've worked so hard getting things ready."

"It can't be helped, with this snow," said Bunpei, smiling. "We'll have it on another day, that's all."

The janitor had come in as Bunpei was speaking. Ginnosuke was so taken up with Ushimatsu and what the others had been saying about him that he did not hear what the janitor said. The gymnastics teacher tapped him on the shoulder.

"Tsuchiya! The principal wants to see you."

"Me?" Ginnosuke looked up, surprised.

## 3

The principal was in the visitors' room with the inspector. When Ginnosuke opened the door and went in, the two men were sitting opposite each other, evidently in the middle of a confidential discussion.

"Ah, it's you, Tsuchiya." The principal got up and offered him a chair. "I've sent for you on account of this queer rumour that's been going round. You've heard it, I'm sure. . . . We can't ignore what's being said in the town. There's no knowing what that kind of thing will lead to if it's allowed to spread unchecked. The inspector's so concerned, he's been good enough to come over especially, in spite of the snow. You seem to have known Segawa longer than any of us, Tsuchiya, so I thought you'd be the best person to ask about these rumours."

"Then I'm sorry I can't help you," Ginnosuke replied with a smile. "Isn't it best to let people say what they choose? Heaven knows where we'd get to if we started taking every bit of gossip seriously."

"That's not quite the point," said the principal, glancing at the inspector. "You don't take much notice of opinion outside the school now, because you're still young. But silly though it may seem sometimes, the world outside can't be ignored, you know."

"Is it necessary to concern ourselves with something that's obviously completely false, just because a handful of people in the town are repeating it?"

"It's precisely that refusal of yours to take any notice that won't do, Tsuchiya. Of course I don't believe the talk either. But where there's smoke, there's bound to be fire of some kind. There must be *something* about Segawa to have made people suspect him, don't you think?"

"No. As far as I'm concerned, I don't think so."

"If you're so positive, there's no more to be said. I should have thought, though, you might have had some idea of what's behind it." The principal lowered his voice. "Segawa looks so solemn these days, as if he were brooding over something all the time. What can have made him so gloomy? He used to come and see me at home quite often, but not anymore. If only he'd talk and laugh with the rest of us, we shouldn't be so much in the dark, but with him always so shut up in himself, anyone who doesn't know what's troubling him is going to suspect something, it seems to me, even if he's no real ground for doing so—"

"No." Ginnosuke interrupted him. "As a matter of fact, there's a quite different reason for his behaving the way he does."

"What do you mean, a different reason?"

"Being the kind of person he is, he doesn't talk about it."

"Then how can you know what it is?"

"One can learn about a person from his actions just as well as from his words. Having known him so long, and seen the change in him, I can tell from his manner just why he seems so thoughtful—so depressed, if you like."

The principal and the inspector pricked up their ears at this claim by Ginnosuke. Puffing at their cigarettes, they waited in silence for him to go on.

According to Ginnosuke, the reason for Ushimatsu's melancholy air was merely a severe case of the emotional upheaval most young men are liable to go through sooner or later. He, Ginnosuke, had a pretty good idea of who the girl was, even though Ushimatsu, being the kind of person he was, had never mentioned his feelings to his friend, or spoken of them to the girl herself, apparently. Compelled by his nature to keep everything to himself, he had sought relief in finding all kinds of ways of helping Keinoshin and Shogo. Beyond all doubt he was suffering deeply from this secret heartache. Admittedly it was only by chance, and quite recently, that Ginnosuke had guessed Ushimatsu's secret. "But once I saw what his trouble was, everything fell into place. Up till then I'd been puzzled, certainly."

"I see. Yes, I suppose there may be something in what you say," said the principal, exchanging glances with the inspector.

## 4

Back in the staff room, Ginnosuke found Ushimatsu and Bunpei hammering away at each other, surrounded by their colleagues. All the other teachers—some standing with folded arms, others leaning on their desks with head resting on hands, others walking about the room—while not contributing to the argument, were following it with intense interest. Some were watching Ushimatsu, evidently on the lookout for clues to confirm what they suspected; others seemed torn between belief and disbelief. From their voices, Ginnosuke sensed the tension between Ushimatsu and Bunpei.

"What's all the argument about?" he asked them, smiling.

Sitting behind the main group, the probationer had begun to sketch the two disputants in a notebook. "Inoko sensei," he said, glancing up at Ginnosuke. "They've just got on to him. That's what the rumpus is about." He licked his pencil, and smiling to himself, went on with his drawing.

"There isn't any rumpus," Bunpei retorted. "I merely asked Segawa how he came to be so interested in Inoko's books, that's all."

"I don't see what Katsuno's getting at." A light burned in Ushimatsu's eyes.

"There must be *some* reason," said Bunpei with open sarcasm.

"Why should there be?" Ushimatsu shrugged his shoulders.

"All right, I'll put it another way," said Bunpei more

seriously. "Let's take an example. Suppose we run into a madman. No normal person will feel any especially deep sympathy for him, which isn't surprising, because a normal person won't be directly affected in any way himself."

"Sounds interesting." Ginnosuke looked from Bunpei to Ushimatsu.

"But then somebody comes along who's in trouble himself and deeply worried about his own life. When he meets this madman, he'll be struck at once by the madman's pathetic, brooding air, by the miserable skeleton despair has reduced him to, by the melancholy expression on his face as he slinks about in the shadows looking as if he can think of nothing but death—and he'll pity what he sees because he's suffering himself. That's how it is with you, Segawa. The reason why you're attracted to Inoko and his struggles when you think seriously about life is that there's some big worry preying on your own mind. Am I right or not?"

"Of course you're right," put in Ginnosuke. "Nobody without some troubles of his own would understand Inoko's books. I've said as much to Segawa myself before now. I know perfectly well, though, why Segawa can't speak freely about all this."

"Why can't he?" asked Bunpei with a meaning look.

"It's the way he's made." Ginnosuke paused. "He's always been like that. I'm different. I give myself away all the time—couldn't hide anything if I tried. It's not because he's trying to hide something that Segawa's so uncommunicative. It's just that he was born that way." He laughed. "I'm sorry for him. But what can you do with a man who's such a congenital brooder?"

Laughter greeted this remark. Interrupting his sketch, the probationer looked round the room at his colleagues. The first-year teacher slipped behind Ushimatsu, and screwing up his face, pretended to be sniffing at his neck.[2]

"As a matter of fact, I've read something of Inoko's myself," said Bunpei, knocking the ash from his cigarette. "I borrowed it from a friend. But just what sort of man is

[2] That is, carrying out the suggestion he made earlier in the discussion; see p. 193.

this fellow Inoko, that's what I'd like to know."

"How do you mean, what sort of man?" Ginnosuke said, not very seriously.

"He's neither philosopher, nor educator, nor priest, nor even a writer, in the ordinary sense of the word. . . ."

"All right, he's a thinker, a thinker in the new style," Ginnosuke replied.

"A thinker, is he?" said Bunpei contemptuously. "An empty-headed dreamer, if you ask me. A—a species of madman in fact."

Laughter broke out again among the listeners, Ginnosuke joining in.

The blood rushed to Ushimatsu's head, and with it a sudden wave of anger, suffusing his pale cheeks and ears and eyelids.

## 5

"You're not far out, either," Ushimatsu came in again. "Inoko sensei *is* a kind of madman, just as you say. Who nowadays, when autobiography means self-advertisement, the stringing together of whatever plausible titbits a man can get together to flatter his own image, would write a *Confessions* like his, so stark and true they make you shiver? It was this society of ours that robbed him of his job, and society that drove him by its persecution to that terrible illness and nearly killed him. Yet it's for this same society's sake that he makes such passionate speeches and writes such moving books, the fire burning him up till his pen breaks in his hand and his voice is worn to a whisper—where else can you find such a crazy, deluded fool? His whole life has been one long confession of his folly, humbly accepting the sneers of 'dreamer' and 'simpleton' the world throws his way. *No man can be called strong who complains of his trials, however cruel or bitter they may be. Let the world jeer at you, and die, if need be, as the wolf dies, in silence, and bravely, like a man.* That's his philosophy. Enough to prove he's crazy, isn't it?"

"Don't get so excited, Segawa." Ginnosuke tried to calm him.

"I'm not in the least excited."

"But this Inoko of yours," said Bunpei, overt contempt in his smile once more, "what is he, after all, but an eta?"

"So what?" Ushimatsu demanded sharply.

"An inferior race isn't going to produce anybody worth taking seriously."

"An inferior race—"

"If a man who can write such filthy, perverted rubbish isn't subhuman, I'd like to know what else to call him. It was a big mistake from the start, his idea of forcing himself on society in this clumsy, brutish way. Sensei, indeed! He should have hidden away in some eta slum and stuck to his cowhides[3]—it's all he's fit for."

"So Mr. Katsuno is the enlightened one, the man of culture, and Inoko sensei is the barbarian, the inferior breed—is that it? The mistake is mine. I always thought both you and he were just human beings—"

"Stop it, the pair of you!" Ginnosuke admonished them. "It's pointless, that kind of talk."

"No, it's not." Ushimatsu would not heed him. "I'm serious. Katsuno says Inoko sensei is inferior, a kind of savage. He's right, and I've been wrong from the start. Oh yes, Inoko should have stuck to his cowhides and kept his mouth shut—if he had, illness wouldn't have nearly killed him. Battling on against society like he did, regardless of his strength or health—sheer madness, wasn't it? Your cultured man has visions of a gold medal sitting proudly on his chest, so he goes in for a solid career in education and things of that sort, but pity the poor barbarian—Inoko sensei could never look to that kind of success, even in his dreams. He knew all along he'd leave no more mark than the dew on the field. He went to the battle expecting death. Isn't it pathetic, that fury of his—and maybe heroic too?" Ushimatsu was trembling. He laughed feverishly, pent-up feelings bursting their bounds: his forehead glistened, his cheeks quivered. Anger and suffering suffused his angular, melancholy face with a new manliness.

Ginnosuke stared at his friend, sensing as he had not done

[3] See Introduction, pp, x. xi.

for a long while Ushimatsu's inner life, young and strong and vital still.

His opponent said nothing, so Ushimatsu did not go on. But Bunpei could not conceal his fury at having been worsted by the man he had been so sure of vilifying. Contempt and hatred showed more plainly than ever in his face, resentment in his eyes—*How dare he, this eta!* After a moment he took the first-year teacher over to the window.

"What did you think of that—given his secret away completely, hasn't he?" he whispered.

The probationer had just finished his sketch. The others crowded round to look at it.

# Chapter 19

## 1

A report that Ichimura and Rentaro had arrived in Iiyama in the middle of the big snowstorm reached Ushimatsu at the school. It was said too that Takayanagi's party, alarmed at the news, had intensified their defensive measures, calling on the electors again, distributing letters of recommendation, and bringing pressure to bear in other, less open ways. A gang of bullies hired to support Takayanagi was rumored to have descended on the town. The election battle was approaching.

Ushimatsu and Ginnosuke had to stay on at school that afternoon, as it was their turn for night-watch duty. Ginnosuke went out, though, after classes finished—he had some business in the town—and still had not come back when darkness fell. Ushimatsu was left for a long while, therefore, in sole charge of the keys and the school diary. Depressed and apprehensive, in the intervals between his various duties he lay on the tatami in the night-watch room to think and wrestle alone with his fears. As this dark mood enveloped him, the wintry afternoon slipped by. When the great bell of Rengeji, tolling sundown, shook the glass windows of the duty room, anxiety for O-Shio set his heart racing. Supposing she discovered what the priest's wife was going to do—or maybe she already knew? If she did, how could she, as her "daughter," let her go and stay on herself at the temple as if nothing had happened? But how should she go back home, either, with that stepmother to face? Perhaps she would die. . . .

Still Ginnosuke did not come back. For a long while Ushimatsu sat with his elbows on the desk, thinking of O-Shio. As he stared at the flame rising from the half-consumed wick, one grim vision succeeding another, exhaustion took over; gradually, still leaning on the desk, he fell asleep. Just then O-Shio came into the room.

## 2

But wasn't this the school? What could have brought her here, of all places? The next instant he realized—she had come to see *him,* and what she wanted to tell him he could read already in those soft, dreamy eyes: *Why are you so kind to my father and my brother and so cold to me? Why, when you live under the same roof, do yon never speak a single kind word to me? Why must your lips be so tightly closed, afraid to say the words they long to say? Why do you tremble so?*

The questions that gave him such delight ceased abruptly, for at that moment Bunpei entered. He spoke to O-Shio urgently, as if he had some special business with her, and when she hesitated, took her by the hand and tried to drag her after him.

"Wait a bit, Katsuno. There's no call to use such force, you know."

Bunpei turned as Ushimatsu tried to stop him. Their eyes met; lightning flashed between them.

"O-Shio! I've something to tell you." Bunpei put his lips to her ear; he was going to whisper to her Ushimatsu's dread secret. . . .

*"Don't tell her!"* Ushimatsu screamed frantically—and woke up. The sudden, white-hot agony left him with the dream, but its core of fear remained. . . . He looked round the room. No sign of O-Shio or of Bunpei. The

door opened; in came Ginnosuke carrying a cloth-wrapped parcel.

"Sorry to be so late. Still up, are you? Let's talk in bed." Kicking off his shoes, Ginnosuke hung up his coat, tossed his collar onto the desk, and slipped off his braces. How often in this room, he could not help recalling, the two of them had talked the night away. In vest and pants instead of a nightshirt, Ginnosuke pulled over him the quilts provided for the teachers on night watch.

"This'll be the last of our nights together," he said with a sigh. "I'll be gone before my turn comes again."

"The last time, is it?" Ushimatsu too got into bed.

"Feels like we were back in the dormitory at the college again. Strange, how it all comes back—how we worked, you and I! What's happened to all our friends, I wonder." Ginnosuke changed his tone. "But there's something I want to ask you, Segawa."

"What might that be?"

"You are your own worst enemy, keeping everything to yourself the way you do. Anyone can *see* you're troubled about something, without your opening your mouth. I'm worried about you, Segawa. If it's that bad, why not get it off your chest? A friend can help a lot sometimes."

## 3

"Why do you have to lock it all up?" Ginnosuke went on, his voice full of sympathy. "Maybe you think it'd be no use telling someone like me, who's always poring over his experiments and scientific books. But I'm not that cold, you know—nor so cruel I can look on with a supercilious smile when someone's lying hurt."

"You say some queer things. Whoever said you were cruel?" said Ushimatsu, his face on his pillow.

"Then tell me."

"What d'you mean, tell me?"

"You don't need to be so secretive! Telling no one makes it worse for you, I'm sure of that. Oh, I've changed myself, I admit. I used to see everything too coldly, too analytically. That's what comes of doing experiments all the time, I suppose. I've learnt a bit of wisdom lately, though, and it's taught me to understand your state of mind. I know why you moved to Rengeji, Segawa, and what the burden is you insist on carrying alone."

Ushimatsu did not answer.

"According to the principal, it's not worth taking seriously—the disease of today's young men, he says. But just imagine—even he must have been young once: and why, when he's sung his own little song in his time, should he expect us to be so solemn and proper? I said as much this morning when they sent for me, the principal and the inspector, and asked me why you seemed to be depressed. Surely you remember yourselves what it was like, I said: everyone's the same when they're young, after all."

"The inspector asked about me, did he?"

"People say the stupidest things about you just because you look so miserable. That must be how this absurd rumour started—"

"What absurd rumour?"

"That you are an eta. Some people will say anything, you know, no matter how ludicrous."

"So it seems." Ushimatsu laughed. "But suppose I were an eta, why on earth should it matter?"

For a long while no voice disturbed the silent room. The light from the lamp, which they had turned down very low, made a faint circle on the wooden ceiling. Staring dreamily up at it, Ginnosuke wondered whether his friend had fallen asleep, he lay so still.

"Segawa—asleep, are you?"

"No, not yet." Ushimatsu was holding his breath to hide his trembling.

"It's funny, but I don't feel like sleep tonight," said Ginnosuke, both hands resting on the coverlet. "Why don't we talk a bit more? When I think of the 'sorrows of youth,' as they call them, I could weep for you, Segawa. Love, and the hope of fame—life gets its meaning from these two for the best of our youth—and death too, sometimes . . . I can guess what you're going through. It's no more than natural, you being the kind of person you are. As for the girl, I know there's nothing to be ashamed of in what you feel for her. I wouldn't have raised the subject otherwise. But if you ask me, you're taking the whole thing a bit too seriously. That's what I wanted to tell you. Can't you see—there's just no *need* to grit your teeth and struggle on alone? A friend may be able to suggest some sort of a way out, provided he's given a chance. If only you can bring yourself to let me in on your troubles, I'll do whatever I possibly can to help."

"You're the only one who'd say as much. I'm grateful." Ushimatsu sighed. "As a matter of fact, what you guessed was true. There *was* a girl. But—"

"Well?"

"You spoke without knowing the whole story. She's dead."

Both were silent for a while; and when Ginnosuke spoke again, his friend did not reply.

## 4

The farewell party for Ginnosuke was held the next day, starting late in the morning and going on till two o'clock in the afternoon. It had been arranged to run through the lunch break because special servings of rice balls done up in neat wooden boxes had been provided for the party in place of the customary lunches brought from home in meal tins. Teachers and pupils got up in turn to make speeches. Sad and gay by turns, a crowd of artless boys and girls did their best to make the occasion unforgettable.

Amid the festivities Ushimatsu alone remained preoccupied. Of what he heard and saw he remembered almost nothing; all that lingered in his mind were the noisy laughter, the clapping after each act or song, and the meaning look in eyes that every now and then furtively glanced his way, even at the height of the party. Tense and nervous from this awareness of being constantly watched, he could feel no interest in what was going on around him; even his body seemed detached from his real self, no longer his own. At times all faded from his consciousness but the memory of his father's commandment. "Tsuchiya's going to get ahead—you'll see," he heard his colleagues whispering among themselves. Thinking of his own dark future, how he envied his friend; he at least had not been branded from birth, like himself. . . .

Ushimatsu hurried back to Rengeji as soon as the party was over. From the courtyard outside the entrance to the living quarters, he noticed the white-robed figure of a nun entering the downstairs living room from the veranda corridor. She would be the priest's wife's sister, he thought, recalling the letter he had written two days before. He went inside.

Kesaji came from the kitchen and handed him a visiting card—Inoko's. He had called that morning, Kesaji told him. He was staying at the Ogiya Inn. His companion, a fat man in a Western suit, had waited outside while Inoko left his card. Ichimura, Ushimatsu guessed at once.

Should he go and call on Rentaro right away, he wondered. Of course he longed to go—a bird would fly no faster, if only there were no need to be careful. He checked his eagerness. Hadn't even reading Inoko's books made him suspect? To go out of his way to call on him so soon after his arrival in the town—no, he must wait till evening, that was it; go after dark, when no one would know. . . .

He went upstairs, anxious also about O-Shio. The day he had moved into Rengeji came back to him suddenly. Nothing had changed: the ancient hibachi, the unpretentious scroll hanging in the alcove, his desk, the bookcase. In comparison, how shifting, how insecure was man's condition! He thought of Ohinara, the rich eta who had been driven from the lodging house in Takajo Street; of the chair that had carried him away by lantern light, just as he himself got back from Rengeji; of his huge servant; of the group of lodgers cursing him and shouting "I told you so!" to one another. . . . A shiver ran from his neck to the very marrow of his being. Ohinata's humiliation was no longer a mere incident, something which he had chanced to witness but which did not really concern him. Ohinata's destiny was the mirror of his own. But *why* should the "new commoners" be so despised and mocked? Why should they not mix with their fellow human beings? Why should the eta alone have no right to live out their lives as members of the community around them? Life for them signified only continual torment, unredeemed even by pity.

He was walking restlessly about the room when the door slid back and the priest's wife entered.

## 5

Obviously very upset, she sat down opposite him.

"I was afraid something like this might happen," she began at once. The evening before, about dusk, O-Shio had gone out—to post a letter, so she said—but had not come back. She had left a letter on top of her chest of drawers, addressed to her mother by adoption. Reading the letter was like listening to her speak, the priest's wife said; there was nothing formal or stilted in it, only natural, sincere affection. Some of the words were smudged with tears. She could not bear to think, O-Shio wrote, that her presence in their household should bring trouble to the two who had looked after her so well since her adoption. She had heard talk of a divorce; if indeed her mother was thinking of any step so drastic, please would she put it out of her mind at once. . . . She would never forget all the kindness they had both shown her during the last five years and wanted nothing more for herself than to live on at Rengeji as their daughter. But her fate would not allow that. She hoped they would accept that she was taking the only way possible, and so forgive her. The letter was addressed simply "To Mother."

"She's so young," said the priest's wife, dabbing her eyes with the sleeve of her under-kimono. "I lay awake all night terrified she'd do something desperate. This morning, though, we sent Sho out to make inquiries, and it turned out she's back at her father's." She paused. "My sister came over from Nagano the moment she got the letter. And this is what she finds . . . it's been a terrible shock to her too, I'm sure." The priest's wife burst into tears, overcome with pity for her unhappy daughter.

What had O-Shio been through, poor girl, as she plodded through the snow, turning her back on the home she had grown so used to and the family to which she was bound by such strong ties of obligation? Ushimatsu tried to imagine what the decision must have cost her.

"Ah well, perhaps this'll make my husband come to his senses at last," said the priest's wife half to herself. Murmuring nenbutsu to try to calm herself, she left the room.

Ushimatsu sat for a while leaning against the ancient wall. Pity brought to life in vivid images the story he had heard. Again and again he pictured her, hurrying away through the snow and thickening darkness yet with many a glance back at the temple as she went. What would become of her in that house, living with her father, prematurely senile and incapable of work or of anything but drinking, fishing, and sleep, with those squabbling, blubbering children—and worst of all, with that inhuman stepmother? Perhaps death—. Once more, and with the same overwhelming sadness as on the previous evening, the grim suspicion crossed his mind.

Ushimatsu jerked himself away from the wall. Jumping up, he put on his hat and ran down the stairs. A moment later he was hurrying through the great gate out into the street.

## 6

Where did he mean to go, he asked himself after he had walked two or three blocks. Trudging aimlessly along the snow-deep road, impelled by terror and despair, he moved as if caught in a nightmare. Men were working here and there clearing up the snow left behind by the big fall, which would not melt now until the spring. Some were sweeping the bigger drifts from the wooden roofs, sending them crashing with a frightening thud onto the street below. More than once Ushimatsu trembled at the sound. And not at that sound alone; for every time he saw people gossiping, he could not stop himself suspecting, with a shiver, that it was him they were discussing.

A poster stuck on the side wall of a corner fish shop caught his eye. The characters on the broad sheet of foreign paper were drawn in thick black strokes, with double circles in red beside some of them for emphasis. A few people were looking up at it curiously. Ushimatsu too stopped to read. The poster announced a political meeting to be held that evening by Ichimura, with Inoko Rentaro in support. The meeting would take place at Hofukuji temple at six o'clock. It was timed to start, obviously, just after most of the townspeople would have finished their evening meal.

After reading the poster, Ushimatsu walked on in the same direction as before. "Fear peoples the darkness with demons," and bright daylight too, as Ushimatsu now discovered. Mocking voices, cruel, gloating faces, innumerable images of disgust and hatred surrounded him on every side. A malevolent raven swept over his head in triumph, croaking contemptuously. Even the birds were on the lookout, it seemed, for any wretched creature that might stumble and perish in the snow. . . .

Before long he came out on the bank of the Chikuma River, overlooking a wide stretch of the riverbed which the water, now confined to a central channel, would not cover till the spring thaw. Lower Ferry, the spot was called, though there was a pontoon bridge now instead of a ferry. Travellers crossing to and from Shimotakai made a long black line against the surrounding snow. Some pulled heavily laden sledges. The exposed section of the riverbed stretched away into the distance like a long white strip of sea; along its edge, reeds and willow trees wilted, half-hidden under a pall of snow. From the mountains to the north, toward Echigo—Kosha, Kazawara, Nakanosawa, and the rest—to the village on the farther bank, and the trees in the forest nearby, everything lay buried under snow, and silent save for the faint clucking of hens from the village opposite.

Such was the scene that confronted him. At one moment, objects he had hardly noticed on other occasions imposed themselves upon his gaze, each one distinct and vivid to the last detail; at another, even their outlines faded, dissolving with everything before him into a shifting, formless mist. What of the future—what could he do? Where could he go? Why had he been born into such a world? Lost in a maze of questions, Ushimatsu stood for a long while on the riverbank staring at the water below.

# 7

Brooding still on the riddle of his whole life, he walked down toward the bridge—nervously, as if he were being followed even here. Two or three times, though he knew the suspicion was absurd, he turned to glance behind him. A strange dizziness came over him at intervals; his legs shook, and he nearly fell in the snow. *You fool!* he cursed himself. *Pull yourself together, can't you?* Clambering over the dunelike mounds of snow that had buried the sandy foreshore, he reached the end of the bridge, from which the eye could see farther up and down each white bank. Everything he saw—a flock of famished crows wheeling low in search of food, river boatmen busy checking their boats before setting out, peasants trudging homeward with a can of kerosene—conveyed the harshness of life in the Shinshu winter. The river water, a sullen, turbid green, murmured derisively as it sped past with the speed of an arrow, in a pitiless display of its power to drown.

The deeper his thoughts probed, the darker they grew. Nothing could soften the horror of total rejection: of dismissal from the school, for instance. The humiliation would follow him to the grave. And how, afterwards, could he make a living? He was still young, with hopes, desires, ambitions. Why should he be singled out as less than human, when all he wanted was to live as others lived? He recalled all the degradation heaped upon his people, the senseless discrimination, the long history of contempt which dismissed them as an inferior race, below even the miserable banta;[1] he thought of the wretchedness of all those men and women who had been expelled from their communities or had hidden themselves away in fear—of his father, of his uncle, of Ohinata, of older men of his own generation, of eta girls who had been secretly sold into prostitution.

Ushimatsu repented. What had possessed him to go in for so much study, why had he hankered so after notions of freedom and justice? If he had never known that he too was a man like other men, contempt and insult might have been easier to bear. Why had he been born so nearly human,

[1] See Introduction, p. x, n. 8.

when a life among the beasts of the moor and mountain would have been freer of pain? Memories grim and gay began to float to the surface of his mind. Memories of events in Iiyama since his appointment to the school, of life at the college, of his home in the mountains; memories of scenes and incidents that for years had lain buried returned with the freshness of yesterday. A wave of self-pity engulfed him for a moment, till the jumble of memories scattered like smoke in a gust of wind and left him confronting the only alternatives the future could hold—dismissal and lifelong humiliation, or death. Surely he must choose the second . . . the shame of exposure would rob him of the will to live.

The brief winter day began to fade. As Ushimatsu, sad at heart, stood on the bridge gazing as if for the last time at the distant landscape, a bank of cloud formed in the western sky—over the hills of his home, surely—umber-coloured, with an edge of gleaming yellow, and surrounded by bright wisps of vapour trailing like elongated sashes. The glow of the dying sun and the icy air of evening bathed the two bleak riverbanks.

Trying to grasp the horror of "death," Ushimatsu walked along the edge of the heaving pontoon. The bell of Rengeji sounded, an unfathomable sadness in its slow, deep tolling. Darkness gathered over the river. In the west, as the sun sank out of sight, the clouds deepened from russet to purple; above them a touch of pale pink illumined the tenuous wisps of vapour before they too vanished into night.

# Chapter 20

## 1

Rentaro, at least, he *would* tell. With him alone, his friend and mentor, he would share his secret. Still standing on the bridge, Ushimatsu made his decision. Their last meeting, it would be. . . .

By the time he was trudging back the way he had come, a week-old moon hung in the evening sky. He did not go straight to Rentaro's inn. The election meeting was due to start any minute, he knew; he would have to wait now till it was over.

Not far away was a little noodle shop where nobody whose presence would embarrass him was likely to go. The smoke from a cooking stove curled upward from under the eaves; appetizing smells drifted into the street outside. Through the open door he could see a fire blazing in the hearth. Suddenly aware of how hungry he was, and in no mood to go all the way back to Rengeji for his supper, Ushimatsu went in. Four or five boatmen were crowded round the fire; another man, a sledge puller perhaps, was eating and drinking by himself. Having time on his hands, Ushimatsu felt he would have to order some saké, though he did not particularly want to drink; so he asked for a single small bottle and a bowl of noodles, as hot as they could make it. It came at once. Breathing with a shiver of pleasure the aroma from the steaming bowl, he ate ravenously, listening meanwhile to the desultory conversation of the group around the fire.

Ruin, disaster—now they stared him in the face. For the first time he felt he understood in full the talk and the sighs of the boatmen and the sledge puller and other such workers, the lowest of the low. Nothing divided him now from these men, living always on the brink of ruin. The fire crackled cheerfully. The boatmen ate and drank and laughed, and Ushimatsu found himself joining forlornly in their laughter.

Time passed too slowly; the long wait was hard to bear. The sledge puller left. Another man came in almost at once, and Ushimatsu could not help hearing as he recounted to the boatmen the desperate tactics Takayanagi and his henchmen were resorting to in the election campaign. How much cash had been laid out on hiring strong-arm men was nobody's business; a whole restaurant had been taken over as Takayanagi's headquarters, with the cook working for him round the clock, saké flowing like water for everyone, and the comings and goings never stopping all day.

But how would tonight's meeting influence the townspeople? Ushimatsu imagined his friend's firm, manly voice echoing through the hall of Hofukuji—just about now, surely, he would be speaking? The meeting must be nearly over. Leaving the money for his soup and saké, and a bit extra besides, he went out into the street.

Above him, the moon and the dark sky. It was a queer sensation, uncanny somehow, as he emerged abruptly from the yellow lamplight inside. Traversing the roofs opposite, the moon's thin light fell on the snow heaped in the middle of the road. On either side, the overhanging eaves cast their shadow. Evening mists were drifting through the streets like wraiths of smoke, making everything appear remote, desolate, mysterious. Slowly, an indescribable terror crept over Ushimatsu. Someone, or something, was approaching him from behind. He tried varying his speed—it followed suit; he longed to look round but dared not. Someone was after him, he was sure, watching for a chance to creep up closer and rush him before he could defend himself. . . . He came to a corner; the footsteps faded. He sighed with relief.

Ahead, too . . . how little help the moonlight, leaving the shapes of things blurred and dim both in its light and out of it, causing all colour to pale into a shadowy obscurity. Through the misty night air, Ushimatsu thought he could make out a figure coming toward him. He shrank back involuntarily, as from the approach of certain danger. The spectral figure peered at him for a moment, then passed on its way and was gone.

The weather had relented a little. The cold was no longer so piercing; a few patches of low cloud showed greyish white against a murky sky, unbroken save for the gleam of one solitary star. The houses lining the street had put up their shutters, though here and there a light shone from smaller windows. His pulse racing at each obscure night sound, Ushimatsu walked through the silent town.

## 2

The speeches had just finished, and the crowd was pouring out of the temple, trampling the snow. Ushimatsu stood near one group and listened as inconspicuously as he could to what they were saying. Every voice he heard was angrily denouncing Takayanagi; one insisted that a man like that should be expelled from Iiyama, another was urging everybody in sight to vote for Ichimura, another was proclaiming his revulsion at the common run of politicians, of whom Takayanagi was so typical. Another group was discussing Rentaro. His speech had not been exactly what you would call brilliant, someone was saying, but there was an extraordinary magnetism about the man: every word he said struck home. Six or seven of Takayanagi's thugs had tried to break up the meeting by constantly interrupting, but in the end even they had given up, and he had been heard out in absolute silence. Passion, feverish at times in its intensity, and a profound seriousness had marked his speech all through. Toward the end, in a final withering attack on Ichimura's opponent, he had spoken of the skeleton in Takayanagi's cupboard—his relationship with Rokuzaemon, and the true motive for his marriage—as a specific example of the inhumanity and deception practised by unscrupulous politicians. Several times during his speech, someone else recalled, Rentaro had coughed blood; when he came down off the platform at the end, the handkerchief in his hand was crimson. There was no doubt the speech had moved its audience deeply. Ushimatsu himself was amazed at the courage—no, the simple *manliness*—of his mentor; yet he could not help feeling worried too. But by now Rentaro would be back at the inn. Ushimatsu set off again, walking as in a dream.

Arriving at the Ogiya, he stopped for a moment under the lanterns hanging from the eaves. There was a strange air of confusion in the entrance hall. Several people were hurrying in and out with a preoccupied air, and a man of fifty or so carrying a lantern, who looked like the proprietor, was hastily slipping on a pair of sandals. Accosting him as he came out, Ushimatsu asked if Rentaro was in—and was thunderstruck by his reply. Rentaro had been attacked and beaten up in the street near the gate of Hofukuji, he was told. Ushimatsu could not believe it. . . . But supposing it were true, it would be Takayanagi, obviously, taking his revenge. Alarmed but still incredulous, not knowing what to think, Ushimatsu ran back to Hofukuji after the proprietor.

But he was too late. Rentaro had died before Ichimura could reach him. Ushimatsu learnt from the lawyer that Rentaro had put on his overcoat and left early, while Ichimura stayed behind to help clear up. Death had been caused by a stone or something similar thrown at him with tremendous force. Weak already from his recent illness and tired out after the meeting, he had probably had no resistance left in him. Blood from the wound was still oozing over the snow.

## 3

It was decided that Rentaro's body must be left as it was, wrapped in his overcoat, until the cause of death had been verified. Hardly conscious of what he was doing, Ushimatsu knelt down and spoke with his lips to Rentaro's ear, as though even now there was still a chance he might be heard.

"Sensei! It's me, Segawa." But Rentaro was past all responding.

A sense of death lay heavy on the air, accentuated by the spectral light of the moon. Bathed in the same cold light, a little crowd of bystanders awaited the arrival of the doctor and the police. Some crouched in the snow like shadows; some walked up and down talking. The lawyer stood silent, with bent head and folded arms.

Before long officials from the town office arrived with a doctor and a policeman and began their examination of the body. In the lantern light Rentaro's face was hardly recognizable, drained of all colour as it was, the nose sharp and thin, the lips tightly closed, and the cheekbones jutting out unnaturally. A shadow of pain accompanied the manly dignity of the expression it still bore, hinting at his tragic end.

The examination over and the officials gone, the innkeeper took charge. The body had first to be taken back to the inn. Ichimura took hold of Rentaro's legs, Ushimatsu pushed his hands under his back, and between them they lifted him onto an improvised stretcher. How cold he was already! And how bitter a farewell for Ushimatsu as he pressed his cheek to Rentaro's, whispering again, *"Sensei! Sensei!"* The innkeeper folded Rentaro's hands over his chest and covered him with his overcoat. Ahead, as the little procession moved off, their lanterns lighting the way through dark streets, the moon was beginning to sink.

Ushimatsu followed, his clogs slicing through the crisp snow. He looked back over the dead man's life. Perhaps, now he thought of it, his friend had foreseen disaster. He remembered how passionately Rentaro had spoken, over dinner at the inn that night in Nezu, of his contempt for Takayanagi, of his anger at the insult to the eta community implied by Takayanagi's marriage. And what was it that he had said on the bridge on the way to Ueda? *However low and dirty we eta may be, there's a limit to the trampling we can take . . . a man like Takayanagi* can't *be allowed to win. It would be a different matter if I hadn't heard all about him. But knowing what I know now, to go home without saying a word—it'd be too cowardly altogether.* Then there was the special tenderness, along with the scolding, with which he had rejected his wife's plea that he should go back with her to Tokyo. Taking all these things together, Ushimatsu was sure Rentaro must have come to Iiyama secretly expecting danger, even death itself.

If only Ushimatsu had known! He would have told him his secret without wasting so much precious time, and Rentaro would at last have understood. But remorse was useless. . . . Shame mingled with his grief.

Through the gate of the inn he had left only a few hours before, chatting with Ichimura, Rentaro was carried on the stretcher. Ushimatsu undertook to send a telegram to his wife in Tokyo. He decided to go at once to the post office. It was late; the streets were empty. He was determined to get the telegram sent, even if the telegraphist had gone to bed and had to be knocked up. But how would she feel when she opened it? What words could he find? He came to a dark, lonely crossroads. Somewhere in the distance a dog was barking incessantly. Ushimatsu could no longer restrain himself: his pent-up grief escaped in a flood of tears, and as he walked he cried aloud.

# 4

The tears refreshed his parched spirit. More calmly, on the way back from the post office, he compared Rentaro's character with his own. Rentaro had lived as a man should—as an eta should. . . . Openly proclaiming his origin wherever he went, he had nevertheless won acceptance and recognition. *I hold it no shame to be of eta birth.* With what power those words were charged! And himself? For the first time Ushimatsu realized the corrosive effect on his character, on the natural self that he had been born with, of the perpetual obsession with concealment. A life of deception, his had been up till now: of *self*-deception. . . . What good did it do, the endless agonizing? *I am an eta.* Why should he not declare the truth, openly and boldly, to all the world? Such was the lesson of Rentaro's death.

When he got back to the inn, his face flushed and swollen from weeping, a number of townspeople, supporters of Ichimura, were gathered in a downstairs room discussing what should be done next. In front of the alcove, with his head to the north, lay the dead man, covered with a brown travelling rug, a handkerchief over his face. A small table stood beside the body with a new earthenware bowl containing sticks of incense—both provided, apparently, by the innkeeper. The room was lit with candles, diffusing a melancholy gleam through the chill, incense-laden air.

Back from the police station, Ichimura had time to talk to Ushimatsu. Everywhere they had been since leaving him at Ueda—Komoro, Iwamurata, Shiga, Nozawa, Usuta, and other places—Rentaro had spoken at meetings on social problems; and through all this time, right up to their return to Nagano and arrival here in Iiyama, he had seemed in excellent health and spirits.

"Even I was surprised," Ichimura went on. "I had no idea, when we started out for Hofukuji, that he would be putting so much of himself into his speech tonight. As a rule he told me beforehand what he meant to say—we'd discuss it over supper usually. But tonight, for the first time, he never mentioned the meeting." He sighed. "You'll think

I'm cruel. Anybody would, I daresay, and I can't blame you. If only I'd sent him back to Tokyo with his wife instead of letting him have his own way! He wasn't strong, as you know. When he first spoke of joining me on this tour, I did my best to stop him, but he wouldn't listen. I wasn't to try to influence him, he said—he had his own good reasons for coming. Whether I was 'using' him or he was helping me was immaterial—all that mattered was that I had my work to do and he had his. He was so keen on coming along, I couldn't refuse. But now—how can I face his wife, when I promised her, before she left, to take good care of him? What can I say to her?" The lawyer sat with bowed head, his massive figure still encased in the tight Western suit he had worn for the meeting. Most of the guests in the inn had gone to bed by now. With the intense, numbing cold of the winter night, an air of desolation pervaded the room.

Rentaro was mourned even by some who would frown with disgust at the mere mention of the words "new commoner"; the cruel manner of his end, in particular, evoked deep sympathy. "The police can't turn a blind eye this time," someone was saying. "They'll be after Takayanagi already, I shouldn't wonder."

With all that he saw and heard, it became clearer to Ushimatsu that in death his friend was taking him by the hand to lead him to a new world. *Confession:* the public confession of his birth, of which he had never dared even to think, the confession he had hesitated to make even to his fellow eta Rentaro. . . . Suddenly a new courage was within his grasp. The man he had been till now was dead. The dreams of love and glory, the pleasures of this world, to taste which most young men would willingly starve themselves of food and sleep together—of what use were they to him, an eta? A "new commoner," that was all Rentaro had been; for himself he wanted nothing more. Hot tears ran down his cheeks, wrung from his life's core as the sweat is wrung from straining muscles.

Tomorrow he would go to school and confess the truth. To his fellow teachers, to the children. That way, they could not laugh at him afterwards; and that way, too, he would cause least trouble to his friends and colleagues. His mind was made up. Thinking of what he would say to his class, of how he would phrase his letter of resignation, he spent the night with Ichimura and the others in vigil beside the body of the dead man.

At last a cock crew. Ushimatsu sensed the approach of a new dawn.

# Chapter 21

## 1

Soon after it was light, Ushimatsu went back to Rengeji to get ready for school. Everyone at the temple, from Simple Sho to the assistant priest, was talking of Rentaro's death and of the likelihood of Takayanagi's arrest; they had been electrified to learn that the murdered man was the one who had called at the temple the morning before, when Ushimatsu was at school.

Her sister had decided to go home, the priest's wife told Ushimatsu. The priest had gone on his knees to her begging her forgiveness, and she had given up, at least for the time being, any thought of a divorce. Telling her beads, she repeated the nenbutsu.

Kesaji brought Ushimatsu's breakfast to his room. It was the first of December. The temple family always breakfasted very early; Ushimatsu was rarely up by then, and by the time he was ready to eat, the rice was invariably half-cold and the soup had boiled so long it had lost its flavour. But today, at least, it was different—the rice was still steaming, and the freshly made soup gave off a delicious aroma. There was a dish of his favourite *natto*[1] too. Sitting at the little table, he thought back over his life with a strange sense of thankfulness. Now that he had resolved to accept that he was what he had been born, a despised, reviled outcast—even as he ate, Ushimatsu could not hold back his tears.

After breakfast he wrote out his letter of resignation. As he did so, he recalled once more his father's commandment:

[1] Fermented soybeans.

*No matter who you meet, no matter what happens to you, never reveal it! Forget this commandment just once, in a moment of anger or misery, and from that moment the world will have rejected you forever. . . . Tell no one!* What it had cost him to obey! *Do not forget,* he had reminded himself again and again; and with every repetition of those words, fear and suspicion had grown within him. His father, had he lived, would surely have thought him mad now. . . . Ushimatsu pictured his anger, and his sorrow, at the change in his son. But he knew now he must break the commandment. No one could stop him.

*Father, forgive me!*

Winter sunlight seeped into the room. Ushimatsu opened the window. Through the bare branches of the gingko tree he looked out over the town in its shroud of snow; every roof was buried in white to the eaves. Between the houses, from the vents below the eaves, the smoke of morning fires rose placidly. The sun had just begun to touch the school buildings. For some moments Ushimatsu stood absorbed and wistful, drinking in the cold, exhilarating air, and assailed by regrets—till the opening words of Rentaro's *Confessions,* returning with new force, swept away all doubts, and he spoke them aloud from the window as if for all the town to hear: *"I am an eta. . . ."*

Ushimatsu began to get ready for school.

## 2

That he should break his father's solemn commandment: as he walked out through the temple gate, the thought filled him with sadness, and with defiant courage, too.

Before he had gone very far, he met a group of four or five men coming from the other direction, roped together and escorted by a policeman. Pale-faced, they shuffled past, avoiding as best they could the eyes of passersby. One was wearing split-toed Japanese socks and a crested haori coat; he hid his face with a raised sleeve, but his clothes gave Takayanagi away. The others, unkempt and suspicious-looking, would be some of the thugs he had hired. Now and again one or another of them would stop, to be cursed each time by the escort.

"Off to jail!" said a man who had stopped by Ushimatsu, staring after them.

"No more than they deserve," said another.

At an order from the policeman, Takayanagi and the rest turned into a side street and disappeared a moment later behind the "snow mountain."

The boys and girls were hurrying to school now. Some, coming in from the hamlets round Iiyama, scampered noisily through the snow, their heads wrapped in flannel mufflers and shawls thrown over their shoulders. In front of Ushimatsu and behind him, town children shouted to their friends and formed in groups as they went. This would be the last time, maybe, that with these innocent, laughing children he would walk the familiar road to school. Everything he saw prompted bittersweet, nostalgic memories. This morning there was charm even in the chattering of the girls, which usually he found so tiresome, and in the drab, faded maroon of their hakama skirts, which soon he would see no more.

On the playground the snow had been swept into a huge mound in the middle, and the vaulting-horses and horizontal bars were still completely buried, so the children were playing inside, where they could move around more freely; laughter filled the entrance hall, the corridors, the big gym. As Ushimatsu walked among them, supervising their play—for the last time—till lessons were due to begin, the children milled around him, calling "Segawa sensei! Segawa sensei!" He loved them for it and wondered how he could bear to cut himself off even from the happy din they made, running, jumping, shouting. Two or three woman teachers standing in the corridor stared at him, sniggered, and exchanged glances. Ushimatsu took no notice. Senta, the third-year eta boy, was standing alone in a corner of the gym—he had come early that morning—looking on enviously at the others. As usual, no one wanted to play with him. Coming up behind Senta, Ushimatsu gave him a hug, not caring who might see or laugh, as he showed unashamed the depth of his pity for the boy born under the same unlucky star as himself. He remembered the game of tennis in which they had shared, Senta and himself, on the Emperor's birthday, after the farewell tea party for Keinoshin. Farther down the corridor some first-year girls were singing:

"Momotaro,
The peach-born boy;
Gentle, yet so strong."

At the sound of their childish, innocent voices, the tears trickled unbidden down Ushimatsu's cheeks.

A moment later the big bell rang out. Their slippers clap-clapping on the wooden floors and raising a small cloud of dust, the children raced from all directions to the gym. The teachers lined up their classes, and the whistle blew for lessons. Teachers and pupils, in proper order, began to file out of the gym. Marching in time, his class of fourth-year boys and girls followed Ushimatsu down the long corridor.

## 3

The principal and the inspector were sitting in the visitors' room awaiting the arrival of three town councillors they had invited to the school to discuss Ushimatsu's position. The inspector, it hardly needs saying, had called on the principal in advance of the time set for the meeting.

In the principal's view, it was not out of any personal animosity on his part that he wanted to remove what he called "foreign elements" from the school. He was an educator of the old style, who belonged to a different age altogether from Ginnosuke and Ushimatsu; he wanted to be able to say that "today" still belonged to himself and his contemporaries, but in fact times had changed without his noticing it. Nothing is so frightening as change. The principal did not like the thought of growing old, of declining into obscurity, of handing over his armour to the succeeding generation. He wanted to keep his position and the status that went with it forever. Hence his inclination to get rid of the most progressive and enterprising of his young teachers. Moreover, Ushimatsu and Ginnosuke tended not to accept his opinions—unlike Bunpei. He often clashed with them in staff meetings. They were a nuisance, in fact, in so many ways. It annoyed him that two such fledglings should be more popular with the pupils than he was. No, in his own estimation he was not acting out of spite; his "duty to the school" to avoid divisions and indiscipline made it inevitable.

"About time they were here," said the inspector, pulling out his watch. "Well, what about this Segawa business? Looks as though something's going to happen at last, don't you think?"

The principal smiled.

"Mind you," the inspector went on, "it mustn't come from us. Oh no, that wouldn't do at all. The town must make the first move."

"Exactly what I was thinking," replied the principal.

"Look—Segawa's going, Tsuchiya's going. When they're both out of the way, we'll have everything as we want it. That nephew of mine will take Segawa's place, for a start, and whenever there's a vacancy, I'll recommend someone suitable. We'll pack the place with our people, eh? That way you can sit tight as long as you want, and I"—he laughed—"I shall feel the time and trouble I've spent on this business haven't been wasted."

The door opened and the janitor came in, followed by the three councillors.

"Gentlemen," the principal greeted them politely, "please sit down."

"Sorry we're late," the councillor with the gold-rimmed spectacles said cheerfully. "It was election business that held us up, of course—with Takayanagi out of action all of a sudden, there's been quite an upset in the campaign."

## 4

Twenty or so students of Nagano Teachers' College, who were visiting the school that day to watch the teaching, filed into Ushimatsu's room. The first lesson, ethics, had just finished, and the class was starting on arithmetic. The pupils were working on a problem Ushimatsu had set them.

For a moment the clatter of the sliding door being opened and the shuffling of feet as the visitors crowded in put them off, but they soon settled down again, and the silence was once more unbroken save for the grating of pencils sliding over slates. Ushimatsu walked up and down between the rows of desks, sadly aware that this was the last time he would ever be looking over their work. Now and then he glanced at the uniformed students standing by the wall; they were watching him, self-confidently critical, as if fully qualified already to pass judgement on whatever they saw. Scenes from his own college days flashed before Ushimatsu's eyes. He and his classmates, accompanied by a lecturer from the college, had made many such school visits, upsetting the teachers in every school they went to by their harsh yet guileless criticisms. He himself had once worn that same uniform. . . .

"Anybody finished? Hands up, those who've finished then!"

Hands rose everywhere, from the class captain in the back row to the really shaky ones in front. Even Shogo, who did not usually make much of a showing in arithmetic, was quick to put a hand up.

"Kazama."

Shogo left his desk and went up to the blackboard. Filtering through the windows, the winter sunlight lent the familiar classroom a lonely air. To Ushimatsu, everything in it seemed new, even the ceiling and the white walls around him, which normally aroused no reaction or feeling in him at all. Seen from behind as he stood writing with chalk on the blackboard, Shogo—in thin, tight-sleeved kimono with a tuck at the shoulders still, and haori coat, his head a little to one side and his left shoulder drooping as he reached up with his right hand, standing on tiptoe, to write at the top of the blackboard—made a picture of boyhood at its most attractive age. He was the hard-working kind and did well in painting, calligraphy, and composition but always fell down in science and arithmetic, which meant that generally he hovered around fifteenth or sixteenth place in the class. Today he was doing unexpectedly well.

"Hands up, those who got the same answer as Kazama."

All the hands in the back row went up. Blushing a little, Shogo went back to his seat. The students looked on, some of them smiling.

The lesson went on in the same way, with Ushimatsu setting problems and explaining when necessary. The pupils were surprisingly quiet that day. Even in the first hour, before the college students came in, no one had been trying any of the usual tricks. The sleepy ones, who invariably dozed off in class, the would-be engineers, who "telephoned" each other surreptitiously under cover of their desks, all sat still and attentive.

Ushimatsu looked at the pupils, at the classroom. Today's lessons would be his last. His pulse quickened; a new earnestness marked his expression as he taught.

## 5

"Ichimura's bound to win now, I suppose," the bearded councillor began, with an air of long experience of the world and its ways. "Popularity's a strange thing. No one'll care a fig for Takayanagi after what's happened to him. Even the support he paid for has gone to Ichimura now."

"It's all because of that fellow Inoko's death. Ichimura has a lot to thank him for," declared his colleague with the gold-rimmed spectacles.

"Looks as though even an eta may have something in him, then," said the inspector, throwing back his head and laughing.

"It does indeed," agreed the bearded councillor, laughing likewise. "Seriously, though, that kind of guts doesn't come easily. But then people like Inoko don't grow on trees, either."

"Exactly. He's one kind of eta, this one's another," said the third councillor, the tradesman with the pockmarked face.

The others laughed. They all knew who was meant by "this one."

"It's 'this one' that we've come to talk about." Gold-rimmed spectacles puffed at his cigarette. "I wonder if we could ask the inspector to take some sort of action before there's too much talk in the town—a transfer perhaps, or indefinite leave?"

"Certainly," replied the inspector, stroking his forehead thoughtfully. "Something of the kind could probably be arranged."

"One is sorry for Segawa, of course, but there's really no other way," said the bearded councillor with a sigh. "You know what Iiyama is like—how strong the feeling is about anything of this sort. If the parents get to find out that Segawa is a new commoner, they'll refuse to send their children to school, I shouldn't wonder. You can see it happening already in the council: complaints have been made to the education committee accusing us of negligence and inaction."

"Nobody feels very happy to hear anything of this sort, least of all people in our position," added the pockmarked tradesman, smiling ingratiatingly.

"It's a very sad business as far as the school is concerned, I must say," said the principal gravely. "You will have heard, I'm sure, how well Segawa has worked here. I've come to rely on him a great deal, more than on any other teacher in fact. He's capable in his work, thoroughly reliable, and popular with the pupils—a rare combination for a young teacher. To get rid of a man of his quality just because of his origin—frankly, gentlemen, it would be cruel, very cruel. I very much hope you will do your best to see that he can stay—"

"Just so." Gold-rimmed spectacles interrupted him. "And hearing you speak of Segawa in those terms, Principal, we all of us feel a sense of shame, I am sure, that we have to discuss this matter with you at all. In the world of learning, as you imply, there should be no such thing as class distinction. That's a noble philosophy. But in a district like this, where old superstitions die so hard, it doesn't have much support, I'm afraid."

"We're very backward still," said the pockmarked councillor.

"When a man is as outstanding as Inoko, people will forgive him anything," put in the beard. "The way he was accepted here proves it. The inn took him in, the temple lent him the hall, and the people went to hear him. What worked in his favour was his never hiding the fact that he was an outcast. Human nature's a curious thing: just because he publicly gave himself out as an eta, people felt sorry for him. It's when they try to hide it, like Segawa, and Takayanagi with his wife, that the trouble really starts."

The inspector nodded agreement.

"Well then—may we suggest a transfer?" said gold-rimmed spectacles, looking round the company.

"A transfer? It wouldn't be so easy to find him another job. And if the real reason were to get out, no school would want him anyway. No, suspension would be better."

"We will leave it to you, then." The bearded councillor rubbed his hands as he spoke. "We have some voices in the council saying it's a scandal he's still teaching. They want him expelled immediately. That's what we're faced with. We'll trust you to deal with the matter in the most appropriate way, Inspector."

## 6

Determined to get through the day's lessons before he made his confession, Ushimatsu suppressed the agitation rising within him. He was teaching calligraphy, the last lesson of the morning. As he stood behind a desk, taking a small hand in his own and guiding it through the strokes of the Chinese characters, the tip of the brush trembled—to a burst of laughter from several inky mouths, whose owners were leaning out of their desks to watch.

When the janitor rang the bell for the end of the third lesson, the inspector and the councillors had left. The students stayed on to watch the afternoon lessons. After lunch Ushimatsu left another teacher to supervise the play and went back to the staff room to clear up his desk. Outwardly at ease as he marked work due for return and checked carefully every doubtful point, so that no criticism could be levelled at him afterwards, within him his heart was pounding. In a corner of the room some teachers with time on their hands were discussing the Hofukuji murder. All kinds of theories were bandied about as to Inoko's motives in deliberately risking his life by such outspokenness: a craze for publicity, the desperation induced by poverty, madness—everyone had his own derisive suggestion to make. If once or twice Rentaro's courage was acknowledged, it was quickly dismissed as artificial, the product of his illness. Listening in spite of himself to their talk, Ushimatsu realized how the world and its ways made such misunderstanding inevitable. Sadly he remembered Rentaro's words: *Die in silence, as the wolf dies, and bravely, like a man.*

The afternoon lessons were geography and Japanese. When Ushimatsu brought into the classroom, along with the two textbooks, a pile of corrected composition books, some fair copies of calligraphy exercises, and some other work he had to return, the children's eyes widened in anticipation.

"We're getting the compositions back!" shouted one.

"And the drawings!"

Ushimatsu put the pile on his desk, opened the textbook, and began the lesson as usual. But when he was little more than halfway through, he shut the book again. They would stop there today, he said, looking down at the rows of faces; there was something special he wanted to tell them.

"Sensei—is it a story?" said a boy at once, one of the talkative ones. Cries of "Story, story!" spread across the room.

Ushimatsu's eyes glistened; a tear he could not check fell on the desk. He gave back the calligraphy exercises, the drawings, and the composition books, some with marks in red figures, some marked simply "excellent" or "good," and some he had not had time to look through. He began by apologizing for the unmarked ones. Of course he had meant to mark them, he said, if only there had been time, but this was the last lesson they would be having with him, for he was going to say goodbye.

"You all know how the people who live up here in the mountain country are divided into five classes." He spoke slowly and with care, so that everyone should understand. "There are the 'samurai,' as they used to be called, the merchants in the towns, the farmers, the priests, and below them the people called eta. You know how the eta still live by themselves, herded together on the edge of the town, where they make leather shoes and drums and samisen, and the sandals you wear to school—or work the fields as peasants, some of them. You know how once a year these eta call on your parents with a sheaf of rice to pay their respects, how when they come they must never step up into any of the rooms where you live but must kneel on the earthen floor of the hall and bow their heads, and take whatever they are given to eat in special bowls kept for them alone. You know the custom there has always been, that when someone from your family goes on some errand to a place where eta live, he must light his pipe with a match, not from the hibachi, and that even if the eta are drinking tea when he comes, they must not offer it to him. There is no class lower, we say, than the eta. Suppose one of these despised outcasts were to come to your classroom and teach you Japanese and geography—what would you think then? What would your parents think? Children, I must tell you: I am such an outcast."

Ushimatsu's arms and legs trembled violently; he steadied himself against the desk. The class was thunderstruck. Open-mouthed, they stared up at him.

"Some of you are fourteen, some fifteen: you know something of the world already. Please listen carefully to what I am saying to you now. When in five years from now, or ten, you look back to your schooldays, I would like you to remember you had a teacher called Segawa once, in the fourth year of the upper school, who taught you in this room—who told you, when he confessed to you that he was an eta and said goodbye to all the class, that each first of January he had welcomed in the New Year with the same sweet wine as you do, that on the Emperor's birthday he had sung "May Thy Glorious Reign" as fervently as you, and wished you well, praying in his heart for your happiness and success. . . . You will feel disgust and loathing for me now that I have told you what I am. But though I was born so low myself, I have done my best each day to teach you only what is right and true. Please remember this, and forgive me if you can for having kept the truth from you till today." He bowed his head humbly before the class. "When you get home, tell your parents what I have said. Tell them that I confessed today, asking your forgiveness . . . *I am an eta, an outcast, an unclean being!*"

Feeling somehow that he still had not humbled himself enough, Ushimatsu stepped back from the desk and knelt on the wooden floor.

"Forgive me! Forgive me!"

Some pupils at the back stood up to see what he was doing. Others, farther forward, followed suit, till all the class was standing; some climbed on their chairs, some left their places, some ran into the corridor shouting.

The bell rang for the end of lessons. Doors opened down the corridor; children and teachers from other classes poured like a wave toward Ushimatsu's room.

* * * * *

Ginnosuke's appointment had ended as of the first of December. But some private business had brought him to school that day, and he was in the middle of a conversation in the staff room when suddenly he learnt what had happened. He ran out and across the hall to the long classroom corridor. Groups of girls in shawls and headscarves were chattering excitedly of Ushimatsu, as if they had forgotten it was time to go home; boys were gathering in the gym talking of nothing else. Pushing his way through a crowd of children hurrying in both directions, Ginnosuke reached Ushimatsu's room. The principal was standing in the corridor with five or six other teachers, Bunpei among them. Ushimatsu's class was crowding round their teacher; the college students looked on, amazed.

Ginnosuke pressed closer. Ushimatsu, on the verge of hysteria, was kneeling abjectly to his colleagues; he bowed his forehead to the floor, burying his shame in the dust and dirt. Pity swept through Ginnosuke from the depths of his being. Going to his friend's side, he helped him up and brushed the dust off his coat. "Forgive me, Tsuchiya! Forgive me!" Ushimatsu repeated over and over again, as if obsessed. Tears streamed down his cheeks.

"Don't worry. I know how you must feel. You've brought your letter of resignation with you? I'll take care of everything here, Segawa. You'd best go straight home. All right? You go home right away."

## 7

Ushimatsu's class stayed behind in the classroom. They were holding a meeting to discuss what they could do for their beloved teacher. The complexities of society might be beyond their grasp still, but with the openness and quick sympathy of their age they understood intuitively how Ushimatsu must feel and longed to find some way of keeping him at the school. They could not just stand by and let it happen—why shouldn't they all go and petition the principal, proposed the class captain, a boy of fifteen. There were cries of approval.

"Let's go now!" shouted another boy, a farmer's son.

The decision was taken. Leaving behind only the pair whose turn it was that day to clean the room, the whole class trooped out into the corridor. Among them was Shogo.

The principal was leaning back in his chair in his office, talking to Bunpei. When the crowd of fourth-year children appeared at his door, he guessed at once what they wanted. But he pretended to be surprised.

"Well, what is it?" he asked.

The class captain went up and stood in front of the big desk. The principal and Bunpei stared at him. The boy was mature for his years—precocious, compared with Shogo. He put forward simply and clearly the feelings of his classmates. Could the principal please make their teacher stay on? They didn't care if he was an eta; there were eta children in the class, nor could they see why an eta shouldn't teach them. All the class wanted him to stay. Please would the principal arrange it? The boy bowed deeply, as did the rest of the class behind him.

The principal got up from his chair. "I understand your feelings," he said, looking round the crowd of children in front of him. "I'll do what I can, if you are so keen to have him stay. But there's a right way and a wrong way of doing things. If you want to make a request to me, there's no objection to that, but you must go about it the proper way—appoint a representative, make out a written petition, and hand it in. It's quite improper, and very bad manners, to come crowding into my office like this, the whole lot of you, when I'm busy."

The boy started to apologize but was silenced by tears.

"Now listen, all of you." The principal picked up a letter from his desk and showed it to them. "I've received this letter of resignation from Segawa sensei. I shall have to show it to the inspector and to the Education Committee. However much I myself may want to keep Segawa sensei on, if the committee doesn't agree, I can do nothing." His voice softened a little. "You must realize that I alone have no power to settle a matter of this kind. And it's not only you that would miss such a good teacher. I should be very sorry myself, too. Now, you've had your say, and I understand how you feel. Go home, all of you, and be sure you don't neglect your studies. The school will deal with this upset in the best possible way, without any meddling from you. The most important thing for you is study."

Bunpei had sat listening throughout with folded arms. In silence, awkwardly, the children withdrew. After seeing the last of them out, the principal shut the door, smiling coldly.

# Chapter 22

## 1

"May I ask if Mr. Segawa has been here?" Anxious about his friend, Ginnosuke had gone to Keinoshin's cottage. O-Shio came running to the door.

"Mr. Segawa? He's just left."

Ginnosuke stared at her. "You don't know where he's gone, I suppose?"

"I—I'm not sure." O-Shio hesitated. "Mrs. Inoko is coming up from Tokyo, I believe. I think he said something about going to see her—at the inn where Mr. Ichimura is staying, that would be."

"The inn? That's good, anyway." Ginnosuke sighed with relief. "I've been very worried. I went to Rengeji first, but all they said was that he hadn't come back from school—and then to the inn, but he wasn't there either. Then I wondered if he mightn't have gone to Mr. Kazama's." He thought for a moment. "So he came here—"

"You just missed him." O-Shio reddened a little. "It's a poor place, as you can see, but won't you come in?"

Ginnosuke followed her inside to the hearth. The tears were not yet dry on her cheeks, which were red and swollen from weeping. From a look at her face, it was not hard for Ginnosuke to imagine what Ushimatsu must have said to her before he left. What it must have cost him, that public confession, in the knowledge of all its consequences! Ginnosuke longed to help his friend, and wanted to tell O-Shio of his longing. But first, he decided, he would ask her about her own position.

O-Shio, harassed as she was now by poverty and other worries, saw at once that Ginnosuke was to be trusted. She knew too that he was Ushimatsu's closest friend. He if anyone would listen sympathetically to her story, she thought gratefully. Yet when he asked her how it was that she had come back to her father's, her feelings were too much for her—should she tell him everything, the whole wretched story, which she could hardly recall without tears, that had led to her deciding that night to run away? Ill at ease, and ashamed, with a young girl's sensitivity, of the shabbiness of the room and the dirty, soot-stained walls, she explained as best she could, now getting up to put more wood on the fire, now nervously adjusting her kimono. She had wept and wept till the tears would come no more, she told him, before finally making up her mind to leave. "Even if they mayn't always treat you as parents should, they cared for you and brought you up, so your duty lies with them. You're the daughter of the temple now. No matter how hard it may be sometimes, you must never come home!" her father had always insisted. So when she had slipped out, unseen, into the twilight, it had been with no clear idea of where to go.

Walking down the snowy road as in some sad dream,

she came across a man lying drunk in the snow. It was her father . . . frozen to death, or so she thought at the time. Just then Otosaku happened to pass by. She called to him; together they lifted Keinoshin and managed to carry him back home—only just in time. He hadn't got up from his bed since. According to the doctor, there was so little resistance left in him that he couldn't be expected to live.

That wasn't all, either. More misfortune awaited O-Shio under her father's roof. Neither her stepmother nor her stepbrother and stepsisters were there, she found. Her father and stepmother had had a violent quarrel the night before; her stepmother had worked herself into a rage over Keinoshin's drinking, accusing him of robbing them all of their living, and next morning when he was out she had gone off with three of her children, apparently to her old home in Shimotakai. She had left behind the youngest girl, O-Sue, who was in fact very little trouble, and taken the difficult, selfish eight-year-old O-Saku with her, presumably with the idea that O-Saku would be more useful. All this O-Shio had heard from a neighbour who had seen them go: her stepmother, with Tomekichi on her back, dragging O-Saku by the hand, and Susumu, walking with a man the neighbour didn't know, turning again and again to look back at his home.

Her only standby in this crisis had been Otosaku and his wife. Every day they both came, bringing food and helping to look after their old master; O-Sue they took to their own cottage, promising to do everything for her that was necessary.

Such, in brief, was the pitiful state of Keinoshin's broken home as O-Shio described it to Ginnosuke.

"So now it's just you and your father and Shogo?" said Ginnosuke, much moved.

"Yes, the three of us." Tears in her eyes, O-Shio pushed back a lock of hair that had strayed over her cheek.

## 2

Presently they began to talk of Ushimatsu. Seeing Ginnosuke's obvious warmth of feeling for his friend, O-Shio could hold nothing back. Pale-faced, his eyes dark with misery, and so tense with emotion he could hardly speak coherently, Ushimatsu had stammered out his farewell. Asking her to think of him—if ever she did think of him again—as a criminal, an offender against society, he had knelt before her and confessed his secret.

"I felt so sorry for him," O-Shio added. "There was such a lot I wanted to ask, but he wouldn't stay. I cried when he left."

Ginnosuke sighed. "Just what I imagined he would do. It must have been a great shock when he told you."

"No." O-Shio was emphatic.

Ginnosuke stared at her.

"Mr. Katsuno heard about it somewhere—he told me some time ago."

Ginnosuke was amazed. Why should Bunpei have spoken of this to O-Shio, of all people?

"The fellow's always babbling," he muttered. Then aloud to O-Shio: "Did he often go to Rengeji, then?"

"Yes, quite often. Mother likes talking, and men say they like to talk to her because she's so frank and straightforward."

"But why do you suppose he told you about Segawa?"

"He said some strange things—" O-Shio hesitated.

"Strange? In what way?"

"About how important his relations were, and how he'd soon be getting promoted himself—"

"Getting promoted!" Ginnosuke laughed scornfully. "He said that, did he?"

"Then he began to say things about Mr. Segawa—horrible things. . . . That was the first time I heard he was an eta."

"I see." He looked at her intently for a moment, then burst out bitterly, "How could he be so heartless, going out of his way to spread such talk!"

"I didn't think he was that sort of man, either. What he said about Mr. Segawa was so *nasty* . . . I was furious."

"You feel sorry for Segawa, then?"

"Of course. Eta or not, isn't a quiet, sensible man better any day than a chatterbox like Mr. Katsuno?" O-Shio said simply. She lowered her eyes, staring down at her rounded, girlish hands.

Ginnosuke sighed. "Why must the world be so harsh? I could cry when I think of Segawa. Can you believe it, just because of his birth he has to throw up his job and let himself be robbed of his good name and all his hopes. . . . Did you ever hear of anything so cruel?"

"But they can't blame *him*—he didn't choose his parents!" O-Shio's bright eyes flashed.

"Exactly. It's no fault of his. I can't tell you how glad I am you say that! I was afraid you might think differently about Segawa when you heard."

"Why?"

"That's what usually happens."

"Other people may change toward him—I shan't."

"Are you sure?"

"How can you ask? I meant what I said."

"That's what I wanted to ask you—"

"And what would 'that' be?" O-Shio looked at him wonderingly, blushing in spite of herself.

## 3

A feeble cough came from the back room. O-Shio listened anxiously for a moment; then, with a gesture of apology to her visitor, she got up and went out. Sitting alone by the fireside watching the burning brushwood, Ginnosuke sensed the youthful resilience that O-Shio must possess to enable her to stand living in such a home without surrendering either in body or spirit to the wretchedness around her. All the women of northern Shinshu, working as they have to in such a severe climate, develop a robust, cheerful disposition; the ability to endure hardship is part of their inheritance, it is not too much to say. O-Shio was no exception. There was an unmistakable hint of firmness behind her gentle manner. Ginnosuke wondered how he could best tell her of his friend's feelings toward her.

Before long she came back.

"How is he—your father?" Ginnosuke asked, his voice full of sympathy.

"Much the same as usual," she said sadly. "He didn't want anything today, he said, except a little rice gruel. He's been sleeping ever since morning. I can't help wondering, when he sleeps so much."

"It must be worrying for you."

"I don't suppose he will last very long now." She sighed. "Mr. Segawa did a lot for him, but even the doctor says now he hasn't much hope." Again, in an unconscious movement, one hand smoothed the straying hair of her side locks.

"What different lives people have to live!" Ginnosuke exclaimed, deeply moved as he pictured to himself what hers must be like. "Some grow up in happy families, without ever knowing what it is to be poor. Others have to face hardship and trouble from childhood, but the buffeting makes them strong. You, for instance: you had to grow up fighting all the way. People like that must have times of depression that nobody else knows of, but even they have their secret days of happiness, I'm sure, to make up for the gloom."

"Days of happiness?" O-Shio smiled forlornly. "Do you think any will ever come to me?"

"Of course they will," replied Ginnosuke emphatically.

"It doesn't seem very likely, judging by what's happened so far. If only I hadn't been adopted by the temple, mother—the temple lady—would never have had to suffer the way she did. It was terrible having to leave her—"

"I can imagine."

"I died then, it seems to me . . . it's only the thought of the kindness I've received that gives me courage to live at all."

"Segawa's lot is a hard one, and so is yours. It's because you've been through so much yourself that you feel sorry for him, isn't it? He's my friend, as you know, and I—to tell you the truth, I came here to ask you if you would be willing to help him—"

"You want *me* to help him?" O-Shio's eyes lit up once more. "Anything that I can do, I will do—anything—"

"You *can* help, I'm sure of that."

For a moment they were both silent.

"I'd better tell you everything," Ginnosuke began

earnestly. "One night when we were on duty together at school, I set myself to find out what was really in his mind. Instead of always suffering in silence, as he seemed to be, why didn't he take me into his confidence, I asked him, and tell me a bit about his troubles. And if he felt that I wouldn't understand, that I wasn't sympathetic enough—well, I said, I wasn't really as unfeeling as he might think. I told him he was taking life too hard altogether. Didn't he realize that sometimes a friend could help? Then at last he spoke about you—for the first time. *There was a girl,* he said—I knew it was you he meant—*but she's dead.* Those were his words. You see—he'd given up all hope, convinced he couldn't ever marry you, because of his birth. He was even determined not to think of you anymore. Can you imagine a more tragic love? That was why he came here to tell you himself the secret he had always kept hidden before. Won't you help him, now that you know what his true feelings are?"

"What more can I say?" O-Shio blushed. "I want to help him, yes—"

"All your life?" Ginnosuke looked her full in the face.

"All my life."

O-Shio's reply astounded Ginnosuke. In those three words were concentrated all her woman's love and tears and resolve.

## 4

Eager to take the good news to his friend, Ginnosuke proposed to go at once to the inn where the lawyer was staying. He promised to come back later to report.

"May I ask a favour?" O-Shio said suddenly as he got up to go. "Could you possibly lend me a copy of *Confessions?* Though I suppose most of it will be beyond me—"

*"Confessions?"*

"You know—Inoko's book."

"Oh, yes. I'm surprised you know about it, though."

"Mr. Segawa was always reading it."

"I'll see what I can do. Segawa will have a copy of his

own, I expect. If not, I'll get him to look out for one and send it to you."

He hurried off to the inn. A small crowd had collected round Inoko's body. The good innkeeper had arranged for a mass to be said for the repose of the dead man's spirit before the body was taken to the crematorium; the elderly priest from Hofukuji, who was officiating, was just now reading from the sutras. The mourners—Rentaro's widow, who had arrived that afternoon from Tokyo, Ichimura, and Ushimatsu—sat in solemn silence, attending to the readings. Perhaps because there was something especially moving about a traveller's death, far from home, the staff of the inn had gathered to pay their respects to the body; some overnight guests even, who had no connection whatever with the proceedings, were standing outside in the corridor, listening to the lonely sound of the wooden gong with which the priest accompanied his reading.

When the incense burning was over and the priest came to an interval in the service, Ushimatsu introduced Ginnosuke to Rentaro's widow. A man from the *Shinano Daily* pushed through the crowd with his notebook in hand.

"You will be Mrs. Inoko, I take it, madam?" He addressed her in the businesslike tones of a reporter. "A terrible shock this must have been for you. I have known your husband's name for a long time—I had a great admiration for him."

Such remarks from the reporter and others soon had the mourners talking once more of the dead man. His widow spoke of the start of their tour, of the strange dream she had had the night before she left for Tokyo, and of the anxiety it had caused her; of the scolding he had given her when she told him of her fears. The more she thought of it, the more certain she felt that he must have known from the start he was going to die. She recalled all that he had said to her then: the late autumn in Shinshu was especially lovely, he was going to enjoy this last part of the trip so much; she was to go home and wait for him there, he'd be sure to bring her some memento, something typical of Shinshu for her to remember their tour by—his last words to her before what was to be their final parting. She expressed her sorrow for the distress and inconvenience this sudden tragedy had caused her husband's friends and the innkeeper and his staff. The depth of her own grief showed through her simple, restrained manner, which aroused the sympathy of her hearers more than any emotional demonstration could have.

The lawyer beckoned Ginnosuke over to a corner of the room to ask him about Ushimatsu. What had happened would make it awkward for Ushimatsu to stay in Iiyama, he presumed, and Mrs. Inoko, for her part, would welcome a man's assistance on her journey back to Tokyo—he himself would have accompanied her if it weren't for the election being so close, but the widow wouldn't hear of it in any case; for him to fight the election with all the energy he possessed, she insisted, would be the greatest comfort he could offer her husband's spirit. Put like that, what she said was right, unquestionably. They would be very grateful, therefore, if Ushimatsu would go with her. He himself would bear all the expenses.

"I have already spoken to Segawa about it," the lawyer added. "But what exactly is the position between him and the school?"

"He'll be 'suspended,' I gather. There's already been some discussion about it. The principal was saying suspension is what the inspector will be recommending. There'll be no objection to his going with Mrs. Inoko, I'm sure. Anyway, I'll take care of the school side of it. The sooner he leaves Iiyama the better, for his own sake."

While they were talking, the coffin arrived. Some moments later the mourners gathered round the coffin to take their last farewell as the priest intoned some final passages from the scriptures. Outside, the light was already fading.

As she watched the coffin being hoisted onto the waiting sledge, the widow broke down at last in a sudden flood of tears.

## 5

When they had come back from the crematorium after

witnessing the lighting of the fire, Ushimatsu and Ginnosuke and the lawyer sat talking round a hibachi in a room at the inn. Fate, so cruel hitherto, began to smile a little on Ushimatsu. Ohinata, the rich eta who had been expelled from the inn in Takajo Street—the humiliation had only inspired him with a fiercer courage and determination—was preparing to start farming in Texas. He had spoken of his plan to the lawyer, who now brought Ushimatsu the first whisper of new hope. Ohinata had asked Ichimura some time ago to recommend a young man to join him, someone of education whom he could trust, Ichimura said. Ohinata would welcome Ushimatsu as a partner, he was sure. If Ushimatsu was interested, he would mention it—did the idea appeal to him? Given the will to succeed, it could be a marvellous experience.

Ginnosuke backed up the lawyer's proposal enthusiastically. "What did I tell you—there are kind gods as well as cruel ones," he said to Ushimatsu.

"Ohinata's coming to see me on business the day after tomorrow, in the morning. That'll be as good an opportunity as any to discuss it with him. You'll see him, won't you?"

The lawyer's words cheered the despondent Ushimatsu and roused in him once more the will to work. He promised to see Ohinata and ask him, if all went well, to be allowed to join him.

That wasn't all. How poignant the shock of delight for Ushimatsu in Ginnosuke's account of O-Shio's quiet, tearful promise! And of pity too, as he thought of the troubles that had crowded on her with her father's illness and her stepmother's flight. To know that there was one who wept for him in secret, when in despair he had forced himself to give up all thought of her—had freely told her his secret and parted from her, as he believed, for the last time; to know that even when she had heard his confession, so humiliating but wrung from the depths of his soul, she was ready still to share her life with a despised eta!

"She's a brave girl, and strong-minded. There's no doubt of that," Ginnosuke concluded.

Next day Ginnosuke went on his friend's behalf to the school, to Rengeji, and to Keinoshin's. It was he who got together Ushimatsu's belongings at Rengeji and sorted them into two bundles, one he would want for the journey to Tokyo and one to be left at the temple till his return. He also made a point of telling the lawyer and Mrs. Inoko about O-Shio. Women have a special sympathy for their own sex, and the girl's unhappy circumstances affected the widow deeply; O-Shio should come and stay with her in Tokyo, she proposed, as soon as possible, and once Ushimatsu's future was decided on, she would take as much pleasure in making the arrangements for the wedding as if O-Shio were her own sister. Ichimura too promised to help them in any way he could. So, leaving everything in the hands of Ginnosuke and the lawyer, Ushimatsu prepared to leave Iiyama.

# Chapter 23

## 1

The day of departure came at last. Sleet had been falling since dawn, intensifying for the party gathered at the inn the mood of sadness that the prospect of a journey always arouses.

Early in the morning a sledge drew up outside the inn. A passenger dismounted, a gentleman, apparently, well wrapped in a thick woollen overcoat. He sent his driver to ask for Mr. Ichimura.

"Ah, it's Ohinata." The lawyer went out to greet him. Ohinata had left Shimotakai while it was still dark to keep the appointment. Ichimura asked him in, but he refused, and put the questions on which he had come to ask the lawyer's professional advice sitting on the raised floor of the porch. Then he spoke of his sorrow at Rentaro's death. He was going to leave, when Ichimura told him of Ushimatsu.

"Do come in! Mrs. Inoko is here, and the young man I've been speaking of. I'd like you to meet him. How can we talk properly, anyway, if you keep sitting out here in the hall?"

But Ohinata would only shake his head with a grim smile, despite all the lawyer's urging. He himself would be going up to Tokyo very soon, he said; he would call on Mrs. Inoko there and see Ushimatsu at her house. If the young man was as promising as Ichimura suggested, joining forces would probably suit them both. But everything would have to wait till he went to Tokyo. Ohinata refused to say any more.

"Are you in such a hurry to get away today?"

"No, it's not that I'm in a hurry—"

The lawyer caught the meaning of Ohinata's obdurate, almost sullen expression. He proposed, therefore, that Ohinata should meet them at the tea house on the other side of the river near Upper Ferry, where they were going to see the travellers off; Ushimatsu's friend Ginnosuke would be with him, and the lawyer could introduce Ushimatsu to Ohinata there. Would he be willing to go on ahead and wait for them at Upper Ferry? Ohinata agreed and left at once, still without having stepped beyond the threshold of the inn. Ichimura went to tell Ushimatsu and Mrs. Inoko, who were making their final preparations.

Another caller was Simple Sho from Rengeji. He brought a parcel of farewell presents, one from the priest's wife and two from himself of his own making—a pair of sandals and another of snowshoes; he begged Ushimatsu to accept them as a small token of his respect. As he looked back over his months at the temple, Ushimatsu knew he would miss Simple Sho as much as anyone at Rengeji. All of them had changed—the priest, his wife, O-Shio, Ushimatsu himself: all but the childlike old man without wife or child or any other relative, to whom he had now to say goodbye—Simple Sho, who tolled the temple bell.

Shogo came too, asking if he could help with the baggage. The whitewood box containing Rentaro's ashes was wrapped first in white cloth, then in black, and placed on the sledge together with a number of Rentaro's belongings and Ushimatsu's bundle. To attract as little notice as possible, Ushimatsu and the widow were to walk as far as Upper Ferry; two passenger sledges would be waiting for them on the other side of the river. To a chorus of farewells from the innkeeper and the maids, the party set out from the inn.

The sleet was still falling steadily. In round wicker hats,

quilted gloves, and close-fitting blue trousers, the two sledge drivers set to work, one pulling in the shafts in front and one pushing from behind, calling to each other "Ho—yo! Ho—yo!" to help them keep in time.

With the others, Ushimatsu followed the ashes of his friend on foot, listening to the sledge as it slid over the snow and quietly thinking over his life. The suspicion, the fear, the mental agony that had never left him, day or night, had eased a little now. He was free, free at last of his burden, free as a bird. . . . Gratefully, unbelievingly, as if recalled from the brink of death, he drank in the cold December air, its taste as sweet to him as that of the sand a sailor falls on his knees to kiss when he steps ashore after a long voyage. Sweeter, yet sadder too. . . .

This world of snow, whispering beneath each step he took—at long last it was *his*. . . .

## 2

As they turned the last corner before Upper Ferry, they found O-Shio waiting with Otosaku to see them off. Otosaku's wife had stayed behind to look after the house. O-Shio and Ushimatsu—this happiest of meetings moved even the onlookers unforgettably. Ushimatsu bowed, O-Shio lifted bright but tear-stained eyes to his; no words could have served them then. To both, it was miracle enough that they had survived thus far—and a greater one that fate had brought them face to face after so many trials, to say goodbye, it was true, but only in the certainty of another meeting.

O-Shio was introduced for the first time to Ichimura and to Mrs. Inoko. At once the two women went ahead together, talking; Otosaku joined Ushimatsu and the lawyer and gave them the latest news of Keinoshin's condition. Loyal as always to his old master, Otosaku spoke with simple peasant directness of the future of the house he had so long served. If Keinoshin were to get worse, he himself, he promised, would do whatever might be necessary; would they take the responsibility for Shogo and O-Shio? O-Sue, the little girl, he and his wife would adopt. They had no children of their own, and Keinoshin had already agreed. They would be happy to bring her up, in memory of their association with her family.

It was not long before they had crossed the pontoon bridge and reached the tea house on the far side. Ginnosuke and Ohinata were waiting there already. When Ushimatsu was introduced to Ohinata, he could not believe at first that this was the man who was planning to start a bold and risky new venture overseas, in Texas—he might have been a country tradesman or herb doctor, he looked so ordinary; but gradually, as they talked, he sensed an unexpected depth in the other's character, as well as a rocklike common sense. Ohinata told him of a "Japanese village" in Texas, and of some young men from Kita-Sakuma who had gone to work there, including one from a quite well-to-do family who had graduated from a well-known middle school in Tokyo.

"So you were staying there too?" he said with a smile as Ushimatsu told him he had seen him being carried out of the lodging house in Takajo Street. "That was a venomous trick they played on me. It was the shock of what happened then, really, that made me think of making a new start abroad. I can laugh about it now, but at the time—I was bitter, I can tell you."

A burst of laughter from the rest of the party, sitting at a table inside the tea house, reminded Ohinata it was hardly the time for recalling painful memories. Smiling wryly, he went with Ushimatsu to join the others.

"We're ready now—bring the order please!" Ginnosuke called to the woman of the place. *O-mitate,* the final exchange of farewell cups of saké before a journey: alike for the travellers and for those who had come to speed them on their way, this moment here in the little riverside tea house, they all knew, would be a treasured memory. Ginnosuke played the host with a gay, studentlike humour that conveyed better than any sadder mood could have the warmth and sincerity of his feeling for his friend. He had come earlier than the others to see that everything was ready.

"I owe you so much, Tsuchiya," said Ushimatsu, his voice trembling with emotion.

"Don't worry, it's mutual!" Ginnosuke laughed. "Though I never guessed I'd be seeing you off like this, I must say—I'm the one that's had a farewell party, and now I'm to be the last to leave! Life's full of surprises, don't you agree?"

"I'll see you in Tokyo anyway, I hope."

"Yes, it won't be long now before I'm on my way too. But it's time to drink—though we've little enough to offer. A cup for you, Segawa!" Ginnosuke turned to O-Shio. "O-Shio! Won't you serve it for us?"

O-Shio poured a cup and offered it to Ushimatsu. Joy and the sadness of parting showed together in the faint trembling of her graceful white hand.

"Now I'll be the server!" Snatching the bottle from her as soon as Ushimatsu had drunk, Ginnosuke tried to pour a cup for her, despite her shyness.

"No thank you! I can't drink saké." She put her hand over the cup.

"Oh, but you must!" Ohinata joined in, laughing. "You can't refuse on a day like this, you know. You needn't drink it all—you can pretend, if you like—but take the cup, please."

"Just a tiny sip," put in the lawyer.

"A sip, then, no more." Blushing, O-Shio raised the cup to her lips.

## 3

Groups of pupils from Ushimatsu's class were gathering outside the tea house. Having heard somehow that the teacher they loved was leaving the town that morning, they had decided, with the delightful sincerity of childhood, that school or no school, the least they could do was see him off. Ushimatsu went out and walked among them, now saying goodbye individually, now giving advice and encouragement for their future, now going down through the sleet to stand on the bank under the willow trees and wait for those who were still on their way across the pontoon bridge.

In the distance the great bell of Rengeji sounded. . . .

A second time it tolled, the deep note reverberating across the water through the silence of the desolate winter day; slowly it spread, and slowly weakened, till as it faded at last, swallowed up in the sleeting sky, the bell boomed once more. A fourth time, and a fifth: Simple Sho's message for Ushimatsu, of farewell and a new life dawning. Ushimatsu bowed his head in spontaneous response.

A sixth time, and a seventh. . . . Listening to the wordless voice as it passed, the travellers and their friends exchanged their thoughts in silence.

The sledges were ready, it was announced. Ushimatsu spoke to Ginnosuke of his uncle and aunt in Nezu. They would be worried, of course, when they heard about his resignation. Supposing some rumour of the real reason were to find its way up to Himekozawa—inevitably it would mean trouble; maybe they would have to leave the village. What should he do?

"Better cross that bridge when you come to it," Ginnosuke answered. "Might be as well to tell Ohinata, though," he went on after a moment's thought. "If they should ever have to leave Nezu, Shimotakai might be a good place to move to. But there's no sense in thinking up new worries now. Things'll work out, you'll see."

"Will you speak to Ohinata, then?"

"Certainly."

After Ushimatsu had promised to send O-Shio a new copy of *Confessions* from Tokyo, the widow and he took leave of their friends. The lawyer, Ohinata, Otosaku, Ginnosuke, and the schoolchildren crowded round the three sledges. O-Shio watched, paler than before and leaning on her brother's shoulder.

"Let's give them a shove-off!" bawled one boy, raising his hands in readiness.

"Sensei! Can we go with you for a bit?" cried another, grabbing the pushing bar at the back of one of the sledges.

Just as they were ready to go, the probationary teacher came running up the bank shouting that the children must get back to school. Ushimatsu and the widow turned in astonishment. The three sledges, headed by the one carrying Rentaro's ashes, had just started to move; the drivers, who had already bent to their work, relaxed suddenly and stood idly waiting.

## 4

"You don't have to be so strict, surely." Ginnosuke confronted the probationer. "Think a bit, can't you? He was their teacher, and they want to go a bit of the way with him because they're fond of him, that's all. A beautiful idea, when you think of it: they deserve to be praised, not told off. And to try and stop them going—no, it's cruel. You shouldn't have come."

"That's not fair," said the probationer, scratching his head. "It wasn't me that said they mustn't go."

Ginnosuke shrugged his shoulders. "Then why does the school forbid it?"

"They can't be allowed to cut lessons just because they feel like it, without asking first. If they've got to go and see him off, the principal says, that's all right, but they have to do it in the proper way and get permission."

"They can explain afterwards."

"Afterwards? Who ever heard of getting permission afterwards? The principal's very angry, and Katsuno—you know Katsuno: according to him, Segawa's class is just plain lazy, and if this sort of thing is repeated, it'll affect the whole standing of the school. If the pupils can't keep the rules, expel them, he says."

"Why do they have to be so rigid? With the principal it's always rules, rules, rules. You don't really think it'll do them any harm to miss half a day? The principal and Katsuno ought to have given them the morning off without being asked and sent you along to encourage them—or come with the children themselves. Segawa's been their colleague for long enough, hasn't he? But to stay away themselves and punish the children for coming without permission—it's too unjust altogether."

But there was something Ginnosuke did not know. The day before, the principal had called the whole school together in the assembly hall and delivered a speech on the reasons for Ushimatsu's suspension, including a violent attack on Ushimatsu's character and conduct. The "clean-up," he claimed, would bring nothing but good to the school. . . . How pitiful that one educator could so hate another! Professional jealousy and racial contempt: the consuming flames pursued Ushimatsu to the very moment of his departure.

Ginnosuke was growing exasperated. Ushimatsu got down off his sledge to try to calm him down.

"Don't be too hard on him, Tsuchiya! He's only the messenger, don't forget."

But Ginnosuke would not listen. "The whole thing's so stupid!" he exclaimed. "Remember my farewell party? That took half a day. If classes were cancelled for my sake, why shouldn't they be for yours?" He turned to the crowd of children. "You go with him and give him a good send-off. If there's any trouble afterwards, I'll answer for it myself."

"We're off!" some of the boys shouted excitedly, waving their hands.

"But that makes it awkward for me, Tsuchiya." Ushimatsu restrained his friend. "Don't think I'm not grateful for their wanting to come. But I shan't feel happy if they're going to get into trouble afterwards. Let them say goodbye here—they've come all this way already, and that's more than I deserve. See that they go back now, will you?"

After a last word to the children, Ushimatsu turned to his sledge. One more "Goodbye!" as he glanced for the last time at O-Shio. To his right, through the branches of the willow trees on the riverbank, he could still see the town of Iiyama stretched under the misty sky: houses lining the opposite bank, here and there a temple, the ruins of the castle, all mantled now in snow. Sleet hid from view the white walls of the school, and Rengeji and its high bell tower, which on a fine day were easily visible from the tea house. Three times Ushimatsu turned to look toward the town. He sighed, a deep sigh of relief and peace. Hot tears trickled unnoticed down his cheek.

The sledges began to move over the snow.